THE BOOK OF PRACTICAL
DREAMCRAFT

THE BOOK OF PRACTICAL
DREAMCRAFT

SAHAR
HUNEIDI
PALMER

SIRIUS

All images courtesy of Shutterstock.

SIRIUS

This edition published in 2024 by Sirius Publishing, a division of
Arcturus Publishing Limited,
26/27 Bickels Yard, 151–153 Bermondsey Street,
London SE1 3HA

ISBN: 978-1-3988-4344-8
AD011322US

Printed in China

CONTENTS

To dreamers everywhere,

may you be always guided by your dreams.

To St. Al Khidr who revealed himself in a dream and
changed the course of my life—thank you.

To my friend, "cousin" and neighbor, Rabie Shawa,
who has a habit of providing timely and
much-needed insights—thank you.

To Jill Woods whose passion for dreaming
inspired a life journey of dreams.

INTRODUCTION

DREAMING AS A SELF-DEVELOPMENT TOOL

"Dreams are messengers to us from the unknown.
They are voices from our collective sub-conscious,
warners of deep inner disturbances in the individual psyche,
bearer of glad tidings of good things to come, or
echoes of happy or sad and long hidden memories."

Dr. Mahmoud Ayoub, Professor of Islamic Studies, Temple University, from his foreword to
Ibn Seerin's Dictionary of Dreams According to Islamic Inner Traditions

Dreams have long captivated humanity, serving as a source of inspiration, reflection, and even foretelling the future. The mystery surrounding the origins and meaning of dreams has sparked the imagination of many great thinkers throughout history, including Sigmund Freud and Carl Jung. Scientific research has shed light on the process of dreaming, revealing that the brain continues to work and process information even while we sleep.

By working with your dreams, we can deepen your understanding of yourself and your place in the world, leading to a more fulfilling and meaningful life. Furthermore, dreams are an important aspect of the human experience and can provide insight into our unconscious desires, fears, and anxieties. They are also thought to play a role in memory consolidation, problem-solving, and emotional regulation. Our brains generate dreams during the Rapid Eye Movement (REM) stage of sleep, when brain activity is like that of wakefulness. The exact process of dream generation remains a topic of scientific investigation, but it is thought to involve the integration of sensory information, memories, and emotions.

In *The Book of Practical Dream Craft*, we will delve into the world of dreams and explore their significance in our lives; through a combination dream-inducing methods, remembering your dreams, identifying "universal" symbols, and deciphering your own dream language. Although any dream may hold some universal symbols within it, the dream represents a unique fingerprint of an individual's mind. As such, the message which a dream communicates would also be unique and specific to the dreamer. Moreover, you will discover how to direct your dreams an develop our own dream dictionary, and with time, you will start interpreting your own dreams.

Additionally, interpreting dreams can be a deeply personal and meaningful process, as it allows us to delve into the inner workings of our own minds and gain insight into our unconscious thoughts and emotions. Through this exploration, we can gain a greater understanding of our own patterns, tendencies, and beliefs, and gain a clearer picture of our life journey.

The intricacies of the human mind are such that even in the realm of dreams, everyone's experiences are uniquely their own. If two individuals were to dream the same sequence of events, the interpretation and significance of those events would differ vastly between the two. This is because each person's mind operates using a personal dictionary of symbols, with its own unique meanings and associations. As a result, the events, people, and symbols present in a dream may hold different interpretations and significance for everyone, shaped by their personal experiences, beliefs, and emotions. In essence, the language of the mind is as unique as the individual themselves.

Dreams are a powerful tool indeed! By working with your dreams, you will become more aware of how you operate in your life, and what you need to address and work on. We will examine how we can use this powerful tool to unlock your creativity, gain insight into your inner self, and lead a more fulfilling life. Did you know that sleep accounts for a third of our lives, and that dreams can provide a vital link between our conscious and unconscious mind? Just imagine overlooking thirty percent of your life's experience. It would be missing out

on valuable insights that dreams offer, the wisdom they bring, and the growth they facilitate. Dreaming is truly a marvel of the human mind.

Moreover, your dreams serve as a window into the inner workings of your unconscious mind, revealing the mysteries of the soul and assisting to understand the unseen aspects of your being. Carl Jung's famous quote, "Until you make the unconscious conscious, it will direct your life and you will call it fate," emphasizes the importance of exploring the unconscious mind, including our dreams. By working with our dreams, we can bring the unconscious into the conscious and gain greater control over our lives and decisions. Therefore, your dreams are a valuable self-empowering tool uncovering insight into your unconscious desires, fears, and anxieties and much more. They are also a safe dimension trying out alternative solutions to problem-solving, taking a virtual holiday, calling in a soul mate, or healing past traumas.

The reality is that our brains never truly rest, even as we slumber. Our brain continues to process and analyze the vast amounts of information we encounter each day. It is during this time that our psyche, or soul, takes center stage, as the brain diverts its attention from its physical responsibilities to attend to the needs of our inner selves. The dream state is a unique opportunity for our physical bodies to rest, and for our spiritual bodies to journey to alternate realities. It is through this process that we can access the wisdom of the soul and bring the invisible into the visible. This makes dreams a crucial tool for integrating the wisdom of our souls with our "earthly" experiences in the physical world.

The following is a beautiful quotation on dreams and spirituality by Shaikh Abdul Ghani Nabulsi, who was a Syrian Islamic scholar born in the city of Nabulsi in Syria in the late 17th century. In his book *Ta'atir-ul Anam* (*The Impression of the People*) he writes: "the soul resides within one's heart, and the functions of the heart are dictated by one's brain. When one falls asleep, his soul becomes like an extended ray of light, or like a sun, where he can see what the angel of dreams reveals to him through the effluent light of his Lord." He continues to write: "when one's senses come to wakefulness, it is as though a cloud has come to cover the sunlight. When one wakes up, he may remember through his soul what the angel of dreams has showed him."

By embracing our dreams and the wisdom they bring, we can embark on a journey of self-discovery, unlocking the full potential of our minds, deepen our understanding of ourselves and our place in the world, and lead a more fulfilling and meaningful life.

STARTING A DREAM JOURNAL

This book is all about helping you create a dream that truly reflects your innermost self and the path you are meant to be on in this lifetime. More importantly, it is a tool to grow your own self-awareness and connect with your own inner guidance by understanding and uncovering the language of your subconscious mind.

Everything you will find in these pages is designed to support and guide you towards that goal. Starting a dream journal is, therefore, an essential tool for anyone who wants to explore their innermost thoughts, feelings, and desires. By recording your dreams in a journal, you are creating a space for yourself to explore your subconscious mind and uncover hidden patterns and beliefs that may be holding you back in your waking life.

As you begin to record your dreams and reflect on their meanings, you will gain a deeper understanding of your own desires and motivations. This self-awareness will help you to craft a dream that is truly aligned with your deepest self and life journey, as mentioned in the paragraph.

Furthermore, by continuing to maintain your dream journal over time, you will be able to track your progress and growth as you work towards achieving your goals and aspirations. This process of self-reflection and self-discovery is an important part of any journey towards personal growth and transformation, and a dream journal is a powerful tool to support you on this journey.

So, take some time to explore and discover, and see where your dreams can take you! Dream journaling can also be an important part of a spiritual practice. It provides a space for introspection and self-reflection. Recording and reflecting on your dreams, enables deeper appreciation for the workings of your own minds and understanding the messages contained in your dreams. With patience, dedication, and a willingness to listen to our own inner voice, the process of exploring and interpreting your dreams begins to unfold in a manner that is relevant to you. It can lead you to a greater sense of self-awareness and a more fulfilling spiritual connection.

As you start the journey of exploring the symbolism within your dreams, keep in mind that this is a process of self-discovery that demands dedication and commitment. Your level of effort will directly influence the benefits you gain from this exploration. So, approach this endeavor with patience, persistence, and a willingness to delve deep into the inner workings of your mind. Remember, uncovering the unique language of your subconscious mind is a lifelong pursuit. The more you explore, the greater understanding you will have of yourself, your desires, and your motivations. So, be persistent in your practice and stay open-minded. The journey of discovering the language of your subconscious is not a destination to be reached, but rather an ongoing exploration. Be gentle with yourself, pace yourself, and take the time you need to fully understand and integrate each new insight.

Therefore, keeping a dream journal is also an important aspect of this exploration.

Writing down your dreams immediately after waking up helps you remember the details and symbols that may be easily forgotten as time passes. This journal will serve as a valuable tool for your self-discovery journey and provide a reference for tracking your progress. Moreover, starting a dream journal is a fantastic way to take your dream exploration to the next level. By keeping track of your dreams, you will be able to see patterns and themes emerging over time, which can provide valuable insights into your subconscious mind.

Here is how to get started:

1. GET A NOTEBOOK

Look for a notebook that inspires you and that you will enjoy writing in. It could be a traditional lined notebook, a fancy journal with a beautiful cover, or even a notebook app on your phone. The key is to choose something that you will be motivated to write in regularly.

Keeping a dream journal can be a fun and creative project too. In addition to writing down your dreams, you can incorporate art and other creative elements to bring your subconscious thoughts to life. Consider drawing sketches of the people, places, or objects that appear in your dreams, or pasting in photographs or magazine clippings that represent

your dreamscape. These visual aids can help bring the dream world to life and provide additional insights into your subconscious mind.

Another option is to make your dream journal into a scrapbook or visual diary, incorporating colors, patterns, and other design elements that reflect your dream experiences. This will not only make the journal a beautiful and unique artifact but will also give you a tangible way to reflect on and remember your dreams. By making your dream journal into an artistic and creative project, you will motivate your own self-discovery, and find that the process of exploring your subconscious mind is even more enriching and rewarding.

2. FIND A PLACE TO KEEP IT

Your journal can be a physical one that you keep by your bedside, or a digital journal that you access on your phone or computer. It is important to choose a format that works for you and that you'll be comfortable using every day. If you are not sure which format to choose, consider starting with a physical journal and then moving to a digital one later, or vice versa. The key is to make sure that the journal is easily accessible so you can record your dreams as soon as you wake up. This will help you to capture the details of your dreams while they are still fresh in your mind. If you opt for a digital journal, make sure you have it easily accessible on your device and ready to use.

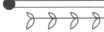

If you chose to voice-record your dreams upon waking up, make sure that you write them down in your physical or digital journal as well. This way you will have a record, and you might discover that will remember more once you start writing your dream. Alternatively, if you choose a physical journal, you might want to consider adding a pen or pencil (opt for one that is fun, attractive and enjoyable to write with) to the bedside table so you can quickly jot down notes if you need to.

Regardless of the format you choose, it is important to make sure that your dream journal is private and secure. You do not want anyone else to have access to your innermost thoughts and feelings; to support you to write freely. So, so make sure your journal is protected by a password or locked away in a safe place.

3. SET ASIDE TIME

Choose a time each day when you are most likely to remember your dreams, such as first thing in the morning. Make it a routine to write down any dreams you can recall as soon as you wake up before you talk to anyone or do anything—dreams tend to "evaporate" quickly if you are not used to capturing them immediately.

Setting aside time to dream journal can be a great way to carve out some quiet, mindful

me-time for yourself. This special time can allow you to disconnect from the outside world and tap into the deeper aspects of your inner self. It is important, for instance, to create a peaceful and relaxed environment. This could mean finding a quiet place to sit and reflect or lighting some candles or incense to set the mood. Whatever you do, make sure it is something that helps you feel calm and cantered.

The act of writing down your dreams can also be a form of mindfulness in and of itself. It requires you to slow down and focus on the present moment, to pay close attention to the details of your dream and reflect on the symbolism and meaning behind it. This focused attention can help you connect more

deeply with your subconscious mind and gain a deeper understanding of your inner self - a bit of self-care and inner reflection.

When you write down your dreams, be as detailed as possible. To start with, write the date down. Include the emotions, thoughts, colors or feelings you woke up with and sensations you experienced in the dream; as well as the characters and symbols that appeared. The more information you can capture, the more you will be able to see patterns and themes emerging over time. Because your dream language will evolve over time as you formulate your own dream dictionary; it is important to record the date of your dream in your journal. This will help you uncover the meaning, and themes of your dreams, even if some time has passed since you first had them.

4. REFLECT

After you have written down your dream, take a moment to reflect on it. Ask yourself questions like, *"what did this dream mean to me?."* For example, it may be about the past, or the present, or what you what was in your mind as you went to sleep the night before. Or *"what emotions did I experience in the dream?"* You might not remember much to begin with; however, you may remember waking up feeling refreshed, or the that the

color blue was on your mind. Whatever it is, this reflection can help you understand the messages your subconscious mind is sending you and it may evoke more details of your dream.

5. IDENTIFY KEY WORDS

After you have recorded the details of your dream, it is time to dig deeper into the content. Highlight or circle key words, colors, names of people, or places where your dream took place. Most importantly write the date down too. By highlighting or circling key words, colors, names of people or places, you can begin to identify patterns and themes that may hold meaning.

These details may seem small or insignificant, but they can often reveal hidden insights into your subconscious mind.

So, take your time, be thorough (as much as possible), and do not be afraid to ask yourself questions about each detail you have recorded to help your own intuition to flow. For example, "what does this color, word, or person, mean to me or what do they stand for in my mind in one word?" Moreover, you can ask yourself "what emotion did this scene, or dream, evoke within me?" Your intuition will answer you. The answers to these questions will be unique to you and will help you uncover the deeper meaning of your dreams.

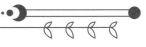

DISCOVER YOUR DREAM THEME EXERCISE

A highly effective approach for uncovering these underlying themes is to condense each dream into a single sentence and then examine the recurring keywords. For instance, you might have a dream like "joyful celebration" or "unsettling sensation of being trapped." Similarly, travel, love, or unique experiences could serve as concise summaries. The goal is to help you recognize the connections between your life experiences and the patterns in your dream language (more details in Chapter 4). This uncomplicated exercise offers valuable insights into the matters occupying your mind and the desires you might not even be consciously aware of, shedding light on the subconscious motivations that influence your thoughts and actions.

Write a few lines, to begin with, and when you are done, go back and summaries each element using one word only.

6. DATE YOUR DREAM

Over time, the act of regularly documenting your dreams will allow you to identify patterns and recurring themes, unlocking deeper insights into your own unique symbolic language. That is why it is also important to record the date of your dream, as this will allow you to track any recurring symbols or themes over time. This can give you a better understanding of your subconscious patterns and help you identify any changes or growth in your thinking and beliefs.

Additionally, reviewing your dream journal regularly can help you identify your own emerging dream symbols and personal themes and become aware of how your dreams are evolved and changing over time according to your personal awareness and growth. Dream interpretation It is a fascinating process that can reveal the depths of your own inner landscape, and the benefits of this exploration are limitless.

7. USE ONE-WORD SUMMARY

Once you write your dreams, start writing down one-word description for key elements that pop out at you. For instance, if your dream took place in a school, when you were younger and your friend Susan was in it, ask yourself "what does the school, the past, and Susan represent or stand for, respectively, in my mind?" and come up with one word.

8. BE CONSISTENT

To get the most out of your dream journal, it is important to be consistent. Consistency is key to unlocking the full potential of your dream journal. Make sure to write down your dreams every day, even if it is just a few sentences. Over time, the insights you'll gain will be well worth the effort.

By making dream journaling a daily habit, no matter how small or insignificant they may seem, you will create a comprehensive record of your subconscious mind's language. Moreover, you might find that your subconscious is more responsive because you are regularly communicating with it by journaling your dreams regularly. This in turn will allow you to track patterns, identify recurring symbols, and gain a deeper understanding of your innermost thoughts and desires.

Being diligent in documenting your dreams, enables you to reflect on your personal growth, and discover insights that may have been hidden to you previously. The process may feel tedious or overwhelming at times, but the rewards you will reap in terms of self-awareness and self-discovery will be well worth the effort. So, make sure to write down your dreams every day and stick with it, the consistency will pay off in the long run.

Starting a dream journal is an exciting and rewarding journey, so embrace it and have fun! With these steps in mind, you will be well on your way to starting a dream journal that you can use to explore your subconscious mind and gain new insights into yourself and your life. Finally, embarking on the journey of interpreting your dreams is a fulfilling and enlightening experience. It requires a patient, persistent, and dedicated approach. Keep up with your dream journaling and remember to have fun with it! By exploring the symbolism in your dreams, you unlock the secrets of your subconscious mind and gain a deeper understanding of yourself. So, be open to the process, and you will reap the benefits of a deeper connection to your innermost thoughts and a more fulfilling life.

May your dreams unlock the mysteries of your life journey and enlighten your path!

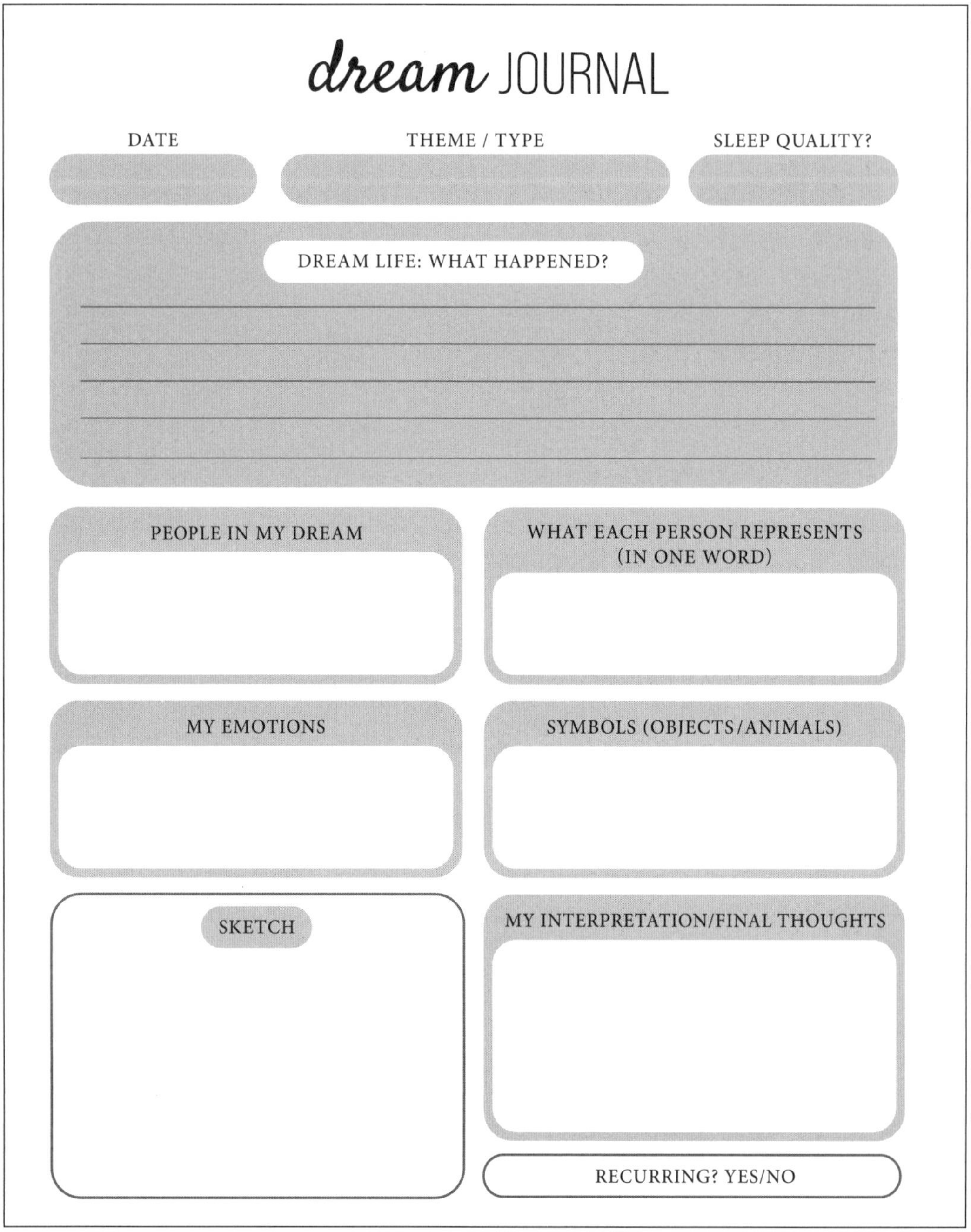

dream JOURNAL

DATE

THEME / TYPE

SLEEP QUALITY?

DREAM LIFE: WHAT HAPPENED?

_____

_____

_____

_____

_____

PEOPLE IN MY DREAM

WHAT EACH PERSON REPRESENTS
(IN ONE WORD)

MY EMOTIONS

SYMBOLS (OBJECTS / ANIMALS)

SKETCH

MY INTERPRETATION/FINAL THOUGHTS

RECURRING? YES/NO

Dream journal elements to note

CHAPTER 1

A LIFETIME OF DREAMS

Dreams and dream interpretation have been a source of fascination and mystery for people across cultures and throughout history. The study of dreams and their meanings has been associated with spirituality and has been used as a tool for self-discovery and personal growth. In many ancient traditions, dreams are often viewed as a spiritual practice, a means of receiving messages from the divine or from a higher power. They are considered as a source of guidance and a way to connect with a deeper sense of purpose and understanding. By paying attention to the symbols and messages contained within their dreams, we can tap into our own inner wisdom and gain a greater understanding of our place in the world.

Moreover, dreams are a crucial tool for integrating the wisdom of the soul with our experiences in the physical world. In other words, a great self-development tool. They offer a glimpse into another reality, where our spiritual body travels and explores, providing insights, knowledge. The dream state, or dream life, is a unique opportunity for our physical bodies to rest and for our spiritual bodies to journey to alternate realities, accessing the wisdom of the soul and bringing "invisible" wisdom into the practical "visible" reality.

ANCIENT TRADITIONS

JUDAIC & CHRISTIAN TRADITIONS

In Judaism, Christianity, and Islam, the three monotheistic religions, for instance, dreams have been seen as a way for God to communicate with human beings, especially prophets. Dreams are viewed as direct messages from God bestowed on chosen "prophets" as a reward for their trust and faith. Their gift is the also the ability to interpret dreams—something that often saved and changed the course of their lives!

Moreover, several key figures such as Joseph and Jacob are known to have received important messages through dreams. Both instances are mentioned in the Torah, Bible, and Qur'an. For example, Joseph and Pharaoh's dreams in Genesis 41. Joseph interpreted Pharaoh's dream about seven skinny cows eating seven fat cows, and seven withered ears of grain eating seven healthy ones. Joseph interpreted the dream as a warning of seven years of famine following seven years of abundant crops. Another example is Jacob's dream, in Genesis 28 is a very interesting and significant one. It is considered one of the most important dreams in the Bible and is often referred to as Jacob's Ladder Dream.

In the dream, Jacob saw a ladder reaching from earth to heaven, with angels ascending and descending on it. This dream was a symbol of God's presence and the communication between heaven and earth. The angels ascending and descending on the ladder represented God's presence in the world and His interaction with humanity. God also spoke to Jacob in the dream, promising to be with him and protect him. This was a significant moment in Jacob's life, as he was on the run from his brother Esau and was feeling very vulnerable and alone. The dream provided comfort and reassurance to

Jacob. To him, it was a sign of God's presence in his life. Moreover, the dream was in a way was formed, or came to answer and address, Jacob's fears and concerns.

After the dream, Jacob woke up and said, "Surely the Lord is in this place, and I was not aware of it." He was filled with awe and reverence for God, and he consecrated the place where he had the dream and set up a stone monument to commemorate it. And you might have experienced this relief when you had a dream about what was in the forefront of your mind! The story also highlights how dreams can bring relief.

Moreover, the story of Jacob's ladder dream is viewed as a powerful reminder of the connection between the physical and spiritual realms. The ladder is seen as a symbol of the journey of the soul, with the angels representing the various stages of spiritual development that one can experience on their journey. Furthermore, the dream is also significant in that it is the first time in the Torah that God speaks to Jacob directly, which is seen as a significant moment in Jacob's spiritual journey and a reminder of the importance of communication with God. Additionally, it also shows that God, or divine inspiration and guidance, can speak to us in many ways, including through dreams. When we are receptive to guidance, we tend to receive it.

Another significant dream mentioned is the dream of Nebuchadnezzar which appears in the book of Daniel. It is a well-known story which is often studied for its prophetic significance. Nebuchadnezzar was the king of Babylon and had a dream about a statue with a head of gold, chest and arms of silver, belly and thighs of bronze, legs of iron and feet of clay. The dream disturbed him so much that he summoned his wise men and magicians to interpret it for him. However, they were unable to provide a satisfactory explanation. Daniel, a Jewish captive in Babylon, was called upon to interpret the dream. He explained to Nebuchadnezzar that the statue represented the succession of kingdoms that would rule the world. The head of gold represented Nebuchadnezzar's Babylonian empire, while the other parts of the statue represented subsequent kingdoms that would rise and fall.

The dream was a vision of the future and provided a powerful message about the limitations and temporary nature of earthly power. "God's" message was that even the greatest kingdoms would eventually come to an end and that God was ultimately in control of the affairs of the world. Additionally, this dream is significant because to the believers, it demonstrated the sovereignty of a higher power, God, and His ability to reveal the future to His prophets. It symbolizes the significance of the receiver of the dream and serves as a reminder to they should always be humble and recognize that God is the ultimate source of power and authority.

The story of Nebuchadnezzar's dream is also a testament to the wisdom and faithfulness of Daniel, who was able to interpret the dream and provide insight into God's plan for the world. What these stories demonstrate, is two things: first that dreams are significant as they represent divine, or spiritual messages. Second, is that the receiver of the dream is also significant; therefore, receivers of dreams, were thought of as "prophets" and wise sages.

ISLAMIC TRADITION

In Islam, dreams play an important role in its history and culture as well. In the Islamic tradition, dreams are considered one of the ways in which Allah (God) can communicate with individuals and considered to be a source of divine guidance and direction.

Dream stories sited in the Qur'an are often prophetic and continue to inspire and remind Muslims of the power of faith, obedience, and good deeds for relief will soon come to the believers and the pure of heart. The dream of prophet Yusuf (Joseph) is one of the most famous dreams in Islam. It is mentioned in Surah Yusuf of the Qur'an (which was also mentioned in the bible). The dream is a significant event in Prophet Yusuf's life and is said to have been a source of inspiration for many generations. In the dream, Prophet Yusuf sees eleven stars, the sun, and the moon, all bowing down to him. The stars represent his eleven brothers, and the sun and the moon represent his parents. The interpretation of this dream is that it represents Prophet Yusuf's future as a leader and a prophet.

Before Prophet Yusuf had the dream

that he would become a leader, he was the youngest son of Jacob and lived with his 11 brothers. According to the Qur'an and Islamic tradition, Prophet Yusuf was a prophet of Allah and had a special relationship with Him. However, Prophet Yusuf's brothers were jealous of him and plotted against him. They threw him into a well and later sold him into slavery. Eventually, where he was bought by a high-ranking official and worked in his household.

Yusuf was eventually taken to Egypt, imprisoned, and then when the Pharaoh had the dream mentioned earlier about the seven cows (this dream is also mentioned in the Qur'an), the pharaoh demanded Yusuf's release so he could interpret the dream. This interpretation saved Egypt from famine, and Yusuf's life. Despite facing many challenges and difficulties in Egypt, Prophet Yusuf was known for his wisdom, unwavering faith and his ability to interpret dreams, according to Islamic heritage.

Additionally, Yusuf also had a dream about the woman he would marry. He saw himself in a dream, pouring water from a pitcher and the woman approached him and took the pitcher from him. This dream was interpreted to mean that he would marry the woman who would take the pitcher from him. The woman in the dream was Zulaikha, the wife of the chief minister of Egypt. She was drawn to Prophet Yusuf's beauty and wisdom and attempted to seduce him, but he refused her advances, as he was a righteous man, a slave and she was his master's wife. However, because of his knowledge of dream interpretation and saving Egypt, Yusuf eventually rose to a position of power in Egypt and was appointed as the chief minister of the country—which subsequently allowed him to marry Zulaikha.

Although marrying Zulaikha seemed impossible, his dream foretold that he would. It brought him a message of relief and reminded to uphold his resolve, faith and trust. It is noteworthy to emphasize that dreams can sometimes serve as a glimpse

into future events, which may unfold in the coming days, weeks or months. For this reason, it is crucial to maintain a dream journal and record your dreams regularly.

Overall, the dream about the woman Yusuf would marry is a significant part of his story and is mentioned in the Qur'an as a reminder of the power of dreams and their ability to foretell the future as they come from a higher and wiser source of guidance. This highlights that dreams are viewed as true divine guidance, and Yusuf was blessed with the knowledge of interpreting dreams, as revealed in the Qur'anic verse (12:16) "Thus will thy Lord choose thee and teach thee the interpretation of stories"—referring to dream interpretation.

Another example is Prophet Ibrahim's (Abraham) dream, which represents a significant event in Islamic history. The dream is mentioned in Surah Al-Baqarah of the Qur'an. In this dream, Prophet Ibrahim sees himself sacrificing his son Ishmael, who represents his unwavering faith and obedience to Allah. In the dream, Allah commands Ibrahim to sacrifice his son, and he is faced with the choice of either following Allah's command or turning away from his faith. Despite the apparent cruelty of the command, Prophet Ibrahim demonstrates his complete trust in Allah by being willing to sacrifice his son, and he raises the knife to carry out the act. However, just as he is about to carry out the sacrifice, Allah stops him and replaces Ishmael with a ram, which is to be offered as a sacrifice instead. This act is seen as a reminder to trust divine intervention and guidance, even in the face of seemingly impossible life's tests and challenges. This act of devotion and obedience to Allah was so profound that it became a tradition in Islam to commemorate the event by sacrificing rams or other animals during the annual Eid al-Adha (Festival of Sacrifice). Additionally, it highlights that for transformation to occur, letting go of something valuable or cherished may be necessary.

The Holy Qur'an narrates this soul-stirring event in these words: "And when he (Isma'il) attained the age to assist him in his (Abraham's) work, he (Abraham) said: O my son! I see in vision that I offer thee

in sacrifice. Now see what thy view is. The son said: O my father, do as thou art commanded. Thou wilt find me, if God so wills, patient. So, when they both had surrendered themselves to (Allah), and he laid him down prostrate on his forehead (for sacrifice), We called out to him: O Abraham, thou hast indeed fulfilled the vision. Thus, do We reward the doers of good. Surely this is a manifest trial. And We ransom- ed him with a great sacrifice" (37:102).

In Islam the act of sacrifice is the symbol of a Muslim's readiness to surrender, and to sacrifice all his interests and desires in the cause of truth or divine guidance. "The purpose of sacrifice is not fulfilled only by shedding the blood of an animal, but it is really fulfilled when a man submits himself completely to the command of Allah" as *Kitab Al Adahi* (Book of Sacrifices explains in Sahih Muslim (a collection of sayings and deeds of Prophet Muhammad). Sura Hajj, verse 37 demonstrates this: "Not their flesh, nor their blood reaches Allah, but it is the piety from you that reaches Him."

This act of surrender is practiced as Istikhara ritual (literally means seeking guidance) in Islamic tradition, when deciding. Istikhara is performed when an individual is faced with an important decision and wants to seek Allah's guidance and wisdom in making the best choice. The process of Istikhara involves making sincere intentions, performing two units of voluntary prayer (salah), and then asking Allah to guide one to what is best for them in their situation. The guidance received through Istikhara is not considered a direct or explicit revelation, but rather a general feeling or impression in one's heart. After performing Istikhara, the individual is encouraged to trust their intuition and decide based on the information and circumstances available to them, while remaining open to Allah's guidance and wisdom.

Furthermore, what is interesting is the specific prayer or invocation that is typically recited when performing Istikhara in the Islamic tradition. The exact wording of the Istikhara prayer may vary slightly based on different interpretations or cultural practices, but the following is a commonly used version:

"Oh Allah, I seek Your guidance [in making this decision]. You are the Most Knowledgeable, and You are the Most Wise. Oh Allah, if You know that this matter [that I am considering] is good for me in my livelihood, and my future; then make it easy for me and bless it for me. And if You know that this matter is not good for me, and harmful to me, then turn me away from it, and choose for me what is good, wherever it may be. And make me content with Your choice."

The invocation requires sacrificing one's desires to arrive at divine "truth" and trust it (and was practiced by ancient Egyptians as you will read later).

Keep in mind that central to seeking guidance through your dreams, is setting a clear intention, and then letting go of any preconceived expectations. This allows your mind to be receptive to guidance without being biased by your desires. Make sure to check out Chapter Four for more comprehensive information.

It is interesting to note that in Judaism, Christianity, and Islam, the significance of piety and surrender is often emphasized in the dream parables mentioned in their scripture. People who were deemed worthy through their piousness and trust were gifted with divine guidance through their dreams. For example, Prophet Zul-Kifl, who is believed to be Prophet Ezekiel in the Bible, is one such prophet whose dream is mentioned in the Qur'an. These dream parables serve as a reminder of the importance of having a pure and surrendered heart when seeking guidance through dreams.

In Surah Al-Kahf of the Qur'an (The Cave), Prophet Zul-Kifl had a dream in which he saw himself in a garden, surrounded by many trees. The dream is seen as a symbol of the abundance and blessings that come from living a righteous life and serving Allah. The interpretation of the dream is that Zul-Kifl saw himself in a state of peace and prosperity, surrounded by the blessings of Allah. The large number of trees represents the abundance of blessings that come from serving Allah, and the garden symbolizes the peace and contentment that comes from living a righteous life.

Another example of dreams heralding a message about future events, is mentioned Mohammad Al-Akili's fascinating book on dream interpretation in Islam entitled, *Ibn Seerin's Dictionary of Dreams According to Islamic Inner Traditions* (Pearl Publishing House, 1992- 2006). The book details a dictionary of dream interpretation according to the Islamic scholar Ibn Seerin of the 8th century. Ibn Seerin was a famous Islamic dream interpreter and psychologist who lived in the Islamic Golden Age and is one of the most prominent figures in the field of dream interpretation. His works are still widely studied and referenced by

scholars and students of Islamic spirituality and psychology.

The significant aspect of Ibn Seerin's approach to dream interpretation, is that he emphasized the importance of considering the context of the dreamer's life and their state of mind. This was essential when interpreting the symbols and themes present in a dream. He believed that the subconscious mind of the dreamer was a powerful tool for exploring the deeper aspects of their inner self, and that the insights gained from dream analysis could be used to help individuals make positive changes in their lives.

Furthermore, the timing of a dream was considered an important aspect of dream interpretation by Ibn Seerin. In his book "The Interpretation of Dreams," he emphasized that the time at which a dream occurs can reveal important information about its meaning. For example, dreams that occur during the day are less significant than those that occur at night, and dreams that occur in the early morning are often seen as more meaningful and symbolic. Timing was just one of many factors that Ibn Seerin took into consideration when interpreting a dream.

In his book, Al Akili mentions that once Mohammed related a dream to his closest companion and served as his closest advisor and friend, Abu Bakr, where he saw in his dream that they were both climbing a ladder. "At the end, I reached two steps further than you did." Abu Bakr replied: "O Messenger of god, God Almighty will call your soul back unto His mercy, and I shall live two- and one-half years after you have departed this world." After the Prophet's death, Abu Bakr was elected as the first leader of the Muslim community, the first Caliph of Islam, and passed away approximately two years and six months after the death of the Prophet Mohammed.

Scholars after Ibn Seerin was influenced by his work (especially on dream interpretation) and expanded on dreams as mystical soul journey in their works. Sheikh Abd Al-Ghani Al-Nabulsi was such an eminent Islamic scholar. Born in Syria in the 17th century, Abd Al-Ghani was an orphan, who later joined the Qādiriyyah and Naqshbandiyyah Islamic mystical orders. He dedicated seven years of his life, in isolation in his house, studying the mystics and their experiences of divinity. Abd Al-Ghani wrote over 200 works in his lifetime, covering a wide range of subjects,

such as Sufism, travel accounts, poetry, eulogies, correspondence, prophecy, dream interpretation (according to Britannica.com, Sufism is "mystical Islamic belief and practice in which Muslims seek to find the truth of divine love and knowledge through direct personal experience of God").

Al-Nabulsi was particularly renowned for his original writing on Sufism, where he explored the concept of waḥdat al-wujūd, "divine existential unity" of God and the universe and, hence, of man. This concept was the main theme in his original Sufi writing and set him apart from other scholars. In his book, *Ta'tir al-anam fi tafsir al-ahlam*, (loosely translates to *Perfuming People with The Interpretation of Dreams, implying that interpreting dreams alleviates or uplifts people); he describes dream time as follows: "the soul resides within one's heart, and the functions of the heart are dictated by one's brain. When one falls asleep, his soul becomes like an extended ray of light, or like a sun, where he can see what the angel of dreams reveals to him through the effulgent light of his Lord. When one's senses come to wakefulness, it is as though a cloud has come to cover the sunlight. When one wakes up, he may remember through his soul what the angel of dreams has showed him."*

Al-Nabulsi held the belief that our dreams are a window into the soul and our consciousness. He mentions in his writings that: "dreams are seen by the soul and are understood by one's consciousness." The concept of the soul venturing beyond the physical world during dream time is a timeless one, as evidenced by the rich history of dream interpretations and practices that have been around since ancient times. People have always sought higher guidance through their dreams to navigate their worldly lives; building temples and performing rituals to enhance their chances of receiving a meaningful message. What a fascinating journey it is to explore the mysteries of the mind and the soul through dreams- read on!

HINDUISM

The idea that dreams can reveal deeper aspects of our inner selves is a common theme in many spiritual beliefs. Dreams are often seen as a way for the subconscious mind to communicate with us, providing us with insight into our deepest desires, fears, and emotions. In the Hindu tradition, the soul is believed to be able to travel outside of the body during sleep and connect with the divine realm through dreams. This is seen as a way for the soul to receive guidance and wisdom from higher spiritual sources. Many Hindu practitioners believe that the messages received in dreams can be interpreted

to gain insight into their lives and help with personal growth and spiritual development.

In Hindu mythology, King Janaka of Mithila is said to have received enlightenment through a dream in which he realized the nature of the self. King Janaka of Mithila is a well-known figure in Hindu mythology who is said to have attained enlightenment through a dream. According to Hindu tradition, King Janaka was a wise and just ruler, but despite his material success, he felt a sense of emptiness and dissatisfaction. One night, he had a dream in which he realized the nature of the self and attained self-realization. This dream is said to have transformed King Janaka and filled him with a sense of peace and fulfillment that he had never experienced before.

King Janaka's dream is considered significant in Hinduism because it highlights the power of self-realization and the importance of understanding the true nature of the self. The story is often interpreted as a reminder that material success and worldly achievements cannot bring true happiness and fulfillment, but rather, it is through a deeper understanding of the self that true peace and contentment can be found.

King Janaka's dream is also seen as an example of how the divine can communicate with individuals through their dreams and provide them with guidance and insight.

It is widely taught and referenced in Hindu philosophy and is considered an important source of inspiration for individuals seeking self-realization and spiritual growth.

Another significant dream in Hinduism is that of Prince Dhruva. Prince Dhruva's story is one of the most well-known stories in Hindu mythology and is often used to teach the importance of devotion and perseverance in the pursuit of spiritual enlightenment. Prince Dhruva was a young prince who was deeply troubled by the fact that his father favored his stepmother over him. In his despair, he turned to his mother for comfort, and she encouraged him to seek the blessings of Lord Vishnu. Prince Dhruva was determined to find Lord Vishnu and gain his blessings, so he set out on a journey of spiritual contemplation and meditation.

During his journey, Prince Dhruva (means unshakable, immovable, or fixed) is said to have had a dream in which Lord Vishnu appeared to him and showed him the path to attain spiritual enlightenment. Lord Vishnu encouraged Prince Dhruva to continue his spiritual quest and promised that he would always be with him. This dream gave Prince Dhruva the strength and determination to continue his journey of spiritual contemplation and meditation, and eventually, he attained self-realization and became a great devotee of Lord Vishnu.

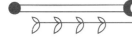 

Additionally, in Hinduism, the concept of "astral travel" during sleep is a significant aspect of spirituality and dream interpretation. It is believed that during sleep, the soul can leave the body and travel to different realms, including the celestial and divine realms. This astral travel is said to be a way for the soul to communicate with the divine and receive guidance, insight, and blessings. For example, it is believed that a person can have a dream in which they meet a deity or receive a message from the divine, which can provide them with guidance and direction in their waking life. The idea of astral travel is also connected to the concept of the "subconscious mind" in Hinduism, which is seen as a storehouse of repressed desires, fears, and unresolved emotional conflicts. By exploring the subconscious mind during astral travel, a person can gain insight into their own thoughts, feelings, and desires, and work towards resolving any emotional conflicts they may have.

Moreover, the dream of Lord Rama, as described in the Hindu epic Ramayana, is another example of the importance of dreams and spiritual enlightenment and self-realization. In the story, Lord Rama has a dream in which Lord Vishnu appears to him and informs him of his divine destiny as the prince of Ayodhya and the future king of India. This dream provided Lord Rama with guidance and direction and helps to strengthen his resolve and determination in his journey as a prince and a future king.

The interpretation of dreams is also considered to be an important aspect of Hindu astrology, known as Jyotish. Jyotish is a system of astrology originating in ancient India. It is based on the idea that the positions of celestial bodies at the time of a person's birth have a direct influence on their life and destiny. Furthermore, Jyotish is one of the six traditional systems of Indian philosophy and is used for a variety of purposes, including predicting the future,

 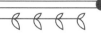

determining compatibility in relationships, and gaining insight into a person's personality and life path. In Jyotish, the positions of the Sun, Moon, and planets at the time of a person's birth are charted and used to create a birth chart, or "horoscope." This horoscope is then used to make predictions and provide guidance in various areas of life, such as career, relationships, health, and spirituality. Jyotish also includes the study of gemstones, mantras, and yantras, which are believed to have the power to enhance the positive effects of the planets and provide protection from negative influences.

Additionally, Jyotish includes the interpretation of dreams, as mentioned earlier, which is an important aspect of Hindu astrology and spirituality. In Jyotish, the timing, frequency, and content of a person's dreams are analyzed to gain insight into their life and future, and to provide guidance and support in their spiritual journey. By paying attention to their dreams and interpreting them, Hindu devotees hope to gain insight into the divine will and receive guidance and blessings in their lives, as was the case with Lord Rama's dream. This, in turn, can lead to personal growth, self-realization, and spiritual enlightenment.

SPIRITUAL DREAMS EXERCISE

Have you ever experienced a dream where a spiritual entity, perhaps an angel or a saint, made an appearance? If so, consider jotting down the details in your dream journal. Take a moment to reflect on the message or interaction that took place. Such dreams can carry profound significance, offering insights or guidance that might be relevant to your waking life. By recording these encounters and exploring their meanings, you create an opportunity to deepen your understanding of your inner self and the connections between your dream experiences and your reality.

DREAMING IN
INDIGENOUS CULTURES

NATIVE AMERICAN TRADITIONS

Many indigenous cultures, such as the Native American tradition, view dreams to receive messages from the spirit world, either from ancestors or other spiritual entities, animals and birds. In these cultures, dream interpretation is a crucial aspect of spiritual life. For example, dreaming about a certain animal can hold symbolic significance and reveal important messages from the spirit world. A dream about a bear for instance might symbolize strength, power, and protection, while a dream about a wolf might symbolize intuition, communication, and loyalty. In this culture, dreams are interpreted based on the individual's personal experiences and cultural beliefs.

For instance, The Dreamcatcher legend is a popular one among the Ojibwe tribe and many other Native American cultures. The symbolism of the dreamcatcher is rooted in Native American spiritual beliefs, and its creation and use are steeped in tradition and symbolism. For many indigenous people, the dreamcatcher is an important symbol of their culture and a reminder of the power of dreams and their connection to the spirit world.

The dreamcatcher is a hoop woven from willow branches and decorated with feathers, beads, and other symbolic items. According to the legend, the dreamcatcher is hung above a person's bed and acts as a filter for their dreams. Good dreams are believed to pass through the holes in the dreamcatcher and slide down the feathers to reach the sleeper, bringing them comfort, insight, and guidance from the spirit world. Meanwhile, bad dreams get tangled in the web of the dreamcatcher and are trapped there, unable to reach the sleeper. When the sun rises, these bad dreams are said to disappear and no longer have any power over the person. The dreamcatcher is often seen as a symbol of protection and is believed to ward off negative energies and help the sleeper have peaceful, restful sleep.

The vision quest is also a traditional Native American spiritual practice. It involves a solitary journey to seek guidance and wisdom from the spirit world. The vision quest is typically undertaken by young people as a rite of passage, or by adults seeking insight and direction in their lives.

During the vision quest, the participant will fast, meditate, and spend time in solitude, usually in a natural setting such as the forest or desert. They may also perform specific rituals or practices to help them enter a deeper state of consciousness and receive messages from the spirit world. One of the key aspects of the vision quest is having powerful dreams. Participants in the vision quest are encouraged to reflect on their dreams and interpret the messages they bring, using the wisdom of their ancestors and their own intuition.

For many indigenous cultures, the vision quest is an important rite of passage and a way to deepen one's connection to the spirit world. The insights gained during the vision quest can have a profound impact on a person's life and help guide their decisions and actions in the future. In this way, the vision quest is seen as a powerful tool for personal growth and spiritual development.

Moreover, The Coyote is a central figure in many Native American stories and is often seen as a trickster, teacher, and shapeshifter. In some cultures, Coyote is a powerful spirit who can bring messages and guidance from the spirit world through dreams. One traditional story about Coyote and dreams is the story of Coyote acquiring the power of flight. According to the story, Coyote dreams that he is soaring through the sky and, when he wakes up, finds that he has the power to fly. From then on, Coyote

uses his newfound power to travel far and wide, teaching and guiding his people and spreading wisdom and laughter.

In this story, Coyote's dream is seen as a powerful source of guidance and insight and is a reminder that dreams can bring important messages from the spirit world. The power of flight symbolizes the ability to move beyond physical limitations and see things from a different perspective and is often interpreted as a metaphor for spiritual growth and transformation. The Coyote, which is a popular figure in Native American folklore, is often used to teach lessons about courage, wisdom, and the importance of being true to oneself.

Animal dreams are a common feature in Native American culture and are often seen to receive messages from the spirit world. Many indigenous cultures believe that animals have unique spiritual qualities and abilities, and that dreaming of specific animals can bring messages that are relevant to a person's life. For example, while dreaming of a bear may symbolize strength and protection, dreaming of an eagle may symbolize spiritual insight and freedom. Dreaming of a snake may symbolize transformation and renewal, while dreaming of a wolf may symbolize loyalty and devotion. Each animal has its own unique symbolism and meaning, and the interpretation of animal dreams can vary depending on the culture and the individual. In general, however, animal dreams are seen to receive guidance and insight from the spirit world and are often interpreted in a positive light.

The buffalo, for instance, is a sacred animal in many Native American cultures, and is seen as a symbol of abundance and nourishment. For example, dreaming of a buffalo may symbolize a new beginning, a sense of abundance in one's life, or the need for strength and protection. In

one traditional story, a young warrior dreams that he is riding on the back of a buffalo, who shows him the path to a great herd of buffalo that will provide for his people. This became known as The Buffalo Dream.

The Buffalo Dream is a term used to describe a powerful and transformative dream that is believed to bring guidance and wisdom from the spirit world. A buffalo dream is often associated with the buffalo hunts, which were a central part of indigenous life and were seen to provide for one's family and community. It symbolizes a new beginning, a sense of abundance in one's life, or the need for strength and protection. It is therefore seen to tap into the strength and abundance of the buffalo, and to receive guidance and support on one's life journey. This connection to the spirit world is vital in native cultures. Dreaming is central to being able to receive guidance and wisdom that can help a person grow and evolve.

THE ABORIGINES OF AUSTRALIA

Similarly, many indigenous cultures have a rich tradition of interpreting dreams and use this understanding to guide their lives. In this tradition, each animal in a dream represents a unique spiritual message, and dream interpretation is a way to gain wisdom and guidance from the spirit world.

Aboriginal people, who have lived in Australia for over 50,000 years, have a rich and diverse cultural heritage, including a deep spiritual connection to the land and a complex belief system cantered around the Dreamtime. The Dreamtime is a term used

to describe a time before time, when the ancestral spirits created the land, animals, and humans, and laid down the laws that govern the world. Dreamtime is believed to be a spiritual realm where the events of the past, present, and future unfold.

The Dreamtime stories, which are passed down from generation to generation through storytelling, songs, and dance, are central to Aboriginal culture and identity. These stories explain the origins of the world and the relationships between people, animals, and the land. They also serve as a source of guidance, teaching important lessons about how to live a good life and care for the land.

Some famous Dreamtime figures and stories include the Rainbow Serpent, who created the rivers and waterways, and Baiame, the Sky Father, who created the first people and gave them their laws. Another famous story is the Tiddalik, the thirsty frog, who drank all the water in the land, causing a drought, until the other animals tricked him into releasing it back into the rivers.

Animals also play a significant role in the Dreamtime stories and are often depicted as spirits or ancestral beings. The Kangaroo, for example, is seen as a powerful and important figure, representing strength and perseverance. The Emu, with its long legs and powerful stride, is seen as a symbol of determination and the ability to cover

great distances. In fact, a link can be assuredly deduced between Aboriginal art and dreams—the creative visual and symbolic interpretation of dreams.

Aboriginal paintings, for example, often use a symbolic language to represent the stories and figures of the Dreamtime. They may use colors, patterns, and shapes to symbolize different elements of the story, such as the land, the ancestral spirits, or the animals. These paintings are often used in rituals and ceremonies and serve to connect with the spiritual world and the ancestral spirits. Folklore art, such as sculptures and carvings, also depict the Dreamtime stories and figures. These works of art are often created for specific purposes, such as to mark a significant event or to serve as a visual representation of a particular story. They may also be used in rituals and ceremonies, serving to connect with the spiritual world and the ancestral spirits.

Through their use of symbolic language and their connection to the spiritual world, these works of art serve to preserve and celebrate the rich cultural heritage of the Aboriginal people. Art serves as a visual language, allowing the artist to convey complex ideas and emotions evoked by a dream. For example, circular shapes are often used to represent the idea of continuity, while straight lines may symbolize the passage of time or the connection between people, animals, and the land. The use of specific colors can also convey different meanings. For example, black may symbolize the Ancestral spirits, while red may represent the earth and the land.

The interpretation of a Dreamtime story through art is a complex and personal process. Each artist has their own unique style and interpretation, and their work may reflect their own cultural background, personal experiences, and beliefs. The art may also reflect the specific cultural traditions of that community, such as the use of specific colors, symbols, and patterns.

SHAPES AND COLORS IN DREAMS EXERCISE

Have you noticed recurring shapes, colors, or animal figures appearing in your dreams? If so, it is a valuable opportunity to embark on the journey of keeping a Dream Journal. As you delve into the following chapters, make sure to record these recurring elements that catch your attention. We will delve deeper into the practice of Dream Journaling in the upcoming chapter, providing you with insights and techniques to unravel the hidden meanings behind these symbols and themes that traverse your dreamscapes. By documenting and reflecting on these consistent motifs, you'll uncover a richer understanding of your inner world and the intricate connections between your dreams and your waking life.

DREAMING IN ANTIQUITY

ANCIENT GREECE

Ancient Greek mythology placed great importance on dreams as a means of communication from the gods. Dreams were believed to be direct messages from the gods and were often interpreted by priests or seers. Many myths and legends feature dream visits from gods such as Zeus, Aphrodite, and Hermes. For example, in the myth of King Midas, Dionysus visits the king in a dream and offers to grant him a wish.

In the myth of King Midas, the king has a dream in which Dionysus appears to him and offers to grant him a wish. King Midas, driven by his greed, wishes that everything he touches would turn to gold. Dionysus grants the wish, but King Midas soon realizes the terrible consequences of his request as he is unable to touch his wife and children or even eat, as everything he touches with his bare hands turns to gold.

The myth of King Midas serves as a cautionary tale about the dangers of wealth and the importance of being careful what one wishes for. King Midas' dream is an example of a powerful dream in ancient Greek mythology that carries a deep message and moral lesson. In another myth, the hero Theseus receives a dream from Athena that guides him on his journey to slay the Minotaur. The dream is a crucial moment in the story of Theseus, as it provides him with the guidance and encouragement, he needs to face the dangerous task ahead.

According to the myth, Theseus is struggling with the decision of whether to embark on the perilous journey to Crete to slay the Minotaur. In his moment of uncertainty, Athena appears to him in a dream and gives him a clear message. She tells him that he is destined to become a great hero and that she will be with him every step of the way,

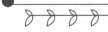

as Odysseus has been away fighting in the Trojan War and then held captive by the nymph Calypso for many years. At the beginning of the Odyssey, Telemachus is a young man who is frustrated with the situation at home and is searching for a way to restore order and find his father. In his moment of uncertainty, Athena appears to Telemachus in a dream and gives him a clear message.

She tells him that he is the son of a great hero and that it is time for him to assert himself and reclaim his heritage. Athena encourages Telemachus to set out on a journey to find news of his father and to gain the knowledge and experience he needs to become the leader that he was born to be.

The interpretation of dreams was a central aspect of ancient Greek religion and culture, and dreams were powerful sources of insight and guidance. It inspires Telemachus to act and sets him on the path towards his goal of finding his father and restoring order to his kingdom.

In addition to dreams, the gods also communicated through oracles, omens, and signs. For example, the famous oracle at Delphi was believed to be a direct link to the gods and was consulted for guidance on important matters.

The Oracle at Delphi was a temple located in the ancient Greek city of Delphi and was one of the most important religious sites in

providing him with the strength and courage he needs to succeed. Theseus is inspired by the dream and sets out on his journey, confident in the knowledge that he has the support of the gods. The dream from Athena serves as a powerful symbol of the intercession of the gods in the lives of mortals and the important role that dreams can play in providing guidance and encouragement.

Dreams were also thought to predict the future. In the Odyssey, the goddess Athena appears to Telemachus in a dream, inspiring him to set out on a journey to find his father, Odysseus.

Telemachus is the son of Odysseus and Penelope and has grown up without a father,

ancient Greece. In addition to its religious significance, the Oracle at Delphi also played a role in the cultural and intellectual life of ancient Greece. Delphi was the center of the known world, and it hosted athletic and musical competitions and served as a gathering place for philosophers and thinkers. The temple at Delphi was dedicated to the god Apollo and was believed to be a direct link to the divine, through which the gods could communicate with mortals.

The Oracle at Delphi was famous for its oracle, a priestess known as the Pythia, who was believed to have the power to receive messages from the gods and to deliver them

to those who sought their guidance. The Pythia would sit on a tripod over a chasm in the temple and enter a trance-like state, during which she would deliver cryptic, often mysterious, messages that were believed to be the words of the gods.

People from all over the ancient world came to Delphi to consult the oracle, seeking guidance on important matters such as wars, political decisions, and personal affairs. The oracle's messages were powerful and authoritative and were often used to make important decisions by both individuals and city-states. However, no matter how significant a dream is, what is even more important about a dream is how it is interpreted! One example of a significant message that was misinterpreted by a king and led to the loss of his kingdom can be found in the myth of King Croesus of Lydia.

According to the myth, King Croesus sought the advice of the Oracle at Delphi to determine whether he should go to war with the neighboring kingdom of Persia. The oracle delivered a cryptic message, saying that "If Croesus goes to war, a great empire will fall." King Croesus misinterpreted the message and believed that the great empire referred to would be that of the Persians, so he went to war confident that he would be victorious. However, the message from the oracle was a warning to King Croesus, as his own empire was the one that would fall. The Persians emerged victorious in the war and King Croesus was captured, leading to the loss of his kingdom and his fall from power.

This myth highlights the importance of interpreting messages from the gods accurately and underscores the dangers of misinterpretation. It serves as a cautionary tale, warning against the dangers of overconfidence and the importance of seeking wisdom and guidance from the gods with humility and respect. However, the interpretations were, to ancient Greeks dreams were seen as messages from the gods, whom they believed that they could visit the dreamer in their sleep. The temple of Aesculapius, the god of medicine, was also a place where people went to receive cures and guidance through dreams.

ANCIENT DREAM THERAPY

Dream therapy was a significant aspect of the healing process at the Temple of Aesculapius, providing patients with guidance, insight, and encouragement as they worked towards healing and self-discovery.

At the Temple of Aesculapius, patients seeking treatment would spend the night in one of the temple's dormitories, where they would receive dreams that were believed to be messages from the god of healing, Aesculapius. These dreams were a crucial part of the healing process, as they provided guidance and insight into the patient's physical and spiritual ailments. Patients would then consult with the temple's priests and practitioners to interpret their dreams and to receive further guidance and treatment.

For example, a patient with a physical ailment might dream of a serpent, which was a symbol of Aesculapius and of healing in ancient Greek culture. This dream might be interpreted as a message from the god, indicating that the patient was on the path to healing. In this way, the dream would serve as a source of encouragement and motivation for the patient, helping them to continue their journey towards recovery.

Similarly, a patient with a spiritual ailment might dream of a labyrinth, symbolizing the complexity of their inner life and the challenges they face. This dream might be interpreted as a message from Aesculapius, encouraging the patient to embark on a journey of self-discovery and to seek help in navigating their inner world.

One example of dream therapy at the Temple of Aesculapius in ancient Greece is the story of a man named Agamemnon. Agamemnon was a soldier who suffered from a persistent and debilitating injury, which left him unable to serve in battle. Desperate for a cure, he turned to the Temple of Aesculapius for help.

DREAM INCUBATION EXERCISE

If you were to spend a few nights at the Temple of Aesculapius for dream therapy, what specific guidance or insights would you seek? Reflect on the areas of your life that you would like to explore or gain clarity on. Are there pressing questions about your career, relationships, personal growth, or any challenges you are facing? Jot down these questions in your dream journal. They will serve as a compass for directing your dreams later. This exercise helps you set a clear intention for your dream experiences and opens the door to receiving valuable insights that can assist you in navigating your waking life.

Agamemnon spent the night in the temple's dormitory, where he received a dream that was believed to be a message from Aesculapius. In his dream, he saw a vision of the god holding a staff, which was a symbol of healing in ancient Greek culture. The dream was interpreted by the temple's priests and practitioners as a message from the god, indicating that Agamemnon was on the path to healing.

Inspired by his dream, Agamemnon underwent a series of treatments at the temple, including physical therapy, herbal remedies, and spiritual guidance. He also spent time in meditation and contemplation, seeking to understand the meaning of his dream and to deepen his connection with the divine.

Through this process of dream therapy, Agamemnon was eventually able to overcome his injury and to return to full health. He was able to resume his duties as a soldier and went on to become a hero of the ancient Greek wars.

Modern "dream therapy," if you like, has its roots in such ancient traditions and

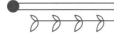

cultures, including Ancient Greece. It is a form of therapy that utilizes the content and symbols of a person's dreams to promote healing and self-discovery.

MESOPOTAMIA

The earliest recorded dream in history can be found in the ancient civilizations of Mesopotamia, which dates to around 2000 BCE. In this civilization, dreams were messages from the gods and were recorded in cuneiform writing on clay tablets. One of the most famous examples of these recorded dreams is the "Epic of Gilgamesh," a Babylonian epic poem that dates to around 2100 BCE. This epic poem contains several dreams experienced by its central character, Gilgamesh, including a dream in which he is visited by the god Shamash, who warns him of an upcoming danger.

Gilgamesh dreamt that an axe fell from the sky. The people gathered around it in admiration and worship. Gilgamesh threw the axe in front of his mother and then he embraced it like a wife. In this dream, the axe symbolizes a powerful person who will initially be seen as a threat to Gilgamesh but will eventually become a close friend and ally. The act of embracing the axe, according to his mother, Ninsun, who interpreted his dream; represents the transformation of

aggression into affection and camaraderie.

This interpretation of the dream is significant because it demonstrates the idea that dreams can provide insight into future events and relationships. It also shows the importance of interpreting symbols and themes in dreams to gain a deeper understanding of their meaning. The idea that a dream can be solved, as Ninsun puts it, highlights the idea that the purpose of a dream

is not only to provide information but also to provide guidance and resolution to the dreamer. Gilgamesh would struggle with him and try to overpower him, but he would not succeed. Eventually they would become close friends and accomplish great things. Ninsun added: "That you embraced him like a wife means he will never forsake you. Thus, your dream is solved."

This approach to dream interpretation is like the contemporary approach to dream analysis, which views dreams to gain insight into one's unconscious thoughts and desires. Ninsun's interpretation also anticipates a contemporary approach. The axe, phallic and aggressive, symbolizes for a male who will start as aggressive but turn into friend. To embrace an axe is to transform aggression into affection and camaraderie. The interpretation of the dream also highlights the idea that dreams can be used as a tool for personal growth and development, and that they can provide important information about one's relationships and prospects.

Moreover, the person that Gilgamesh eventually befriended in the "Epic of Gilgamesh" is Enkidu. Enkidu was originally created as a wild man to challenge and distract Gilgamesh, but after a series of adventures together, the two eventually become close friends and allies.

Together, Gilgamesh and Enkidu undertake several heroic feats, including defeating the monster Humbaba and killing the Bull of Heaven. Their friendship and adventures are considered one of the central themes of the story and demonstrate the idea that dreams can provide insight into future relationships and events. The friendship between Gilgamesh and Enkidu is often seen as a symbol of the power of friendship and the transformative nature of dreams.

However, after the death of his friend, Gilgamesh embarks on a quest seeking the secret of immortality. Even then, as early as 2000 BC humanity was curious about a spiritual connection, visions of the afterlife and the source of spiritual guidance. The Epic of Gilgamesh says that this quest leads Gilgamesh to the realm of the gods, which is depicted as a place of great beauty and power, where the gods live in luxury and have access to the secrets of the universe. It is also a place of danger and challenge, as Gilgamesh must overcome many obstacles to reach Utnapishtim and learn the secret of immortality.

In the epic, the secret of immortality is guarded by Utnapishtim, a wise and ancient king who was granted immortality by the god Ea as a reward for his virtuous deeds. Gilgamesh travels to the realm of the gods and meets Utnapishtim, who tells him the story of a great flood that devastated the world and how he (Utnapishtim) was able to survive it and attain immortality as a reward for his resolve and good deeds.

After the death of his friend Enkidu, Gilgamesh becomes obsessed with the idea of finding the secret of immortality and sets out on a journey to find it. He faces many challenges and obstacles along the way, but he remains determined to find the secret of immortality and overcome his own mortality. Despite his efforts, however, Gilgamesh ultimately fails to attain immortality and returns to the mortal world, where he must come to terms with his own mortality.

The story of Gilgamesh's quest for immortality is often seen as a meditation on the themes of mortality and the human condition and serves as an important example of ancient Mesopotamian mythology and storytelling. Through his journey, Gilgamesh learns important lessons about life and death, and ultimately must come to terms with his own mortality. Additionally, what is interesting is that the "Epic of Gilgamesh" makes a distinction between dreams and visions, and these are portrayed as distinct and separate phenomena in the epic. Dreams are depicted as more passive and unconscious experiences, often coming to a person as they sleep. Visions, on the other hand, are portrayed as more active and deliberate experiences that are often the result of direct divine intervention.

For instance, Gilgamesh has a vision of the underworld and the spirits of the dead. In this vision, he sees the ghosts of those who have died and are now condemned to live out their existence in the realm of the dead. This vision is significant because it serves to emphasize the idea of mortality and the inevitability of death, and it also provides Gilgamesh with a sense of the transience of life.

Another example of a vision in the epic is when Utnapishtim, the survivor of the great flood, has a vision of a great bird that comes to him bearing an olive branch. This vision is seen as a message from the gods and is interpreted to mean that the gods have repented of their decision to destroy the world with the great flood. This vision is significant because it serves to provide hope and a sense

of renewal, and it also suggests that the gods are willing to listen to the prayers and pleas of mortals.

ANCIENT EGYPT

Dreams have been an important part of Ancient Egyptian culture too, for thousands of years. The earliest recorded dreams from Ancient Egypt date back to the Old Kingdom (26th-22nd centuries BCE). They were documented on a variety of different materials including papyri, tomb inscriptions, and temple walls. According to J.S. Lincoln, author of *The Dream In Primitive Cultures* (London, Cressett, 1935), People with vivid and significant dreams were thought to be blessed and were considered special.

One of the most famous examples of an Ancient Egyptian dream is that of the prince Thutmose IV, recorded on the Dream Stele, which was erected in front of the Sphinx at Giza. According to the inscriptions on the stele, Thutmose IV dreamt that the Sphinx spoke to him, promising to make him pharaoh if he cleared away the sand that was burying his statue.

In Ancient Egypt, dreams were often considered to be messages from the gods or a way for the deceased to communicate with the living. Many people would consult with dream interpreters or scribes to decipher the meaning of their dreams, and some even believed that certain dreams had the power to predict the future.

Another recorded dream in Ancient Egypt which was believed to predict the future, is the dream of King Thutmose III. Recorded on the Temple of Amun at Karnak, in the dream, the god Amun appeared to Thutmose III and told him that he would become the next ruler of Egypt, even though he was not the first in line to the throne at the time. The interpretation of this dream was seen as a divine confirmation of Thutmose III's future rule, and he went on to become one of the most successful pharaohs in Egyptian history.

These examples show how dreams were often interpreted as oracles, direct messages from the gods. The Ancient Egyptians

believed that by paying attention to their dreams, they could gain important insights and guidance, which could shape the course of their personal and political lives. "They thought that the best way to receive divine revelation was through dreaming and thus they would induce, or "incubate" dreams.

People would often go to temples to seek guidance through dreams and to sleep in the hopes of having a dream that would provide insight or direction. It was quite common for an Egyptian to go to a sanctuary, sleep on special "dream beds" and hope to receive advice, comfort, or healing from the gods; according to *Languages of dreaming: Anthropological approaches to the study of dreaming In other cultures*, by J. Gackenback, and A. Sheikh (New York 1991, Baywood).

DREAM INCUBATION

Dream incubation was an important aspect of ancient Egyptian religious and cultural life, and these dream temples played a significant role in this practice. They were seen as places where people could receive divine guidance through their dreams, and they were often associated with specific gods or goddesses who were associated with dreams, healing, and divination.

The practice of dream incubation involved several steps. Firstly, the dreamer would visit a temple or sacred site and make an offering or perform a ritual to the gods, asking for a dream that would provide guidance or healing. Then, the dreamer would sleep in the temple or sacred site, often on a specially designated sleeping platform or bed. Finally, the dreamer would record their dream upon waking and seek interpretation from a priest or oracle.

These temples were known as "dream temples" because they

were associated with the practice of dream incubation. This involved people sleeping in the temple with the intention of having a dream that would provide guidance or healing. Dream temples were dedicated to a variety god as people did not attribute the power of their dreams to just one deity. Dream temples were open to everyone, regardless of their social status. The only requirement was to believe in their chosen god and a to be in a state of purity.

The process of purification could have involved engaging in rituals like fasting or cleansing to prepare for the dream journey. They believed by preparing for the dream, they would be closer to the gods and would be more likely to receive a divine message through their dreams. Purification, in some cases, would include having the dreamer perform rituals or offerings to the gods in the hopes of receiving a dream that would provide insight or guidance. Afterwards, the priests at the temples would often interpret the dreams and offer guidance or treatment based on the dream's symbolism.

The interpretation of the dream was a crucial part of the dream incubation process. The priests or oracles would use symbols, images, puns and word meanings. Additionally, the examination of the dreamer's physical and emotional state, and the comparison of the dream to other events and experiences in the dreamer's life. They dream would then be "decoded" to provide guidance or treatment. The treatment could include offerings, sacrifices, or other rituals to the gods, or practical advice for the dreamer's life.

There were several dream Temples in ancient Egypt, such as The Temple of Ptah at Memphis, which was dedicated to the god Ptah and was known as a place for dream incubation. Also, The Temple of Aesculapius at Per-Wadjet (known today as Edfu), which was dedicated to the god Aesculapius, the Greek god of medicine, and was known for its dream healing practices. Moreover, The Temple of Imhotep at Saqqara, which was dedicated to the god Imhotep, the patron saint of medicine and architecture, and was also known for its dream healing practices. In addition to The Temple of Hathor at Dendera, which was dedicated to the goddess Hathor and was known for its dream oracle practices. These are just a few examples of the dream temples in ancient Egypt. These temples played an important role in ancient Egyptian religious and cultural life, and they were often associated with specific gods or goddesses who were associated with dreams, healing, and divination.

An ancient Egyptian would say a prayer, or a spell to induce a dream. The spell was often recited before sleeping, and it called

upon various gods, including Thoth, the moon god Khonsu, and the goddess of sleep and dreams, Nephthys, to grant vivid and meaningful dreams. The spell also included specific requests for specific types of dreams, such as dreams of healing or dreams of guidance.

However, ancient Egyptians were known to be polytheists. That is, they believed in the existence of many gods, each with their own specific responsibilities, powers and personalities. These gods were believed to control various aspects of nature and human life, such as the sun, the moon, the sky, fertility, health, and the afterlife. Ancient Egyptians would pray to different gods for different purposes, such as asking for protection, guidance, blessings, or healing. They also believed that the gods could be appeased or pleased through offerings, sacrifices, and other acts of worship. These religious practices were an integral part of daily life in ancient Egypt, and many temples and shrines were built to honor the gods.

For example, they would pray to Ra, the sun god, for light, life, and wisdom, and to Osiris, the god of the underworld, for a safe journey through the afterlife. They would also pray to Anubis, the god of mummification, for protection during death and to help preserve the body for the afterlife. Additionally, they would pray to Hathor, the goddess of fertility, for blessings in childbirth and to Sobek, the god of the Nile, for abundance and prosperity.

Furthermore, there were several gods associated with dreams in Ancient Egyptian religion. Examples include Khnum, who was a creator god who was responsible for the formation of children in the womb. He was also believed to help people sleep, and dreams were said to be a way of communicating with him.

Serapis, who was the god of dreams and was thought to have the power to prophesize the future. People would visit his temple to sleep and ask him for dream guidance. Additionally, Rem, who was the god of dreams and sleep. He was believed to have the power to send messages through dreams. And Iah, who was the god of the moon and was also associated with dreams, sleep, and protection during the night. However, they had a rich pantheon of gods and goddesses, and each deity was associated with specific aspects of life, such as the sun, the moon, fertility, death, and so on.

They believed that the gods had the power to influence their daily lives, so they prayed to several gods for various purposes, such as asking for protection, guidance, and blessings. For example, they would pray to Ra, the sun god, for light, life, and wisdom, and to Osiris, the god of the underworld, for a safe journey through the afterlife. They

would also pray to Anubis, the god of mummification, for protection during death and to help preserve the body for the afterlife. Additionally, they would pray to Hathor, the goddess of fertility, for blessings in childbirth and to Sobek, the god of the Nile, for abundance and prosperity.

DREAM SPELLS

Ancient Egyptians were deeply religious, and prayer was an integral part of their daily lives, as they sought the favor and guidance of their gods. They would compose a dream prayer, or a spell, asking their favorite God to send guidance in a dream. While the exact text of a dream spell or prayer, is not well-preserved nor documented, if one were to compose such a prayer, by drawing on similar references found in several ancient Egyptian texts, especially *The Book of The Dead*, a dream invocation would be something like this, beginning with the name of the god appealed to (Thoth was the god of knowledge):

Oh Thoth, scribe of the gods,
Who writes the dreams of all who sleep,
Grant me a dream that I may know
The secrets hidden in my heart.

Oh Khonsu, lord of the moon,
Who governs sleep and dreams,
Bless me with sweet and peaceful slumber,
That my dreams may be bright and clear.

Oh Nephthys, protectress of sleep,
Who guides the dreamers on their journey,
Lead me to the truths I seek,
And reveal to me the secrets of the night.

May I dream of healing, of joy, of peace,
And may my dreams bring me knowledge
    and light.
So be it.

DREAM INVOCATION EXERCISE

While the preceding example of an invocation is crafted for illustrative purposes, a personalized dream invocation can serve as a powerful tool to channel your intentions towards the guidance you seek through your dreams. Take a moment to create a dream invocation that resonates with your unique language and style.

Craft a statement that clearly articulates the insights or answers you wish to receive during your dream journey. You can use this opportunity to express your intentions, whether they revolve around solving a particular challenge, gaining insight into a relationship, or tapping into your creativity. Writing this invocation in your own words and storing it in your Dream Journal further solidifies your commitment to seeking meaningful guidance through your dreams.

_____

_____

_____

_____

_____

CHAPTER 2

HOW YOUR DREAM IS FORMED

Dreams serve as a profound bridge between the realms of the physical and the spiritual, allowing us to bring the wisdom of our eternal souls into the visible realm of our everyday lives. When we delve into the realm of dreams, our physical body takes a backseat, temporarily relinquishing its dominance to our invisible, spiritual or astral body. It is within this ethereal state that we embark on journeys beyond the confines of our physical reality. During these dream journeys, we explore alternative scenarios and encounter different dimensions, transcending the limitations imposed by our waking existence. In these mystical realms, we receive invaluable information and insights that often elude us in our conscious state. Our dreams become a channel through which we recharge our spirits, gain wisdom, and ultimately comprehend the hidden facets of our own souls.

By venturing into the land of dreams, we establish a profound connection with our spiritual selves. It is a space where the invisible becomes visible, and the intangible aspects of our being manifest in tangible ways. Through this extraordinary connection, we begin to unravel the secrets held within our souls, gaining a deeper understanding of our true essence and purpose. Dreams are not merely fleeting night-time occurrences; they hold immense power and significance. Ignoring or neglecting them means missing out on a significant portion of our life's potential. By acknowledging and embracing the messages and revelations brought forth by our dreams, we unlock the door to a world where the invisible and visible intertwine, offering us boundless opportunities for growth, self-discovery, and spiritual development.

When we enter the realm of sleep, a remarkable shift occurs within our brains. No longer burdened with the immediate task of safeguarding our physical well-being, the brain redirects its focus towards a different endeavor—reorganizing and restructuring itself. While awake, the brain is constantly engaged in protecting and preserving our bodily functions, ensuring our survival in the external world. However, during sleep, it seizes the opportunity to prioritize internal processes, such as consolidating memories, integrating new information, and making sense of the vast array of experiences we encounter while awake.

As the conscious mind takes a temporary leave, the sleeping brain becomes a bustling hub of activity, tirelessly sorting and categorizing the influx of data it has received throughout the day. It sifts through memories, discards what is deemed insignificant, and strengthens the neural connections associated with important information.

Moreover, this reorganization is essential for enhancing our cognitive abilities, optimizing learning, and facilitating problem-solving. Additionally, research indicates that the brain undergoes distinct changes in circuitry and brainwave patterns during sleep, reflecting different states of consciousness. While awake, the brain operates in a state characterized by beta and gamma brainwave frequencies, associated with active cognition and external focus. However, as we transition into sleep, the brain enters specific stages, such as non-rapid eye movement (NREM) and rapid eye movement (REM) sleep, each with its own characteristic brainwave patterns.

If you like, the brain's nocturnal efforts extend beyond mere reorganization. It delves into the realm of the subconscious, where hidden insights and dormant knowledge reside. By tapping into these depths, the sleeping brain unravels connections and patterns that may have eluded us during wakefulness. It weaves together fragments of information and experiences, shedding light on intricate aspects of ourselves and our world that may have remained hidden in the wake of our bustling lives. During NREM sleep, the brain exhibits slower brainwave frequencies, such as theta and delta waves, signifying deep relaxation, memory consolidation, and restoration. In REM sleep, which involves rapid eye movements and vivid dreaming, the brain shows brainwave patterns like wakefulness, with faster frequencies resembling beta waves. These distinct brainwave patterns reflect the brain's shift in circuitry and neural connectivity during sleep.

These changes in brainwave patterns and circuitry allow different regions of the brain to communicate and synchronize, forming unique networks that facilitate crucial functions such as memory consolidation, emotional processing, and information integration. By adapting to different brainwave frequencies and circuitry during sleep, the brain can engage in internal processing and analysis without the immediate demands of external sensory input and motor responses. Moreover, brainwaves are like the rhythmic electrical pulses that flow through your brain, evidence of its constant activity. These waves emerge when groups of neurons communicate by sending bursts of electrical signals to one another. This communication is happening all the time as your brain engages in various functions like thinking, concentrating, and remembering.

These brainwave patterns, or rhythms, reflect different states of consciousness, ranging from deep dreamless sleep to moments of blissful ecstasy. They can be both fast and slow, with fast waves having low magnitude or power, known as amplitude, and slower waves having larger amplitude. The speed of brainwaves is measured in frequency, expressed as cycles per second, or Hertz. Researchers have discovered that a fully functioning brain can generate up to 10 watts of electrical power. When you are awake and alert, your brain is buzzing with activity, resulting in faster brainwaves. However, when you feel sleepy or bored, the waves tend to slow down. In terms of amplitude, fast brainwaves have low amplitude, while slower waves have higher amplitude.

Understanding the different frequencies and amplitudes of brainwaves provides insights into the dynamic nature of your brain's activity. It reveals the varying levels of engagement and attentiveness throughout your waking and sleeping states. By delving into the intricacies of brainwave patterns, we gain a deeper understanding of the remarkable power and potential of the human mind (see figure 1).

These findings emphasize the intricate nature of our sleep-wake cycles and highlight the brain's multifaceted role in supporting cognitive processes, memory consolidation, and overall well-being. Understanding these changes in brain activity during sleep provides valuable insights into the brain's remarkable capacity to adapt and perform vital functions throughout our sleep cycles.

Moreover, brainwaves are measured using Electroencephalography (EEG) and magnetoencephalography (MEG). The procedure entails placing electrodes or sensors into your head to measure brain activity. All humans have the same four brainwave states. Men, women, and children of all ages all experience the same characteristic brainwaves.

(λ)
WAVELENGTH

AMPLITUDE
(POWER)

TIME

ONE OSCILLATION
(FREQUENCY IS NUMBER OF
OSCILLATIONS PER SECOND)

Brainwaves frequency and amplitude

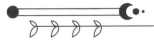 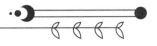
Brainwaves are like a universal language that transcends cultural boundaries and nationalities. They represent different states of consciousness, each with its own unique characteristics. Let's explore these brainwave states from slowest to quickest:

TYPES OF BRAINWAVES		
GAMMA WAVES 40 to 100 Hz.	Process information from various brain areas, conscious perception, high focus and concentration, learning.	These are the fastest of the brainwaves. Highly focused. • Cognitive enhancement • Attention to detail, aids memory recall. • Encourages a different way of thinking, which is a sign of creativity.
BETA WAVES 12 to 40 Hz. These are the most common daytime brainwaves.	Beta waves are dominant in normal wakeful states, and when you are focused on cognitive tasks, such as problem-solving or decision making.	Awake, focused, daily activity, attention; anxiety (higher 22Hz). • Focused attention. • Solving problems. • Stimulates action. • High-level cognition.
ALPHA WAVES 8 to 12 Hz	Alpha waves are involved in how we think, feel, communicate, sleep and generally function.	Very relaxed, awake, passive attention. • Reduces stress. • Encourages positive thinking. • Increased learning abilities • Engagement with environment, feeling in the flow.
THETA WAVES 4 to 8 Hz	Theta waves also occur during sleep, and in very deep states of meditation.	• Deep relaxation. • Meditation. • Creativity.
DELTA WAVES 0.5 to 4 Hz	Delta waves are the slowest brainwaves and occur in the deepest states of sleep.	• Deep Sleep. • Healing & pain relief. • Meditation • Anti-aging: decreases cortisol/increases DHEA. • Accessing unconscious.

Types of brainwaves

Delta State

This is the slowest brainwave frequency during deep dreamless sleep. Delta waves have the lowest frequency, typically ranging from 1.5 to 4 cycles per second. They are strongest during this state, reflecting a state of restful slumber.

Theta State

When you are fully relaxed or lightly asleep, your brain produces theta waves. These waves have a slower frequency, ranging from 5 to 8 cycles per second. Theta waves are associated with deep relaxation, daydreaming, and creative thought. It is a state where fresh ideas often emerge, such as when driving on the highway or engaging in repetitive tasks.

Alpha State

Alpha waves are generated when you are in a calm and relaxed state. They have a cycle rate of 9-14 cycles per second, with larger amplitudes. Alpha waves are present when you take a break from a task, meditate, or engage in leisurely activities. They reflect a state of calmness and relaxation.

Beta State

Beta waves occur when your brain is stimulated and mentally active. They have a frequency range between 12 and 40 Hz, indicating a focused mind. Beta waves are dominant during awake and alert states when you are engaged in everyday routines, decision-making, or having conversations.

Gamma State

The fastest brainwave frequency is gamma waves, which reflect peak concentration and intense mental activity. They are challenging to measure with current equipment but indicate that your brain is actively processing information and seeking solutions. Gamma waves are associated with states of deep concentration, problem-solving, and heightened cognitive functioning.

Understanding these brainwave states allows us to train ourselves to enter specific states of consciousness. For example, by slowing down our breathing and focusing our attention, we can enter a meditative state such as alpha, which enables us to tap into our psychic abilities. Research suggests that practices like meditation and binaural sound beats can help increase gamma wave production.

It is important to note that different meditation techniques and breathing rhythms can produce various results. By tracking your experiences and progress in a psychic development journal, you can determine which meditation style and brainwave state benefits

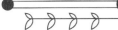 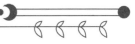
you the most. Additionally, meditation has numerous health benefits, including stress reduction and improved well-being.

Throughout the day, your brain produces different types of brainwaves depending on your level of consciousness and attention. By becoming aware of these brainwave states, you can learn to relax, activate your dream-inducing abilities, and harness the power of your mind.

Finally, Dream formation is a complex and fascinating process that occurs during sleep, specifically during the rapid eye movement (REM) stage of sleep. While the exact mechanisms are not fully understood, researchers have put forth several theories to explain how dreams are formed.

One prominent theory is the activation-synthesis theory proposed by psychiatrists J. Allan Hobson and Robert McCarley. According to this theory, dreams are the result of random neural activity in the brain stem and other areas of the brain during REM sleep. This activity triggers the activation of various brain regions, including those associated with emotions, memories, and sensory experiences.

As these different brain regions are activated, the cerebral cortex, which is responsible for higher cognitive functions, attempts to make sense of these neural signals. It creates a narrative or story by synthesizing the random neural activity and integrating it with stored memories, emotions, and experiences. This process gives rise to the vivid and often surreal experiences we perceive as dreams.

Another theory, known as the cognitive theory of dreaming, suggests that dreams serve a purpose in processing and consolidating information from our waking experiences. According to this theory, dreams reflect our thoughts, concerns, and emotions, and they help us make sense of and integrate new information into our existing knowledge and memories. Dreams may also provide a way for the brain to problem-solve, explore different scenarios, and simulate potential future events.

Neuroscientific research has also revealed the involvement of various neurotransmitters and brain structures in dream formation. For example, the release of certain neurotransmitters, such as acetylcholine, serotonin, and norepinephrine, plays a role in regulating REM sleep and influencing dream content.

Dream formation is therefore a dynamic process that involves the interplay of neural activity, memory consolidation, emotions, and cognitive processes. While the precise nature and purpose of dreams continue to be explored and debated, they remain a fascinating and mysterious aspect of human consciousness.

YOUR PERSONAL
DREAM PROCESS

The way your dreams are formed is personal to you. Dreams reflect your own fears and hopes, your mental construct or belief system, emotions and understanding of your life's experiences. In other words, the wisdom you gained as you live your life. This process of understanding takes place in your subconscious mind and forms the language of your dreams. Your brain continues to process as you sleep. It never stops working! And, as you dream, your subconscious mind communicates with you. If you like, your conscious mind is out of the way, and the unconscious begins to communicate with you freely. It brings up issues that have made an impression on your mind, but you did register them! So, your dreams, bring to your attentions experiences that have not been "archived" or processed consciously within your mind.

Indeed, the interpretation and meaning of dreams can vary significantly from person to person. Each dream is a personal experience, and its significance is influenced by an individual's unique thoughts, emotions, memories, and life experiences. The mind's language, or internal symbolism, differs from person to person, leading to diverse interpretations of the same dream content.

When we dream, our subconscious mind creates a symbolic language to convey messages, emotions, and subconscious desires. This symbolic language is based on our personal associations and experiences. For example, a dream about a cat may hold different meanings for different individuals. For one person, it may symbolize independence and intuition, while for another person, it may represent fear or anxiety due to a childhood trauma involving a cat.

The mind's dictionary or internal symbolism is built over a lifetime through personal experiences, cultural influences,

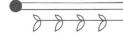 
and individual beliefs. It includes symbols, events, and people that hold specific meaning to everyone. Therefore, when two people have an identical dream, their interpretations may diverge because the symbols and events in the dream are filtered through their unique internal symbolism.

Additionally, dreams are highly subjective experiences. They reflect an individual's inner world, emotions, conflicts, and desires. The same dream can evoke different emotions and reactions in different people based on their personal circumstances. For example, a dream about falling may be exhilarating and exciting for one person, symbolizing a sense of adventure, while it may evoke fear and anxiety for another person, reflecting a fear of losing control.

To fully understand and interpret a dream, it is essential to consider the dreamer's personal associations, feelings, and life context. Dream analysis techniques, such as

keeping a dream journal, exploring personal symbols, and engaging in self-reflection, can help individuals uncover the deeper meanings and insights embedded in their dreams. Therefore, the uniqueness of everyone's mind and their personal experiences shapes the interpretation and meaning of dreams. The mind's language, or internal symbolism, varies from person to person, making each dream a personal and individualized experience with its own significance

and interpretation. This is also because your brain does a process referred to as "chunking" which is personal to your brain.

Chunking is a cognitive process that involves organizing and grouping information in your brain into meaningful units, or "chunks," to enhance memory and cognitive efficiency. It allows you as an individual to overcome the limitations of your working memory by grouping related pieces of information together, reducing the cognitive load and facilitating easier recall and processing. When we encounter large amounts of information, such as a long series of numbers or a complex set of words, our working memory can become overwhelmed. However, by employing chunking, we can break down the information into smaller, more manageable chunks.

Chunking, moreover, relies on our ability to identify patterns, relationships, or meaningful associations within the information. By grouping individual items together based on these associations, we can remember and process larger amounts of information more effectively. For example, when trying to remember a long string of numbers like "7-1-9-4-1-6-8-2-5," we can chunk them into meaningful groups like "719," "416," and "825," which are easier to remember. It is often used in various domains, including mathematics, music, language learning,

and problem-solving. It allows individuals to organize information in a way that aligns with their existing knowledge and mental frameworks, making it easier to encode, store, and retrieve the information later.

Furthermore, chunking can enhance our understanding and comprehension of complex concepts by highlighting the relationships and connections between different pieces of information. It enables us to focus on the underlying meaning and structure rather than getting overwhelmed by individual details. Just as chunking helps us process and remember information in our waking lives, it also plays a fascinating role in the formation of our dreams. When we dream, our minds draw upon the vast reservoir of knowledge and experiences we have accumulated throughout our lives. Just like chunking relies on existing information to create meaningful chunks, dreams often incorporate familiar symbols, events, and people that are deeply rooted in our personal dictionaries. This allows our dreams to make use of what we have acquired, weaving together a tapestry of images and narratives that reflect our individuality.

In the realm of dreams, chunking becomes a subconscious process of organizing and connecting the fragments of our experiences both conscious and unconscious. The mind seamlessly combines various elements from our memories, emotions, and perceptions to construct dream scenarios. As we sleep, our brains engage in a remarkable dance of chunking, linking related pieces of information to create cohesive dream narratives. Just as chunking helps us make sense of complex information in our waking state, it aids in the formation of dream sequences, allowing our minds to weave together a rich tapestry of symbols and meanings unique to everyone. Remembering that the main objective of our brain is to preserve our safety and help us predict outcomes to obstacles by finding solutions; dreams serve as a playground for the mind, where chunking takes center stage.

The mind's language, built upon our personal dictionaries, shapes the symbols and events that appear in our dreams. By utilizing what we have acquired, dreams become a collage of our memories, emotions, desires, and fears. In the mysterious realm of dreams, chunking helps our minds process and connect the fragments of our consciousness, unveiling hidden meanings, insights, and even creative solutions. It is through this process of chunking, drawing upon our personal mental resources, that dreams become a deeply personal and transformative experience, allowing us to explore the depths of our subconscious and gain a deeper understanding of ourselves.

DREAM FORMATION
–A SIMPLIFIED PERSPECTIVE

To simply how dreams are formed, we can say that they are a product of:

1. Your beliefs

2. Your memories

3. Your emotional blueprint (or emotional dynamic), and

4. Your personal perspective (or level of awareness).

5. Current life experiences.

YOUR BELIEFS

Beliefs serve as the foundation upon which our life experiences are constructed. Right from the moment we come into this world, our beliefs start taking shape through the encounters and situations we face. Some of these beliefs are obvious to us, while others remain hidden beneath the surface of our consciousness. During our childhood, when our understanding is still developing, our beliefs start forming based on our emotional encounters and they generate. For instance, if we experience care and nurturing when we're hungry, we begin to develop beliefs like "I am loved" and "I can trust life." These positive experiences lay the groundwork for beliefs that create feelings of security and affection.

On the flip side, encountering neglect or loss at a young age might lead to beliefs rooted in mistrust, a sense of being unsafe

or unloved, or a belief that life is inherently challenging or lacking. As these experiences repeat themselves, they solidify into core beliefs that shape our viewpoints and actions as adults. These beliefs function as filters through which we perceive the world around us. They impact our thoughts, emotions, choices, and behaviors, often operating on a subconscious level. These deeply embedded beliefs, whether positive or negative, influence our relationships, self-image, and overall sense of well-being.

Furthermore, understanding and becoming aware of our beliefs is a pivotal step toward personal growth and transformation. By scrutinizing the fundamental beliefs, we carry, especially those that reside in our subconscious, we can recognize any limiting or harmful patterns that might be constraining us. Through self-examination, dream therapy, or other methods, we possess the ability to challenge and reshape our beliefs, thereby opening ourselves up to fresh possibilities and cultivating a more empowering and gratifying life. More on how to direct your dreams to heal emotionally and mentally in chapter five.

In addition, just as beliefs shape our experiences while awake, they also play a significant role in constructing the narratives of our dreams. Our dreams mirror the beliefs, emotions, desires, fears, and perceptions we hold, both consciously and subconsciously. While navigating the dream realm, our beliefs act as a lens through which we interpret the symbols, situations, and storylines that unfold. The beliefs we have gathered over our lifetime impact the themes, emotions, and meanings that manifest in our dreams, imbuing them with an intensely personal and subjective essence. For instance, when you learn to let go of anxiety and stress, your dreams may evolve into more positive scenarios, altering the very themes that play out in your dreams.

Dreams can offer a unique window into our subconscious beliefs. They grant us insights into the concealed layers of our mind. Fueled by beliefs we might not even be consciously aware of; the subconscious constructs dream scenarios that reflect our deeply ingrained convictions. If, for example, we harbor a subconscious belief that we are unworthy of love, our dreams could manifest as scenarios where we confront rejection or feelings of inadequacy. By paying heed to recurring themes and emotions in our dreams, we can initiate the process of uncovering and delving into the underlying beliefs that form our perceptions of ourselves and the world. Furthermore, dreams hold the potential to challenge and transform our beliefs. During the dream state, we might encounter symbols, events, or characters that

call into question our existing belief systems, inviting us to reconsider our viewpoints and consider different possibilities. Dreams serve as a safe arena to explore and experiment with new beliefs, enabling us to step beyond the confines of our waking reality.

In essence, our beliefs, whether conscious or subconscious, actively shape the structure and content of our dreams. They dictate the themes, emotions, and symbols that materialize in our dream experiences, weaving together a rich tapestry of individual significance. By investigating the correlation between our beliefs and our dreams, we can access valuable insights into our subconscious, challenge limiting beliefs, and embark on a voyage of self-discovery and transformation.

Your Dream Attitude

If you do not usually remember your dreams, it can be that your personal beliefs around dreams, their meaning, or significance are blocking you.

If you often find yourself struggling to remember your dreams, it is worth considering whether your personal beliefs about dreams could be playing a role. Our perspectives on dreams, their meanings, and their importance can affect our ability to recall them. For instance, if you believe that dreams are insignificant or lack

meaning, you might unintentionally disregard them upon waking, making them harder to remember. Similarly, if you think that dreams are random and do not hold any valuable insights, you might not try to remember them.

These beliefs can create a mental barrier that hinders dream recall. By examining and adjusting your beliefs about dreams, you might find that it becomes easier to remember them. Being open to the idea that dreams can offer valuable insights or messages can encourage you to pay more attention to them upon waking. This shift in perspective could lead to a more consistent ability to recall and explore your dreams, potentially unlocking a source of self-discovery and understanding.

Dream Attitude Exercise

The following dream journal exercise can offer a unique window into your own subconscious beliefs. Potentially it can help shed light on your individual perspective about dreams. By paying attention to your immediate reactions, you are tapping into your intuitive responses. The latter, often carry valuable information that might be otherwise overlooked. As you accumulate these insights in your dream journal, you are laying the groundwork for better understanding your own beliefs. This in turn could be impacting your dream experiences.

Your responses can serve as a valuable tool for self-discovery, allowing you to uncover layers of your thought processes and potentially fostering a shift in how you approach and engage with your dreams. For example, one can have negative attitude in any of the following five, or more aspects about dreams:

Skepticism

Believing that dreams are meaningless or random mental processes without any significance or value.

Negative Attitude Statement: "I believe that dreams are meaningless and random."

Dismissiveness

Dismissing dream content as irrelevant or unimportant, failing to explore the potential insights they may offer.

Negative Attitude Statement: "My dreams do not offer any meaningful guidance"

Fear

Being afraid of one's own dreams, particularly nightmares or unsettling dream experiences, and avoiding them altogether.

Negative Attitude Statement: "I am afraid to dream."

Apathy

Demonstrating indifference towards dreams and not making any effort to remember, analyze, or engage with them.

Negative Attitude Statement: "I do not bother to understand the meaning of my dreams."

Lack of Self-Reflection

Failing to see how dreams might reflect aspects of one's own life, emotions, or subconscious thoughts, and ignoring their potential for self-discovery.

Negative Attitude Statement: "My dreams have nothing to do with my real life."

Take a moment to jot down your own doubting attitudes about dreaming. Turn each attitude into a negative statement. Next, read aloud each of your statements and then carefully observe your reaction or response. Then, jot down below, or in your dream journal, your impressions and feelings, and responses within your body as you read or say each negative attitude. Remember that

Aspect	Dream Attitude Statement	Mental response	Emotional response	Physical Experience
Skepticism				
Dismissiveness				
Fear				
Apathy				
Lack of Self-Reflection				

Dream attitude exercise

responses to these common beliefs can be expressed in various ways:

Mentally: what is the first thought that popped into your mind about that statement?

Emotionally: What feeling did it evoke within you as you read the above negative attitude statement?

Physically: What response did you experience

Negative Dream Attitude Statement	Turned Around Dream Affirmation
Example: I believe that dreams are meaningless and random.	My dreams always provide me with clear guidance that I need
(Write your negative attitudes and turn them around into positive affirmations).	

Negative dream attitude turn around

in your body? Where exactly did you feel the response?

You will notice that your responses essentially mirror your attitude. These beliefs play a role in shaping your feelings about dreams, guiding your attention toward areas that have room for improvement. If you discover that certain beliefs are not contributing positively, remember that you can modify them. This is where affirmations come into play. Affirmations are fresh and optimistic statements that represent a new belief. By repeating an affirmation until it integrates into your thought process, you can genuinely influence your dream mindset. For instance, you can turn the above negative attitude statement into positive affirmations that you enforce by repeating as you fall asleep. Work on one statement at a time, then move to turning

around your next negative attitude statement into a positive affirmation (see table above).

Finally, maintaining an open mind and a willingness to explore the meanings and benefits of dreams is crucial. Any negative attitudes can indeed restrict the valuable insights and personal growth that dreams can offer you. On the other hand, embracing a positive and receptive approach to dreams can lead to a deeper understanding of yourself and the world within and around you.

YOUR MEMORIES

Memories are not merely fragments of our past; they are life events that leave imprints on our minds, shaping our perception and influencing our beliefs. From the moment we are born, we begin to formulate beliefs

based on our experiences. Some beliefs are consciously recognized, while others remain hidden in the depths of our subconscious.

As we grow up, we often find ourselves caught up in the busyness of life, leaving little time for reflection and processing of these memories. Especially when it comes to negative memories, we tend to push them to the back of our mental filing cabinet, hoping to forget or avoid them.

However, when our memories and life experiences are not integrated into our conscious understanding, the thoughts associated with them become "disassociated".

These thoughts circle in our minds like an unsettled bee and fling back at us when we least expect them like a ball around the Maypole, especially when we are in a relatively happy or stable phase in our lives, as our mind is ready to deal and cope with the painful stuff (see figure 6)!

These disassociated thoughts, though varied, often lead us to similar conclusions. For example, if we have disassociated thoughts around a negative memory of a break-up, our minds may form a pattern where we repeatedly conclude that we are unworthy of love or that relationships always end in disappointment. Over time, these patterns solidify into what psychotherapy refers to as "main images" or "main beliefs" making those beliefs good material

to explored by your dreams. It is your subconscious mind asking you to integrate this disassociated (painful) past memory to help you make better decisions about the future.

Dreams play a crucial role in the formation and exploration of these memories and beliefs. When experiences are not fully processed or understood, our minds seek to integrate them through the language of dreams. Dreams bring these unresolved experiences to the forefront, offering us a chance to examine them from a new perspective. They serve as a symbolic representation of our inner world, often revealing insights and truths that our conscious mind may have overlooked.

Disassociated thoughts

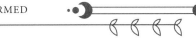

To share a personal example that illustrates this process, in my late thirties, I was involved in a relationship that seemed to be going nowhere. The man I was with was elusive and ambiguous, and yet, I found myself trying to make it work. Unbeknown to me, this dynamic stemmed from an earlier failed relationship that had left an unhealed emotional scar. One night, I had a dream that perfectly encapsulated my underlying feelings and provided a crystal-clear insight. In the dream, the man came over to my place for dinner, but when he saw my family seated around the table, he became surprised, confused, and hastily escaped through the window without acknowledging them. This dream shook me, as it revealed his true character that I had been oblivious to in waking life. It connected with a saying my father used to share: "There are two types of men, a man who comes through the door, and a man who comes through the window." The dream vividly mirrored my internal conflict and validated my intuition.

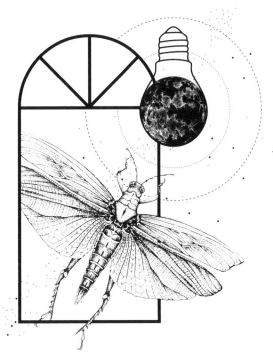

This dream experience exemplifies how our minds utilize dreams to bring unresolved memories and beliefs to the surface. Dreams serve as a gateway for us to explore and understand the hidden layers of our consciousness. By paying attention to our dreams and reflecting on their messages, we can uncover valuable insights, make connections to our past experiences, and initiate transformative healing and growth.

Your memories and your dreams are, therefore, intertwined aspects of your inner landscape. Memories shape and express our beliefs and experiences; while dreams offer a pathway to explore and integrate these memories. Through dream analysis and reflection, we can gain valuable insights, heal unresolved emotions, and transform our beliefs to align with our true selves. Dreams, therefore, serve as a powerful tool for self-discovery and personal growth, inviting you to delve deeper into the realms of your mind and unlock the wisdom within. Simply put, when there is an experience that you have not "filed" yet in the right place, your brain "urges" you to integrate it by throw it at you in the form of a dream, or even a nightmare - if you are not paying attention. Do not be surprised if that happens when you are generally feeling good about your life. I often hear my clients say, *"all of a sudden I had a nightmare, although I feel good, and things are going great."* However, is there a better time to tackle a difficult issue in an objective way than when your life is going well, and you feel safe and secure? Embrace your dreams, they are guiding you to your own self-development and evolution.

YOUR EMOTIONAL BLUEPRINT

Your "emotional blueprint" is a profound concept, a representation of how your brain processes and engraves emotional reactions from your life experiences. Over time, these patterns weave together to form a unique architectural design, akin to a blueprint, that intricately captures the dynamic interplay between your emotions and your mind. This blueprint acts as a living record, reflecting how your responses sculpt the intricate neural pathways, subtly etching emotional marks onto the pages of your life's story. These emotional imprints, much like scars,

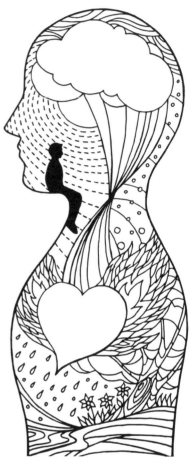

can wield considerable influence over your future decisions, as your brain diligently seeks to steer you away from revisiting painful episodes.

For instance, the chapters of your life narrative may be a blend of achievements and setbacks, leaving you with feelings of disillusionment and a sense of wariness.

Alternatively, you might have frequently encountered instances of abandonment or a lack of support in various realms, whether at work or in relationships. These experiences, even if you are not consciously aware of them, act as an undercurrent that shapes your decision-making. This can manifest as an instinctive tendency to steer clear of committing to new partnerships or venturing into uncharted projects, a natural defense mechanism to shield yourself from potential emotional pain. Unattended, these emotional imprints can subtly lay the foundation for negative mental programming, leading you to make choices that may not align with your best interests, all the while being oblivious to the underlying reasons. Nonetheless, these emotional scars, as intriguing as they are, also provide fertile ground for exploration within your dreams.

Within the realm of dreams, these emotional imprints manifest in captivating and intricate ways. Dreams become a stage where you can subconsciously grapple with these scars, delving into their significance and uncovering hidden meanings. They offer an opportunity to revisit the emotional architecture of your experiences, to analyze, understand, and ultimately rewrite the narrative. By navigating this dream landscape, you embark on a journey of self-discovery, gradually untangling the threads that weave the fabric of your emotional responses, and in doing so, opening the potential for healing, growth, and the creation of a more empowered emotional blueprint for the chapters that lie ahead in your life's story.

Essentially, dreams serve as a powerful workshop for examining and reshaping the intricate contours of your emotional blueprint. Within the realm of dreams, you are provided a unique canvas where you can experiment with diverse scenarios, test alternative responses, and work through unresolved emotional conflicts. This dream landscape becomes a sanctuary, a haven to confront the emotional wounds that might otherwise lurk beneath the surface of your conscious awareness. Through this dream journey, you embark on a transformative adventure, uncovering hidden insights and shedding light on aspects of your emotional architecture that may have remained obscured.

Moreover, it is important to recognize that, much like architectural plans can be adjusted, your emotional blueprint is malleable and can be intentionally modified. Dreams offer a powerful toolkit in this endeavor, granting you the ability to break free from the gravitational pull of repetitive patterns that may have held you captive. The insights gleaned from your dreams can

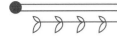

be harnessed to challenge and reshape limiting beliefs, ultimately reconfiguring the course of your emotional responses. This is an empowering process, one that invites you to seize the reins of your emotional narrative and guide it towards a more empowering, fulfilling direction.

So, your emotional blueprint, a cumulative result of your unconscious emotional reactions to life's myriad events, can wield significant influence over your decision-making and overall life trajectory. However, the beauty lies in the fact that dreams offer an accessible pathway for exploration, understanding, and transformation

of this blueprint. By actively engaging with the messages woven into your dreams, you initiate a process of breaking free from negative programming, a journey of emotional healing where old scars can be mended, and where the vast landscape of new possibilities emerges. Embrace the profound potential of your dreams as a catalyst, an agent of change that propels you towards personal growth, enabling you to rewrite your emotional blueprint and craft a life imbued with greater fulfillment and self-awareness.

YOUR PERSPECTIVE

Your perspective is a powerful force, a unique lens that shapes your understanding of life's experiences and determines the meanings you attach to them. This lens is the amalgamation of your conscious thoughts, unconscious biases, and deeply held beliefs (see figure 7). It acts as the filter through which you view the world, influencing not only how you perceive events but also how you react to them emotionally and how you navigate the ever-changing currents of life.

Your perspective is like a lens that helps you make sense of your life experiences, providing a sense of stability and familiarity. However, it's essential to recognize that this lens has its limitations—it's akin to peering through a keyhole, offering a narrow view

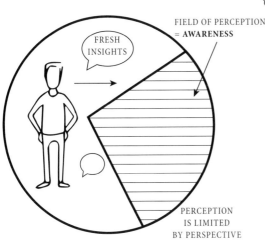

Perspective and field of vision

of the larger reality. Imagine you're looking through a telescope; the lens can focus on one specific part of the night sky, but you might miss the beauty of the entire cosmos. In the same way, your perspective can provide comfort, yet it can also hinder your ability to fully embrace alternative viewpoints or new insights. It serves as both a guide and a potential barrier to exploration.

To overcome these limitations, it is crucial to intentionally expand your field of view, much like widening the lens of your telescope. Creating room for introspection and self-reflection allows you to break free from the confines of your current perspective. Consider this as a mental journey where you venture into uncharted territories of your mind. It involves questioning assumptions, considering diverse interpretations,

and welcoming new information. By actively engaging in this practice, you empower your perspective to evolve, opening to a broader range of viewpoints.

This shift in perspective is not confined to your waking life. It seamlessly extends to the realm of your dreams. When you consciously stretch your mental horizons, you transform your nightly dreamscapes into a dynamic canvas for exploration and self-discovery. Think of your dreams as a vast landscape. By expanding your perspective, you are opening new pathways through it. As you free your mind from the confines of past beliefs, your dreams turn into an interactive playground; where you can unearth deep-rooted patterns, gain profound insights, and even stumble upon ingenious solutions to real-life challenges.

For instance, let us say you have been struggling with self-doubt in your waking life. Your perspective might have you stuck in a cycle of negativity, unable to see your true potential. By intentionally broadening your perspective through activities like journaling or meditation, you begin to realize that your self-doubt stems from limiting beliefs formed during childhood. You may even ask for guidance in your dreams on how to resolve this. The revelation in your dreams, might help you conquer your fears. The opposite is also true. Your self-exploration in

real life, will also be reflected in the stories of your dreams. You might dream of soaring to new heights, for example. Suddenly, your dreams are infused with newfound courage and possibilities, all because you consciously expanded your perspective.

Furthermore, this expanded viewpoint invites you to embrace alternative angles and welcome diverse insights, propelling you into uncharted territories of personal growth. Just as an artist experiment with various colors to create a masterpiece, you too can paint the canvas of your dreams with a multitude of perspectives. This expanded lens enriches your self-awareness, elevates your understanding of emotions, and deepens your appreciation of life's intricacies. It empowers you to see the world from a higher vantage point, catalyzing personal evolution and transformation.

Therefore, your perspective, while comforting, can also be constraining. By intentionally making space for reflection and growth, you are like an explorer charting new territory. This expansion is not limited to your waking hours. This newfound self-awareness seamlessly extends to the dream realm. By widening your perspective, you unlock doors to profound insights and fresh pathways for exploration. As you continuously embrace and challenge your perspective, you open a world of ongoing growth, transformation, and a deeper connection to both your waking and dreaming realities. Finally, when you actively engage in the process of exploring different perspectives and challenging your existing beliefs, you open a treasure trove of possibilities for dream exploration by:

Asking the right questions

Asking the right questions is like activating a search engine for your mind. When you ask meaningful questions about a challenge you're grappling with, you are sending a signal to your subconscious to dig deeper. It is like opening a door to a room full of hidden answers and possibilities. For example, consider a situation where you are uncertain about your career direction. Instead of staying stuck in uncertainty, you begin posing specific questions: *"What other job paths could I explore?"* or *"Which aspects of my current job bring me satisfaction?"*, and *"which ones do not?"* These questions work as signposts, guiding your dreams toward fresh perspectives and potential solutions.

Simply said, when your mind is prompted with questions before sleep, you are setting a target for your dreams. You are essentially saying, "Show me something related to this topic," and your unconscious mind pays attention. Your dream story, in

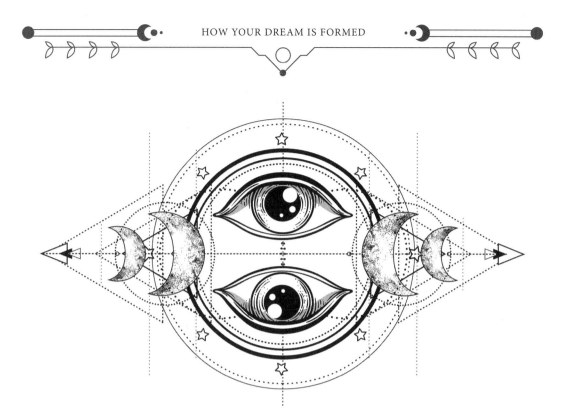

response, might present scenes or symbols that offer insights into your queries. So, by introducing questions into your thoughts before falling asleep, you are steering your dreams towards healing through self-exploration and self-guidance. Effectively, you are asking your mind to seek out insights that might otherwise stay hidden while you are awake, and pre-occupied living your "real life". These insights could materialize as dream scenarios that correspond to your questions. Questioning is not limited to waking hours. It is an effect dream generating tool, that unlocks the vault of your mind's creations.

Seeing the issue from the other point of view

Looking at things from a different angle can be surprisingly enlightening, especially when it comes to your dreams. One powerful technique to provoke unique dream perspectives is, to explore your issue through the eyes of different characters or archetypes. In the realm of dreams, you are not limited to one role—you can step into various shoes to gain fresh insights.

For instance, imagine that you are facing a challenge in a relationship. Instead of just seeing it from your standpoint, you can ask your mind to guide your dreams from the

viewpoint of another person, a friend or a partner. You might dream as if you were your partner, your best friend, or even a neutral bystander. This shift in perspective is like holding a lantern to illuminate hidden corners of your situation. By walking in another's shoes, you can unravel underlying dynamics and unlock creative solutions that might have eluded you before. Suddenly, you would be privy to their thoughts, emotions, and concerns. Such elements might have been obscured in your waking state. This newfound understanding opens doors to insights that can strengthen your relationship or provide clarity on how to address your challenge.

Through this powerful technique, you are not only generating diverse dream experiences, but also broadening your real-world perspective and discovering innovative ways to navigate your life's complexities.

Asking for symbols

Exploring dreams from a metaphorical angle opens an intriguing journey. Dreams often communicate through symbols and metaphors, conveying messages from your subconscious. When you craft questions that invite these symbolic interpretations, your dreams start to reveal their wisdom in a unique way.

If you are considering a personal goal, for example, instead of taking it at face value, ask yourself, "What does this goal symbolize to me?" or "What dream symbols might provide insight into achieving this goal?" These questions set the stage for delving into your dreams, where symbols and metaphors become your guides. It is like solving a puzzle, with each symbol revealing a deeper truth. Moreover, when you pose the right questions, your dreams become a canvas of symbols and metaphors. Think of it as an artist's palette, filled with insights that guide you in solving problems and growing personally. Through this process, your dreams become allies as you navigate your daily life.

For instance, think about a tough decision you are facing. Instead of just thinking about it, ask yourself, "Which dream symbol represents taking this decision?", or "give me a dream where a cup represents the best choice." Such manner of phrasing questions leads your dreams to weave stories rich in symbols. If you recognize or remember the symbol, understand that your dream is pointing you toward the best choice.

By incorporating these techniques into your approach to exploring dreams, you unlock new aspects of self-discovery and effective problem-solving. Embrace different viewpoints, take on various roles, and decipher symbolic language to gain valuable insights. Your dreams become a source of wisdom, offering guidance and clarity as you

navigate life's challenges. By mastering the art of crafting dreams for solving problems, you equip yourself with a powerful tool to unravel life's mysteries.

CURRENT LIFE EXPERIENCES

Your current life experiences, the ongoing situations and events that shape your reality, have a direct influence on your dreams. These experiences leave a fresh imprint on your mind, significantly impacting the content of your dreams. These real-life moments can encompass a broad spectrum of events, ranging from major life changes to transformative phases in your life's journey. They might also include significant milestones such as a new job, marriage, or the loss of a dear one.

In your dreams, these tangible life occurrences often show up as symbols or icons, essential elements that convey messages related to both the physical and emotional aspects of your current state. These dream symbols can take on diverse forms, representing places, people, objects, or even the emotions connected to these real-life situations. For instance, consider the symbolism of a pair of rings, standing for marriage or symbolizing a significant connection to an event.

Given this, it is essential to note down the date and a brief description of what's happening in your "real life" (R.L.) when you document a dream or intend to generate one in response to a specific issue you're aiming to explore. Recognize that when individuals appear in your dreams, the central focus of the dream often isn't solely about those people themselves. Instead, they often serve as symbols or representations of qualities or emotions they signify in your consciousness. Sometimes, they even reflect facets of your own personality.

When analyzing a dream, it is helpful to reflect on the personal significance of the person in the dream and what they represent to you. Your mind frequently chooses these dream figures as a gentle way to convey messages indirectly. However, if these messages go unnoticed, your mind might intensify its efforts, leading to more vivid and occasionally unsettling dreams or nightmares.

For instance, when I first embarked on my journey as a professional psychic over three decades ago, I faced challenges in fully embracing my "gift". In one dream, I found myself in a celebration, handed a deck of Tarot cards by a trusted friend. As I turned, I noticed a woman giving me a disapproving look. I had no familiarity with her, yet her image lingered vividly. Reflecting on the dream, I understood that she symbolized a part of me not entirely at ease with my chosen path, perhaps even harboring some negativity towards it. The contrast between the festive atmosphere and the unsettling gaze made this dream image stand out upon waking.

Clearly, your current life experiences significantly shape your dreams. Symbols and icons rooted in these experiences become vital components within your dreams, delivering messages and insights about the situations you're navigating. The individuals appearing in your dreams often symbolize aspects of your own self or carry metaphorical meanings linked to their roles in your life. By delving into and comprehending these dream messages, you gain valuable insights into your emotions, perceptions, and personal growth. Dreams act as a bridge connecting your conscious and unconscious minds, facilitating deep processing and integration of your experiences.

The Awareness Pyramid

As your understanding grows and you integrate your life experiences, your field of vision expands, leading to a shift in perspective. More will become apparent to you as you change your point of view. Imagine yourself, for example, ascending a metaphorical pyramid of awareness, where each step represents a higher level of consciousness and personal How Dreams Are Formed awareness.

With each upward step, your viewpoint elevates, broadening your perspective and increasing your field of vision.

The awareness pyramid in figure 8 visualizes this growth. It symbolizes the levels

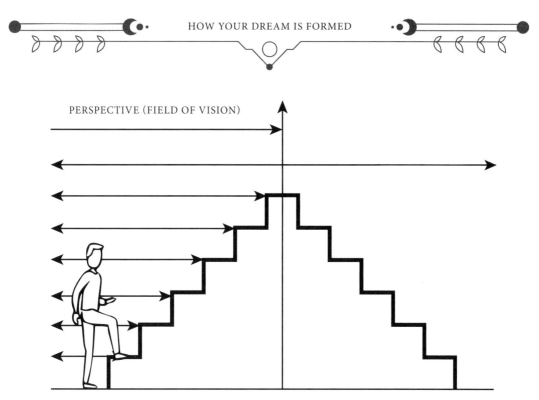

PERSPECTIVE (FIELD OF VISION)

The awareness pyramid

of consciousness you can attain. As you climb higher on the awareness pyramid, your dreams reflect this growth and transformation.

If you like, it is like witnessing the emergence of the mighty Nile River, referring to the pyramids in Egypt, from a distant vantage point as you climb upwards. Initially, you might doubt its existence because it lies beyond the scope of your current viewpoint. However, as your awareness develops as you ascend the pyramid, the Nile gradually reveals itself until it becomes fully visible from the top. It is a moment of celebration

and discovery, as you realize that the Nile has always been there, waiting for you to expand your perspective to see it.

Therefore, as your perspective grows, your sense of reality expands, encompassing more than what was previously within your peripheral vision. Keeping a dream journal can reveal the evolution of your dreams, and therefore your mind and awareness, over time. You will notice a change in the subject matter and symbols within your dreams as your perspective expands. The emotional blueprint, as described in the earlier section, plays a significant role in shaping your

experiences. It sets the tone for attracting similar positive or negative experiences into your life. This blueprint becomes reinforced and takes on a tangible form, resulting in blocks or recurring patterns of misfortune. In essence, you create a theme or "main image" that shapes your perception of yourself, forming your assumed character or false self. This becomes your reality because it aligns with the awareness level you have experienced so far.

By consciously elevating your perspective and expanding your awareness, you can break free from the limitations of your emotional blueprint and transcend recurring patterns. The more you explore and ascend the awareness pyramid, the more interconnected everything becomes, as if you are witnessing the interconnected threads of a cosmic web weaving together the fabric of reality. For instance, you can start directing your dreams by asking questions to your mind before going to sleep; and noting down your dreams upon waking up. The practice of dream journaling helps you to tap into your subconscious mind and begin to understand its symbolic language. Essentially, making you more self-aware. Moreover, when you dream you are outside the laws of physics. An epic dream seems to last a few hours, but in fact you could have been dreaming for ten minutes! This makes

dream time a fertile ground for exploring options around any issue you are struggling with in real life.

When you experience a dream, it is as if you enter a realm where the constraints of the physical world, governed by the laws of physics, no longer hold sway. It is a fascinating journey where your mind crafts scenarios and narratives, sometimes seemingly stretching out over hours, yet just a fraction of that time has passed in the waking world—a mere ten minutes, perhaps. This unique phenomenon of dream time creates a remarkable opportunity for delving into the depths of your thoughts and emotions, giving you a fertile ground to explore the various aspects of issues you may be grappling with in your real life. As you navigate these dreamscapes, you may find yourself confronting challenges, interacting with intriguing characters, or even unraveling mysteries that mirror the concerns and dilemmas you face during your waking hours.

The uncanny ability of dreams to provide a space unbounded by the physical laws of reality allows your mind to roam free, experimenting with alternative solutions, trying out different approaches, and gaining fresh perspectives on the very issues that might be causing you distress or confusion. It is like a playground for your thoughts, where the

boundaries are malleable, and the outcomes are as limitless as your imagination.

Suppose that you had a dream where you are grappling with a difficult decision, caught between conflicting choices. As you dream, your mind might construct a vivid landscape where these choices manifest in tangible ways. You might witness the consequences of each option, experiencing them first hand, and gaining insights into the potential outcomes. This dream exploration can provide you with a wealth of information, helping you weigh the pros and cons, and ultimately guiding you toward a more informed decision when you return to the waking world.

Dreams, in their enigmatic and abstract nature, hold the power to unveil the hidden corners of your psyche, shedding light on the subconscious, and offering a fresh lens through which you can view your everyday challenges. By embracing the surreal, timeless, and boundary-breaking essence of dream time, you open yourself up to a realm of creative problem-solving, self-discovery, and personal growth that transcends the confines of our physical reality.

Moreover, as your awareness blossoms, you will also find that it ripples through the various aspects of your life. Relationships deepen, goals become clearer, and your ability to navigate challenges evolves. This expanded perspective allows you to see the bigger picture, empowering you to make more informed choices and to appreciate the beauty and complexity of the world around you. Embracing this journey of growth and self-discovery in your dreams, allows you to transform your reality and create a more expansive and fulfilling life.

Growing Personal Awareness Through Dreams

When we elevate our perspective to a new vantage point, a remarkable transformation

unfolds within our understanding of the events that have transpired. Our previous certainties and absolutes take on a relative nature, expanding our view of life and offering a newfound flexibility and resilience. We find ourselves on a journey of self-discovery, recognizing that what we once held as truth is but a fraction of the vast tapestry of reality. The boundaries of our immediate perception stretch, revealing a richer, more nuanced understanding of ourselves and the myriad experiences that shape our existence. This expansion in our awareness, this broadening of our vista, imparts a heightened sense of wisdom that evolves in harmony with our ever-expanding perspective. It is as if we recalibrate our emotional blueprint, enabling us to traverse the twists and turns of life with greater clarity and equilibrium.

As you embark on this illuminating journey of self-awareness, you will likely observe significant shifts in the narratives woven within your dreams. Your mind becomes attuned to fresh inquiries, and the landscapes of your dreamscapes mirror this evolution. Past experiences, once isolated fragments, now harmoniously merge with the backdrop of your newfound understanding. Extracting wisdom from even the most unfortunate situations becomes a profound healing process, enhancing personal growth and initiating transformation.

The awareness pyramid, like a beacon of guidance, symbolizes the hierarchical and evolutionary nature of consciousness. It maps our quest for individuation, demanding that we shed old beliefs and paradigms to ascend towards the next tier of awareness. Releasing the weight of emotional baggage becomes a fundamental step, clearing the way for a smooth ascent up the pyramid, and laying the groundwork for our personal evolution.

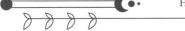

In this remarkable journey of self-discovery and awareness expansion, our dreams become our companions, reflecting the evolving landscape of our inner growth. Each dream serves as a mirror, revealing the integration of past experiences into the tapestry of our expanding understanding. The awareness pyramid, as a metaphor, invites us to rise above the limitations of old perspectives, guiding us to a higher vantage point where we can embrace a more comprehensive, enlightened view of ourselves and the world. In this process, we shed the burdens of emotional history, creating a path that ushers in personal transformation, aligning us with the ever-unfolding currents of our own evolution.

Moreover, it is important to recognize that everyone's journey of raising awareness is unique and can begin from any side of the pyramid. Love, work, business, health, creativity, and various other themes serve as vehicles for growth and evolution, guiding us towards higher levels of consciousness. As we reach the pinnacle of the awareness pyramid, we not only gain a deeper understanding of our lives but also realize that there are multiple paths to creating and experiencing it. This newfound awareness empowers us with a range of choices and opportunities that were previously inaccessible, opening doors to a more fulfilling and purposeful life.

Throughout this self-discovery process, we come to understand the interplay between emotional responses, belief formation, and attracting corresponding experiences that confirm our beliefs. Unprocessed and unresolved experiences linger as dissociated thought forms in our mental map. Our minds create symbols and representations of these situations and experiences in dreams, calling our attention to "unfinished business" and providing an opportunity for healing, understanding, and integration. Remember that dreams represent thirty percent of our lives. Dream craft allows us to evolve our responses, actions, and decision-making processes, empowering us to consciously create desirable outcomes when similar experiences arise in our waking lives. It is a transformative journey of self-discovery and self-mastery, where we reclaim our ability to shape our reality and live authentically.

DREAMS AS MIRRORS THAT REFLECT OUR PERSPECTIVE

As we continue our journey of personal growth and self-awareness, our dreams serve as intricate mirrors, reflecting the ongoing transformation of our perspective and the expansion of our consciousness. The very fabric of our dreams evolves, much like a tapestry, to mirror our ascending climb up the awareness pyramid. It is akin to witnessing a shift in the scenery from a confined maze to an expanse of open landscapes or soaring heights. These evolving dreamscapes symbolize the newfound freedom weave embraced, a liberation from the shackles of limitation that previously constrained us. By mindfully observing these subtle changes

in dream symbols and themes, we gain a tangible sense of our progress on the path of personal growth, recognizing the beautiful alignment between the messages of our dreams and the experiences unfolding in our waking life.

As we embark on this journey of heightened self-reflection, our dreams do not merely remain stagnant; they take on a vibrant, symbolic language that communicates the profound changes occurring within us. As we work diligently to heal past wounds and nurture self-compassion, our dreams may portray epic quests through treacherous landscapes, each obstacle a representation of our inner struggles. These dream narratives serve as a powerful reminder of our resilience, and by delving into the depths of these symbols, we unearth profound insights that guide our personal development. These dream symbols act as lanterns, illuminating the path ahead, casting light upon the aspects of our journey that require attention and nurturing.

Furthermore, our expanded perspective, like a magnifying glass, allows us to examine intricate details and explore the uncharted territories of our dreamscapes. Dreams offer a unique platform where we can unravel complex issues and examine them from multiple angles, much like a vibrant brainstorming session. When faced

with a daunting decision in our waking life, our dreams offer a diverse array of scenarios and outcomes, each a potential piece of the puzzle, allowing us to consider the implications of our choices from various perspectives. It is as if our dreaming mind becomes a guide, offering a multitude of vantage points, enabling us to navigate the intricate web of decision-making with a heightened sense of clarity and insight.

In a nutshell, our dreams remain faithful companions on our journey of personal growth, reflecting the expansion of our perspective and the unfolding chapters of our self-awareness. Through dream symbolism, we witness the evolution of our consciousness, from constrained mazes to open landscapes, from inner struggles to newfound resilience. By understanding our own dream language, we receive the guidance we need for our ongoing development, a precious gift that aligns our dreams with the experiences of our waking life. With this expanded perspective, we not only gain insights into our progress but also transform our dreams into a fertile ground for exploration, a realm where we can grapple with complex issues and discover innovative viewpoints, enriching our understanding and guiding us towards a more fulfilling and meaningful existence.

DREAMING TO INTEGRATE THE PAST

The process of integrating past experiences into your evolving understanding is a pivotal facet of raising awareness. Dreams serve as a secure and transformative arena where this integration can take place. For example, consider a recent challenging breakup you have experienced. The emotions and memories tied to this relationship might manifest in your dreams, presenting vivid imagery and emotionally charged scenarios. These dream experiences act as a fertile ground for processing lingering emotions, seeking closure, and weaving the valuable lessons learned from this relationship into the fabric of your consciousness. When you work with your dreams, you actively participating in the process of your healing and personal growth, a conscious choice that propels your perspective to expand even further. You can induce a dream that help you understand what has happened and why, or how to heal, or what lessons have you learned from that experience.

In a broader context, let us explore how dreams can serve as a conduit for integrating diverse life experiences. Suppose you have embarked on a journey of self-discovery and have been diligently working on bolstering your self-confidence. Your dreams may manifest symbolic situations where you are facing challenges, asserting yourself, and

triumphing over obstacles. These dreams, as intricate narratives, are like workshops, offering you a safe space to confront the barriers that once held you back, providing a stage to hone your newfound confidence and resilience. As you engage with these dream scenarios, you subconsciously integrate this bolstered self-assurance into your self-concept, effectively upgrading your emotional blueprint.

Additionally, dreams can assist in integrating moments of joy and triumph. Imagine you have recently achieved a significant professional milestone, like securing a long-desired job. Your dreams may be filled with celebratory scenes, symbolic representations of success, and empowering imagery. These dream experiences serve to celebrate your achievements on a deeper level, reinforcing your sense of accomplishment and further embedding the positive emotions associated with your success into your psyche. This integration of positive experiences amplifies your emotional repertoire, providing you with a reservoir of inner strength to draw upon during challenging times.

You can, therefore, harness the power of dreams to heal and deepen your understanding. Dreams are dynamic arenas where the integration of past experiences takes place, offering a secure and transformative setting.

Whether it is processing the aftermath of a breakup, fostering self-confidence, or internalizing moments of triumph, your dreams act as a catalyst for this integration. When you actively engage with and reflect on the messages within your dreams, you take charge of your healing and growth journey. And this process continuously expands your perspective and enriching your understanding of the intricate tapestry of life.

DREAMING TO CO-CREATE DESIRABLE OUTCOMES

Your dreams can help you design your next step or platform in life. They hold the potential to act as visionary architects, designing the steppingstones and platforms that propel you forward in life. When viewed from an elevated perspective, with an awareness that stretches beyond the confines of the mundane, your dreams transform into potent co-creators, capable of shaping desirable outcomes in your waking reality. You hold the reins of this incredible process. As you deliberately shape your perspective and anchor empowering beliefs, you can consciously program your dreams to act in harmony with your goals and aspirations.

For instance, consider a scenario where you are striving to enhance your public speaking prowess. Before drifting into slumber, you

set a clear intention, a gentle directive, to have a dream that empower you to exude confidence and communicate eloquently. You can ask for a dream that demonstrates what you need to full more confident. As a result, your dreams may be about experiencing yourself standing on a stage where you find yourself addressing vast audiences with unwavering confidence or engaging in captivating, inspiring conversations. Even though it is a dream, your emotional threshold has expanded, you may gradually get used addressing the public and the fear or anxiety you experience in real life may even subside and disappear altogether. Your dreams effectively, act as a "real" experience which your mind verifies.

It is essential to remember that, just as the sun's rays gradually illuminate the horizon during dawn, your expanding perspective and deepening awareness are mirrored in the dreams that grace your nights. These dreams, like gentle mentors, provide valuable insights into the ongoing evolution of your inner self. They extend a hand, offering opportunities for integration, emotional healing, and intentional co-creation. Each dream becomes a brushstroke, contributing to the masterpiece of your personal growth, each revealing a facet of the magnificent mosaic that makes you who you are.

Hopefully by now, you began to perceive dreamtime as a potent platform for visualization and practice possible solutions. Get ready to tap into the immense transformative potential of your subconscious mind, aligning your dreams harmoniously with the objectives you seek to achieve in your waking life. As you continue to nurture this symbiotic relationship with your dreams, you forge a deeper connection with your subconscious, enabling you to tap into the hidden reservoirs of wisdom that reside within you. With each dream, you weave the threads of intention, fostering a bridge between the realms of the subconscious and the waking. This bridge, like a beacon, guides you, illuminating the path towards the realization of your goals and the embodiment of your aspirations.

It's a dynamic dance between the waking and dreaming realms, a beautiful ballet of self-exploration and creative manifestation. Through this partnership with your dreams, you embark on a journey of empowerment, crafting your destiny with each intention set before slumber, and awakening to the vibrant, harmonious symphony of a life well-lived, where dreams and reality converge.

DREAMING TO UNVEIL DEEPER INSIGHTS

Your life experiences are not haphazard or random occurrences. They hold significant meaning and purpose in the grand tapestry of your personal growth and evolution. When you pay attention to your experiences, your mind begins to process and integrate them, weaving them together to offer you a deeper understanding of yourself and the world around you. Your dreams play a vital role in this process by providing a platform for your mind to process and make sense of these experiences.

By integrating your different experiences and placing them into context, you gain a greater sense of coherence and meaning in your life. This understanding leads to wisdom, allowing you to become a conscious creator of the life you desire rather than a mere victim of circumstances. Moreover, it is important to recognize that your life experiences serve a purpose, acting as catalysts for the transformation of your mental constructs and the expansion of your perception. Each experience you go through, whether pleasant or challenging, contributes to your growth and self-awareness. Putting

experiences into context allows you to "make sense" of your life. Understanding leads to wisdom. Wisdom means you become a better creator of the life you want, and not a victim. Your Life experiences are not ad hock! They are what you need to go through to recreate your mental construct, change your perception, and evolve as a person. In the same way, we each experience what we need to experience. And this allows us to become more conscious, more self-aware. That is why one can never judge the life of others. We each have our own unique life-path to raising our awareness.

One powerful tool for gaining insights into the deeper meaning of your experiences is through your dreams. Your dreams are a direct reflection of your inner world, expressed through the unique language of symbolism and metaphor. They offer a window into your subconscious mind, where hidden truths and unresolved issues reside. Nightmares should not be ignored, as they often carry important messages and urgent prompts for resolution. Moreover, your dreams are the gateway to becoming conscious of your unconscious mind, emotions, and unresolved experiences. When you take the time to listen to your inner self and engage with understanding the language of your unconscious through your dreams, you tap into a wellspring of self-knowledge

and guidance. Your dreams are created by you, using the language of your own subconscious mind.

Understanding the meanings and messages of your dreams is invaluable. It can provide insights that enrich your waking life. The key is to try to decipher them. Moreover, your life experiences are purposeful and meaningful. They serve as building blocks for your personal growth and self-awareness. By actively engaging with your dreams and recognizing their significance, you unlock a powerful tool for self-reflection and understanding. Embrace the wisdom of your dreams, for they hold the keys to unlocking your true potential and guiding you towards a more fulfilling and purposeful life. Maintaining a dream journal, you help you realize that your dreams play a pivotal role in the process of integrating and making sense of your life experiences.

When you enter the realm of dreams, your subconscious mind takes center stage, providing a rich landscape for exploration and insight. You can see by now how dreams are a natural extension of your waking life, offering a platform for your mind to process emotions, conflicts, and unresolved issues. Furthermore, as you sleep, your mind weaves together fragment of memories, emotions, and symbols to create intricate dream narratives(chunking). These narratives often

reflect the themes and patterns of your waking life, but they also can transcend ordinary boundaries and delve into the depths of your subconscious. Through dreams, your mind communicates with you in a language that is deeply personal and symbolic, aiming to shed light on hidden aspects of yourself and offer solutions to unresolved dilemmas.

Dreams can serve as a powerful tool for resolving inner conflicts and gaining deeper understanding. They allow you to explore different perspectives, alternative scenarios, and uncharted territories of your consciousness. For example, if you have been grappling with a particular issue or seeking clarity on a decision, your dreams may present you with symbolic representations or metaphoric narratives that hold the key to unlocking new insights and perspectives. By paying attention to the symbols, emotions, and recurring themes in your dreams, you can uncover the underlying messages and guidance they hold. Additionally, dreams can reveal patterns, highlight areas of growth, and even provide glimpses of future possibilities. They act as a bridge between your conscious and unconscious mind, offering a unique opportunity for self-reflection, self-discovery, and personal transformation.

Finally, keeping a dream journal, practicing dream recall, or exploring dream symbolism, opens a channel of communication with your subconscious. This active participation in the dream realm strengthens your ability to remember and understand your dreams, allowing for a more profound integration of their wisdom into your waking life. As you delve deeper into the language of your dreams, you cultivate a richer and more nuanced relationship with your own psyche, unlocking the potential for greater self-awareness and personal growth.

This symbolic, intuitive as well as creative language through which your mind communicates, offers you insights, solutions, and self-guidance. By attentively exploring and deciphering the messages within your dream, you tap into a wellspring of self-knowledge and expand your understanding of yourself and the world. Dreams do have a transformative power, for they hold the key to unlocking your inner wisdom and guiding you towards a more fulfilling and meaningful life.

CHAPTER 3

THE WONDER OF DREAMING

Dreams, like the stars that adorn the night sky, come in a multitude of forms and hold an exquisite diversity of meanings. As explored earlier, each dream is a tapestry woven with threads of personal experiences, emotions, and beliefs, creating a vivid and intricate landscape within the realm of the subconscious. While dreams may share certain common themes or motifs, it is crucial to recognize that every dream is inherently unique, shaped by the individual dreamer's intricate web of thoughts, feelings, and life encounters. Through the kaleidoscope of dream types, we embark on a journey of exploration, where the mysteries of the mind unfold and offer glimpses into the depths of our inner worlds.

Within the realm of dreams, an expansive canvas unfolds, presenting an array of dream types that span the spectrum of human experience. These dreams, like the facets of a multifaceted gem, showcase various dimensions of the human psyche. They reflect the individual dreamer's subconscious tapestry, intricately interwoven with memories, desires, fears, and aspirations. From prophetic dreams that whisper fragments of the future, to lucid dreams that grant us the power to shape our nocturnal adventures, and even vivid nightmares that jolt us awake, each dream type carries its own significance, offering profound insights and opportunities for personal growth.

Imagine a vast library of dreams, with each dream type representing a unique book, waiting to be discovered and deciphered. These dreams, born from the depths of our minds, possess the power to transport us to alternate realities, illuminate hidden truths, and ignite the embers of imagination. As we navigate the labyrinthine corridors of our dreamscapes, we encounter

a diverse collection of dream types, each adorned with its own symbolism and narrative. Whether it be the surreal landscapes of fantastical dreams, the symbolic theatre of archetypal dreams, or the therapeutic journey of healing dreams, each dream type invites us to explore the vast terrain of our inner selves and venture into the realm of the extraordinary.

As we embark on this exploration of dreams, grouping them into types might help recognize why are you having a dream and aid in interpreting your dreams. The types below are by no means conclusive. You can add your own in your dream journal. The essence of each dream resides within the unique tapestry of your own being. Every dream you have is unique to you and will have its own meaningful interpretation to you personally as it is shaped by your individual experiences, emotions,

and beliefs—your own dream dictionary. However, depending on what phase in life you are at, the nature, or themes, of your dreams may vary. For example, during a very traumatic period of my life having been displaced from the country I grew up in due to war, my dreams were mostly about living in crumbled homes with no ceiling or roof. The other common theme was dreaming about the immediate as well as extended family members. At that time, my dreams reflected the profound instability I was experiencing feeling insecure, and away from immediate family and any form of support or guidance. As I restarted my life in a new country, found what I wanted to do, and started making friends my dreams changed. I felt more settled in my new life and began dreaming about the future possibilities, places I could travel to, and subjects I wanted to learn.

DREAM THEMES

Have you ever considered the idea of categorizing your dreams into different types or themes? It might significantly enhance your ability to recall your dreams. As you maintain your dream journal (more details in chapter seven), aim to summarize what the dream is about in one word. This straightforward approach can offer you valuable insights as you work on interpreting the language of your dreams. Moreover, there is an added benefit to this technique. Beyond enhancing your dream journaling, categorizing your dreams can actively guide your dreams in a direction that aids in better interpretation. It is almost like providing your subconscious mind with a road map to unlock its potential.

Think of categorizing your dreams as a tool to begin deciphering your dream language. By classifying your dreams into categories such as adventurous, humorous, or relationships or education; you create a structured framework that leads you to understanding the dream dictionary of your own unconscious mind. This framework becomes a reliable aid, helping you capture essential elements like emotions, symbols, and recurring themes. Consequently, your dream journal evolves into a valuable resource that allows you to discern trends, explore your subconscious, and gradually unearth hidden insights.

The next time you awaken with a dream fresh in your mind, take a moment to reflect on which category it might fall under. Was it a dream involving soaring through the sky? That could be categorized as an "adventure" dream. Did your dream feature reunions with old school friends? It might find its place in the "past" category. By adopting this approach, you not only refine your dream recall but also craft a dream journal that gradually reveals profound insights about yourself.

Moreover, categorization empowers us to actively direct our dreams, tapping into

the vast potential of the subconscious mind. When we understand the different dream types, we gain the ability to set intentions for our dream experiences. This intentional dreaming, or dream direction, allows us to explore specific themes, solve problems, or seek guidance from our inner selves. By asking for a particular type of dream, we are essentially programming our subconscious to deliver a dream experience that aligns with our desires or inquiries. This process

of directing dreams can be a powerful technique for personal growth, creative exploration, and emotional healing, harnessing the vast capabilities of our mind while we sleep.

For instance, if you find yourself waking up with the sensation that your dream has vanished without a trace, no need to fret. There is a dream hack that can help you recapture those elusive fragments. Take a moment to tune into your immediate post-wakeup feelings. Do you experience a subtle sense of relief, as if you have shed a perplexing burden? Or does it feel more like you have been on an extraordinary journey to a realm where the laws of physics do not apply? Additionally, do you detect a faint trace of reuniting with loved ones who are no longer present? These emotions serve as hints, breadcrumbs deliberately left by your dreaming mind as it explores the realm of dreams.

Even if you cannot remember all the nitty-gritty details of the dream, these emotions are like gold nuggets of insight. Us them to describe the type of dream you had. Classifying your dreams by their type, is a starting point of remembering and directing your dreams. Just jot down a few words that capture that sense of relief, the vibe of the adventure, or the feeling of meeting those familiar folks. Keep at it, and these soft

echoes, these fleeting feelings, can be stepping stones to better dream recall. Over time, this little practice, along with your genuine desire to remember, will weave together a tapestry of dream experiences, shining a light on the fascinating depths of your subconscious, one emotion at a time.

Categorizing dreams facilitates effective dream journaling, making it easier to capture and analyze the nuances of your dream experiences. Furthermore, it empowers you to actively engage with your subconscious mind, leading to intentional dream exploration, or direction, and the potential to gain profound insights, all while harnessing the incredible creative and problem-solving capabilities that your dreams can offer. The following types are a suggestion. You can create your own dream-type categories as you engage more deeply in this practice.

HEALING DREAMS

These are the dreams that have a therapeutic or a therapeutic effect, helping the dreamer to process emotions, or resolve conflicts, as well as make positive changes in their life. Additionally, healing dreams can take many forms. They can include nightmares, lucid dreams, and ordinary dreams where the dreamer may experience an emotional relief, if you like, because of that dream.

Moreover, many indigenous cultures, such as the Aborigines in Australia, have a tradition of using dreams for healing purposes. In the traditional healing practices of the Aborigines in Australia, dreams were believed to have a powerful impact on the physical and emotional well-being of the dreamer. They believed that the dreamer's spiritual journey in the dream state was a powerful tool for healing and growth, as it allowed them to connect with the spiritual world and receive guidance and support. For example, a person would go to a sacred site, such as a rock or a tree, and spend the night dreaming to receive a healing message from the spirits.

Furthermore, the person would sleep facing the east, the direction associated with new beginnings and the rising sun and would

seek guidance from their ancestors or guides in their dream. The dreamer would then interpret the dream and use the guidance received to make positive changes in their life, such as resolving conflicts, overcoming fears, or healing physical ailments. By incorporating the messages received in their dream into their waking life, the dreamer was able to bring balance and harmony to their physical and emotional health.

Moreover, when you start directing your dreams, you can ask your mind to give you a healing dream. You might receive a dream that heals whatever you are going through, without the need to interpret it. Directing your dreams, is about directing your subconscious mind to help you balance as you live your life. The more you consciously

work with your unconscious, the more aware you will become of how to direct your own life, understand human nature more deeply, and have the resources you need to solve life problems.

ENCOUNTERING SPIRIT IN DREAMS

Seeing the spirit of deceased loved ones, can be a healing dream too. For instance, the famous author and creator of Sherlock Holmes is said to have had a dream in which he saw his own deceased son. In the dream, his son appeared healthy and happy, and he told Doyle not to worry about him. This dream was reportedly a source of comfort for Doyle and helped him to come to terms with his son's death. Furthermore, as a dream type, seeing spirits in a dream tends to have a unique, perhaps even potent, "flavor". Meeting with the spirit of that person, feels more realistic. Often, spirit dreams leave an impression on the mind. You are likely to remember it when you wake up, or remember the message contained within it. In Middle Eastern, culture spirit dreams are referred to as visitation—meaning that the dreamer had a visit from spirit.

Over thirty years ago, I had such a visit! My sister was about to have her first born. I went to be with her, while my mother stayed with my father who was very ill. Soon after

I arrived, I had a dream that my father was driving his car, parked the car inside the garage, switched the engines off, dropped his head and died. Ten days after the baby was born, my father passed away calmly in his sleep. My dream had, in a way, prepared me to cope with the trauma of his death. In my dream, he was in the driver's seat, which indicated to me that it was his soul's choice to depart. My dream brought a comforting message to me and my mother: all that was done to help him recover, has been done. Now his soul wanted to continue its journey.

TRAVEL AND HOLIDAY DREAMS

Sometimes, in our busy lives, a daily stressor can take a toll on our physical and emotional health. In these cases, a travel or a holiday dream can provide a much-needed escape, giving our minds and bodies a chance to recharge and rejuvenate. In these dreams, the dreamer may imagine visiting a beautiful or exotic location or taking a relaxing vacation. These dreams can bring feelings of peace, happiness, and relaxation, and can help the dreamer to feel refreshed and revitalized when they wake up. For instance, a person who has been working long hours and feeling overwhelmed might dream of taking a trip to a tropical beach, where they can soak up the sun, swim in the ocean, and

enjoy some well-deserved rest and relaxation. The feelings of peace and rejuvenation they experience in the dream can carry over into their waking life, helping them to feel more refreshed and ready to tackle the challenges of their daily life. Another example is a person who has been feeling stressed and anxious about a forthcoming event might dream of taking a leisurely hike through a scenic countryside. The dream could help the dreamer to feel more relaxed and at peace and may give them new perspectives on their worries and anxieties.

You can ask your mind for a travel and holiday dream (more about that in the Dream Wheel Section to follow). Such a dream can be a valuable form of healing providing a much-needed escape from the stress and demands of daily life and allowing us to recharge and rejuvenate our minds and bodies. Other times, you might just go to sleep without having anything specific in mind. You may

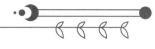
wake up with a healing dream because your body, mind or soul required such a dream to balance and rejuvenate. When you begin dream journaling, it is a good idea to ask for a dream each night during the week. However, do give your mind a break over the weekend, where you ask for a holiday dream, for example, or a healing dream and you do not need to interpret it. The feel and energy of the dream will be embedded on your unconscious mind, and you would receive the benefit of that dream.

PROPHETIC DREAMS

Prophetic dreams are dreams that appear to provide information or predictions about the future. Sometimes, a prophetic dream appears out of nowhere when you least expect it. Often, it is might not be related That is why it is a good practice to journal your dream and their meaning will become apparent later.

While some people believe that prophetic dreams are messages from a higher power, others view them as a manifestation of the dreamer's intuition or unconscious mind. The previous examples from scripture, for instance Joseph's dreams which later came true. President Lincoln, for instance, is said to have had a dream in which he saw his own funeral, including the faces of those

who were mourning him. This dream was reportedly so vivid that it stayed with him for days, and he shared it with close friends and family. Many people believe that this dream was a premonition of his own death, as he was assassinated just a few years later.

Furthermore, History.com recounts this dream describing it in more detail. President Abraham Lincoln dreams on this night in 1865 of "the subdued sobs of mourners" and a body lying on a catafalque in the White House East Room, according to Ward Hill Lamon, one of his friends. Lincoln asked a guarding soldier in his dream, "Who is dead in the White House?" The soldier responded, "The President." He was assassinated, that's how. Then Lincoln began to

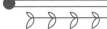 

stir. He revealed to Lamon on April 11 that the dream had "strangely annoyed" him ever since. Lincoln was assassinated while attending a theatre ten days after having the dream. Oddly enough, President Kennedy is said to have had a similar dream in which he saw himself being shot and killed. Sadly, his dream became a reality when he was assassinated in Dallas, Texas, in 1963.

Additionally, the famous civil rights leader is said to have had a dream that he would lead his people to freedom and equality. This dream became a driving force in his activism and ultimately helped to bring about significant change in the United States. Mother Teresa, the revered humanitarian and founder of the Missionaries of Charity is said to have had a dream in which she saw the suffering of the poor and sick, and felt called to help them. This dream inspired her to devote her life to serving the less fortunate, and her work has inspired countless others to do the same.

Determining if a dream is prophetic can be a challenging and subjective process. Usually, the interpretation transpires later! Prophetic dreams often relate to events or experiences that are relevant to your current life or future. They may foretell future events or provide insight into your own thoughts and feelings. However, it can be said that they have distinctive characteristics. For example,

a prophetic dream can be out of the ordinary, "un-invited" or "odd". Generally, there is a vivid quality to them (like High definition, or vivid details) to the extent that they attract your attention and can stay with you long after you have woken up. Emotionally, they feel more significant and meaningful than other types of dreams. Furthermore, prophetic dreams may repeat themselves over time, or they may be like dreams you have had in the past. This repetition can indicate that the dream is trying to convey a specific message or impart a certain insight. They may hold a personal significance for the dreamer, and may relate to their own experiences, feelings, or goals. Moreover, prophetic dreams may contain unusual or unexpected elements, such as symbols, visions, or experiences that do not seem to fit with the dreamer's normal reality.

LUCID DREAMS

Lucid dreaming is a state in which a person becomes aware that they are dreaming while they are still asleep. In this state, the dreamer has a heightened sense of self-awareness and control over their dream experiences. They can make conscious decisions, influence the dream's outcome, and have a sense of agency within the dream. Lucid dreaming is a natural occurrence that happens spontaneously, but

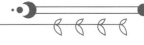

it can also be cultivated through various techniques such as dream journaling, reality testing, and lucid dream induction methods. By becoming more aware of their dreams and learning to recognize the dream state, individuals can increase the likelihood of having lucid dreams.

Ben Apringett, or University of Bristol in the United Kingdom, makes an interesting point about an aspect distinguished lucid dreaming in his article entitled "Philosophy of Dreaming" (Internet Encyclopaedia of Philosophy). He writes that "ordinary dreams are commonly thought to not actually involve choices and corresponding agency. Lucid dreaming invokes our ability to make choices, often to the same extent as in waking life." He likens lucid dreaming to being able to live and act in a "virtual reality".

If you are a lucid dreamer, you can train yourself to direct your dream (while you are dreaming) to "practice" different scenarios to a situation and play out various probabilities to help you make a better choice in real waking life. No wonder that interest in virtual reality on computers is on the rise! A lucid dream is effectively, a dream within a dream and is shown to have many benefits, including improved emotional regulation, enhanced problem-solving skills, and increased creativity. It can also provide a sense of liberation and freedom, as the

dreamer is able to explore their inner world and create their own reality within the dream. By becoming more aware of your dreams through dream journaling, for example, you will come to recognize this dream state.

Reality testing techniques

Essentially, lucid dreaming is a wondrous realm where the boundaries between imagination and reality blur. It invites us to explore the infinite possibilities of our dreamscapes. One powerful tool in our arsenal to enhance

lucidity is the practice of reality testing. These techniques serve as a bridge between the dream world and our waking consciousness, allowing us to discern whether we are in the realm of dreams or the realm of waking life. By cultivating a habit of reality testing, we can awaken within our dreams, grasp the reins of our nocturnal adventures, and unlock the limitless potential that awaits.

Reality testing techniques serve as a compass that guides us through the ethereal landscapes of lucid dreaming. As an example, one effective technique is the classic "reality check." To train yourself, throughout your waking hours, develop a habit of questioning the nature of reality by performing simple tests. Pause and ask yourself, "Am I dreaming?" Moreover, engage in actions that challenge the expected outcomes of reality, such as attempting to push your finger through your palm or trying to read a line of text twice. In the realm of dreams, these reality checks often yield peculiar results, serving as a signpost that signals your lucid state. By regularly conducting reality checks during waking life, you will train your mind to perform them instinctively within the realm of dreams.

Another valuable technique in the realm of reality testing is mindfulness. Cultivate a state of heightened awareness in both waking life and within your dreamscape.

Pay attention to the details of your surroundings, the sensations coursing through your body, and the subtle nuances of your experiences. By nurturing this mindfulness, you create a foundation for recognizing the subtle inconsistencies and peculiarities that often arise within dreams. This heightened state of awareness becomes an ally on your lucid dreaming journey, as it sharpens your perception and acts as a beacon that signals the departure from the ordinary into the extraordinary.

Furthermore, as you embrace the realm of lucid dreaming, remember that reality testing techniques are the keys that unlock the door to your conscious presence within the dream world. With practice and dedication, you will develop the ability to traverse the ethereal landscapes with ease, embracing the exhilarating freedom to shape your dreams and unravel the mysteries that lie within. Reality testing can become your guiding light, illuminating the path towards lucidity, and empowering you to embark on extraordinary adventures within the boundless realm of your dreams.

Inducing a lucid dream

As soon as you are awake, try not to move. Stay still for a few moments as you recall whatever you can from your dream, be it feelings or details. Afterwards, try to write

something down in your dream journal. Maintaining a dream journal may help an affirmation if that helps, to assert to your unconscious mind that you are ready to explore that realm. You would remember your dreams more clearly and become more adept at recognizing signs that indicate you are indeed dreaming and having a lucid dream.

The art of dream journaling plays a vital role in the pursuit of lucid dreaming. So, keep a journal by your bedside and commit to recording your dreams upon awakening. As you document the details, emotions, and symbols woven within each dream, you cultivate a deeper connection to your subconscious mind. By immersing yourself in the realm of your dreams through journaling, you become more attuned to the patterns, themes, and peculiarities that arise. This heightened awareness serves as a stepping stone to lucidity, as you become intimately acquainted with the landscape of your dreams.

So, with intention, reality testing, and the power of journaling, you pave the way to the enchanted realm of lucid dreaming. Embrace these practices with dedication and patience, for they are the keys that unlock the gateway to lucidity inviting you to step into a world where imagination and reality intertwine. Remember, if you dream, for example, that you are talking to your pets, and they answer they answer you back, seeing floating cars; or a small box that contains the universe which you travel through (it happened to me once!), or talking to the dead, etc. then you are having a lucid dream. The idea is that you will perceive these things as an indication that you are lucid dreaming; and you will become more lucid.

Another method to induce a lucid dream is meditation. Before drifting off to sleep, immerse yourself in a meditative state, let go and breathe deeply for a few times. Set a clear intention to become lucid within your dreams. Visualize yourself recognizing the dream state, vividly imagining the exhilaration, freedom, and empowerment that accompanies lucidity. By harnessing the power of intention and visualization, you pave the way for the doors of lucid dreaming to swing wide open. Once you have crossed the threshold of lucidity and find yourself aware within the realm of dreams, remember that you possess the extraordinary power to shape and form the dream as you desire. So, be prepared to explore the limitless expanse of your imagination. It lies within your grasp!

Changing a lucid dream

In this ethereal playground of lucid dreaming, you can become the author, the artist, and the director of your own dream narrative.

You can try changing the dream while you are in it. So, embrace this newfound awareness and unleash your creative abilities and imagination. If you like, you hold the pen that rewrites the script of your dreams. As you become more conscious of your lucid state, seize the opportunity to manifest your imagination and manifest your desires with each brushstroke of your dream canvas. Through the power of your thoughts, you can direct your journey in a lucid dream.

As soon as you have a thought you might see manifest in your lucid dream. Once you recognize that you are dreaming, let go of any limitations that may have confined your waking reality. Embrace this boundless potential as it unfolds before you and summon the courage to challenge the laws of physics, alter the environment, and transmute the very fabric of the dream itself. For instance, you may wish to soar through starlit skies, walk through ancient realms, or converse with fantastical beings; remember that you can shape-shift the dream at will. Embrace the exhilarating freedom of this surreal landscape and allow your imagination to flourish without constraint. As you delve deeper into the realm of lucid dreaming, tap into the reservoir of your creativity and explore the art of dream manipulation. With a gentle flicker of intention, watch as the dream world bends to your will,

transforming into a canvas awaiting your artistic touch.

Experiment with your ability to morph landscapes, summon objects, and even alter the very laws of time. This can be exhilarating as you reinvent your dream environment and craft new possibilities with every thought- the only limit is the scope of your imagination. Allow your imagination to soar, challenge the boundaries of the dream world, and revel in the joy of being the ultimate creator of your dream narrative. May your lucid adventures be filled with endless exploration and boundless creativity, as you rewrite the script of your dreams and craft a symphony of wonder within the realm of lucidity. Whatever you lucid dreaming experience may be, remember that a lucid dream defies the natural laws of physics. You are entering the mind's creative zone. So, have fun with them, dare to be creative, and experiment with possibilities.

ASTRAL TRAVEL

While lucid dreaming and astral travel share some similarities, they are not identical concepts. Lucid dreaming refers to being aware and in control within the dream state. The dreamer can exercise a degree of control over the dream experience and make conscious decisions within the dream; while

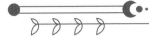

astral travel involves the belief in the ability to travel outside of the physical body and explore other realms or dimensions.

Astral travel is often related to dreaming because it involves the idea of the consciousness being able to separate from the physical body and explore other realms or dimensions or timelines. Some believe that astral travel can occur spontaneously during dreaming, when the consciousness is already in a state of separation from the physical body. Others see astral travel as a deliberate and intentional act, in which the individual practices techniques to consciously project their consciousness outside of their physical body. In this sense, astral travel is seen as a type of lucid dreaming, where the dreamer is aware that they are dreaming and has some control over their dream experiences.

Furthermore, astral travel is often considered a type of out-of-body experience (OBE) are largely recognized within the medical community and have been the subject of many studies and is sometimes associated with spiritual or mystical experiences. According to Healthline.com, astral projection is a spiritual practice. Regardless of how it occurs, astral travel is often described as a profound and transformative experience, allowing individuals to explore the inner dimensions of their mind, as well as other realms beyond the physical.

NIGHTMARES

Bad dreams, often referred to as nightmares, can be seen as poignant messages from the depths of your unconscious mind, urging you to confront and conquer irrational fears that might be impeding your progress in life. These unsettling dreams are like beacons, pointing out matters that sap your energy and hinder your forward movement. Think of them as an alarm, a red flag raised by your mind, signaling a need for

attention and resolution. Nightmares often serve as the psyche's way of processing and integrating adverse situations you may have encountered. They are the mind's workshop, where it dismantles the elements of fear, anxiety, and unresolved conflicts, working tirelessly to bring about healing and growth. While they may appear distressing or even terrifying, nightmares act as a sort of emotional pressure valve, allowing you to release bottled-up anxieties and address underlying concerns.

In the realm of nightmares, you might find recurring themes, such as the feeling of danger, being chased, or even the sensation of falling off a cliff. These motifs are like coded messages, each carrying a unique emotional weight, revealing the dreamer's anxieties and fears. Nightmares reflect the darker corners of our psyche, places where unresolved conflicts or unresolved emotions linger. They serve as mirrors, showing us the aspects of our inner landscape that require attention and transformation. Additionally, there is an intriguing phenomenon often experienced, known as "paralysis," where upon waking, the body remains immobilized. This occurrence, especially after significant traumatic situations or periods of excessive worry, is like a physical manifestation of the emotional weight you carry. It is your subconscious, through this temporary

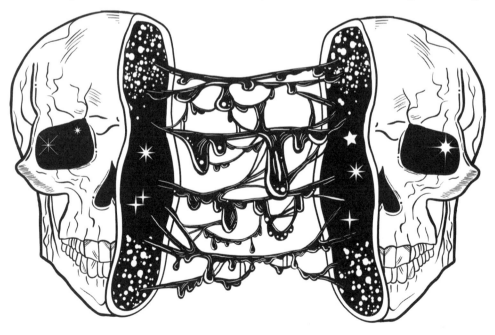

immobilization, asking you to pause, to process, and to grant yourself the time and space needed to heal.

The fascinating aspect of this intricate dance between the conscious and subconscious mind is the responsiveness of the latter. It is a beautiful conversation where the subconscious listens intently and responds to our thoughts, fears, and hopes. When you embark on the journey of transforming your mindset, of seeking happiness, and genuinely enjoying the beauty of life, you will find these experiences gradually receding and eventually disappearing altogether. As you reshape your perspective, replacing fear with courage and negativity with positivity, you will notice a shift in the dream landscape. The nightmares that once haunted your nights will lose their grip, and instead, you will find dreams that mirror the newfound vibrancy of your waking life. This incredible interplay between the conscious and the subconscious underscores the immense potential for personal growth and transformation, reminding us of the intricate interconnectedness that shapes our inner and outer worlds.

DAYDREAMS

Unlike night dreams, daydreams occur during our waking hours and allow us to mentally explore new possibilities, scenarios, and experiences. They are a form of spontaneous and imaginative thought that can occur when our minds wander from the present moment. They can be triggered by external stimuli, such as a scenic view, music or a movie, or they can arise from within our own thoughts and emotions.

Daydreaming can serve as a temporary escape from stress, boredom, or monotony, and can provide a sense of pleasure, enjoyment, and relaxation. However, what you daydream about is indicative of what is on your mind! In addition to being a form of escapism, daydreams can also serve a purpose in inspiring and motivating us to pursue our goals and aspirations. For example, an athlete may daydream about winning a gold medal, a writer may daydream about publishing a best-selling novel, and a musician may daydream about performing in front of a large crowd.

Moreover, daydreams can help us visualize our desires and make them feel more real and achievable. They can also spark our creativity and lead to new ideas, perspectives, and solutions to problems. For instance, when you daydream visualizing o something you desire to solve or manifest, your subconscious is listening and might help you induce a dream on how to achieve the result you seek. However, please note that excessive

daydreaming may also become a form of procrastination and interfere with our ability to act and achieve our goals in the real world.

It is not just during night-time slumber that our minds can weave the fabric of dreams. Daydreaming, too, holds a remarkable potential—a potent tool to intentionally shape the dreamscape or even to "rewrite" past dreams with a touch of conscious influence. This act of intentional daydreaming

becomes a canvas where we can paint our desired outcomes or engineer positive shifts in our mindset. Imagine this: you are yearning to meet the right partner, or you are poised to launch a successful business venture. This is the moment when your daydreaming time becomes invaluable. Your body needs to taste the sensations, to soak in the emotional essence of what it feels like to meet that perfect match, to bask in the glow of a thriving business. It is the emotional charge, the vivid imprint of that experience, that registers deeply in the chambers of your mind, etching itself into the pages of your emotional blueprint (recall how that was described earlier). This emotional memory, crafted through daydreaming, takes on a tangible form in your mind, becoming, in a sense, a parallel or a possible reality.

Once you have experienced it, not just as a fleeting thought but as a visceral, emotional immersion that permeates every cell of your being, something profound occurs. Your mind, in its ever-adaptive brilliance, begins to believe in the possibility. The once-distant dream now seems within reach. Your subconscious, always the diligent orchestrator of your inner world, now steps in. It assembles the intricate pieces, crafting a dream that offers more insights—perhaps a dream that unveils the steps needed to reach that partner or outlines the strategies to make your business thrive. It is as if your subconscious becomes the ultimate problem-solving partner, guiding you with dream narratives that hold the keys to your aspirations.

Let us consider a different scenario: imagine you are seeking to overcome a challenge, perhaps the apprehension of embarking on a solo travel adventure to an unfamiliar destination. Through purposeful daydreaming, you visualize yourself confidently navigating the streets of an exotic locale, embracing the thrill of new experiences, and immersing yourself in the vibrant culture around you. You welcome the emotions of this imaginary journey, feeling the liberation, the empowerment, and the sense of accomplishment. This emotional surge becomes a guiding light of possibility, resonating deep within. Your mind, now infused with the belief that you can indeed conquer this fear, weaves a dream that unveils the blueprint for success. It may conjure scenes where you confidently explore foreign markets, engage with locals, and boldly venture off the beaten path. This orchestrated dream acts as a mentor, offering invaluable insights, providing a tantalizing glimpse of the potential route to overcoming your apprehension of solo travel.

In essence, daydreaming becomes the fertile soil where the seeds of our desires are planted, and through the nurturing act of emotional immersion, these seeds germinate into vibrant dreams that align with our aspirations (much like the process of manifesting. You cannot manifest what your mind does not believe!). Our minds, ever the faithful partners in this intricate dance of life, respond to the emotions we feed them. By consciously harnessing the power of daydreaming, we leverage the language of emotion to communicate with our subconscious, nudging it in the direction of our dreams. It is a harmonious collaboration, if you like, between the conscious and the subconscious—a dance of intention and response—that reveals the incredible potential within us to shape our dreamscape, one daydream at a time.

RECURRING DREAMS

Recurring dreams are a common experience for many people. There are several reasons why we may have recurring dreams. One possibility is that our subconscious mind is trying to bring our attention to a particular issue or problem that we have not yet resolved in our waking life. The dream may recur until we address this issue and find a solution. Quite frequently, that happens when you are most relaxed into your life and things are going smoothly. This is because you are feeling well, and your conscious

mind can cope deal with the issue successfully. So, do not be alarmed when recurring dreams begin to happen, or when you have what refer to as a "rubbish" or nonsensical dream (see the next section).

Another possibility is that the recurring dream is a manifestation of a deep-seated fear or anxiety that we have not yet been able to overcome. The dream may be a way for our mind to process and release these emotions, allowing us to work through them and eventually let go of them. Additionally, some recurring dreams may simply be a result of our brain processing and consolidating memories from our daily life. In these cases, the dream may continue to recur until our brain has processed the memory fully.

Keep in mind that recurring dreams can be a way for our subconscious mind to communicate with us and help us work through unresolved issues or emotions. Maintaining a dream journal and reflecting on the recurring dream can help us gain insight into its meaning and find ways to address it in our waking life. You can also direct your dreams (see chapter five) by asking your mind to explain the reason or the meaning of the recurring dream. You can also use my Dream Wheel technique to allow revelations around the recurring dream to unfold naturally (see chapter six) over a few days. Whatever the reason may be, your mind is

weaving together an important message in a dream. You would do well to pay attention to it.

"RUBBISH" DREAMS

There are various factors that can contribute to having dreams that are difficult to interpret or feel like "rubbish" dreams that do not make sense. One possible factor is chemical overactivity in the brain, which can be caused by consuming certain substances, or going to bed with a full stomach! This is not as strange as it sounds, for eating a large or heavy meal before bed, for example, can cause the body to produce more digestive enzymes and increase metabolic activity, which can stimulate the brain and lead to more vivid or strange dreams. Similarly, consuming alcohol or drugs before bed can affect brain chemistry and disrupt normal sleep cycles, leading to more fragmented or nonsensical dreams.

Other factors that can contribute to difficult or nonsensical dreams include stress, anxiety, and sleep disturbances such as insomnia or sleep apnea. In which case your unconscious mind is simply trying to wake you up, through your dreams, so you can breathe! In some cases, certain medications or medical conditions also affect the quality of sleep and content of dreams. It is worth

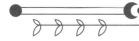 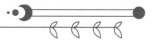
noting that while some dreams may seem meaningless or difficult to interpret, they can still offer valuable insights and information about our subconscious thoughts and emotions. Even if a dream does not seem to have an obvious message or meaning, it can still reflect our current state of mind and offer clues about areas of our life that may need attention or reflection.

For instance, a client of mine had what she called a weird dream the night before she decided to leave her husband and end their marriage. She dreamt that she was sleeping on the floor, and her back hurt. Then her sister asked her to get up, and placed a layer of pink flowers made of cardboard on the floor underneath the sheets and told her that now she can sleep. I asked her to identify what were the significant elements to her and what they meant for her. She said that her back pain represents all the marital struggle

she was going through in her marriage, and that her sister represents support, home, love and safety. The pink flowers stood for happiness and feeling nice.

Sleeping on the floor probably represented avoiding their marital bed, sleeping on the floor stood for "lying low" avoiding conflict; back pain stood for having no support. Her safety system asked her to "insulate" herself from the marriage (cardboard and to practice self-love (pink flowers). What is interesting is that she did not go back to bed in her dream but continued to sleep on the floor. The following morning a significant communication took place between her and her husband the result of which she decided to leave the marriage for good having been struggling for a while without making any progress. So, your "rubbish" dreams are worth making a note of. So, keep your dream journal nearby.

REWRITING A DREAM

Dreams often arise from a blend of our beliefs, emotions, thoughts, and life experiences. Often, our dreams carry emotional charge. Our minds automatically associate a thought to the way we feel having had a dream. But what if the dream leaves a negative emotion which leads to a negative belief. How can we address this? Well, by rewriting the dream. Whether right after you wake up, or later during a day-dreaming session.

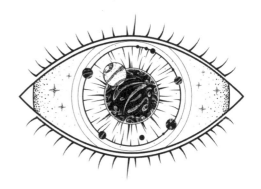

Consider a personal experience: shortly after my brother's painful passing, I had a distressing dream where my sister-in-law, whom I deeply care for, faced a similar fate. My brother's death was profoundly traumatic as we shared a close sibling bond, a friendship that ran deep. The emotional turmoil was overwhelming. I feared losing more people whom I loved and cared about. At that moment, my spiritual mentor proposed a unique solution: revisiting the dream with the aim of visualizing a different ending. The goal was to break the cycle of excessive worry, preventing the birth of negative scenarios that could attract more negativity.

By going back into the dream, through "daydreaming," I took an active role in reshaping its outcome. I rewrote the dream with hope, resilience, and positive outcomes in mind. I felt an exhilaration knowing that my sister-in-law was alive and healthy, and I imagined sharing many happy memories together. This intentional act of altering the dream served as a countermeasure against the unconscious anxiety was experiencing which transpired in the initial dream. It was also a way to prevent further harmful beliefs from forming. Sort of like ordering my mind to stop! This process was a transformative one within my own mind. I felt empowered having redefined the narrative my subconscious mid was playing out in the dream. I focused more on the healing path I desired.

This example underscores the remarkable power within us to reshape the course of our dreams, rewriting their conclusions and, in turn, influencing our waking experiences. It highlights the link between dreams and our real-life perception, reminding us that our minds are not fixed but adaptable landscapes where we can make positive changes. By consciously engaging with our dreams, we take control of our mindset, steering it away from negativity. Through dream exploration and

revision, we discover our ability to create narratives infused with hope, healing, and the strength to rise above life's challenges.

DIRECTING DREAMS

Directed, or intentional dreaming, can be a powerful tool for personal growth and transformation. Directed dreams allow you to tap your subconscious mind and access deeper levels of insight and creativity. They can be used for a variety of purposes, such as gaining clarity on a particular issue, overcoming fears and phobias, enhancing creativity and inspiration, exploring different various outcomes to a situation you are struggling with, and improving overall well-being.

So, when you write a question in your dream journal, for example, asking your mind to give you a dream on a certain issue; you are directing your dreams. In a sense, directed dreams are dreams that are intentionally influenced by directing your mind towards a particular topic or theme. In other words, they are dreams that are focused on a specific goal or intention you set such as problem-solving, self-improvement, or creative inspiration.

The purpose of a directed dream is to seek guidance, insights, and answers, to specific questions or challenges that you are currently facing in your life. Therefore, the interpretation of a directed dream must relate to the question you asked before going to sleep. For example, if you asked for guidance on how to handle a difficult situation at work, and you dream of being lost in a maze, the interpretation could be related to finding your way through the obstacles and challenges at work to reach your goal.

However, if you do not remember your dream or the dream seems unrelated to your question, it could be a sign that you need to rephrase or clarify your intention before going to sleep. Moreover, it is also possible that you were too preoccupied with other thoughts, feelings, or concerns that night, causing your subconscious to bring up unrelated content in the dream. You may wish to address this other issue first and return to requesting your directed dream once more afterwards. Remember that the interpretation of a directed dream is highly personal and subjective, and it is up to you to discern the meaning and relevance of your dream to your waking life.

There are various techniques and methods used to induce directed dreams, such as visualization exercises, affirmation practices, and guided meditations. These techniques are designed to enhance the dreamer's ability to consciously direct their dream content towards a desired outcome. It is worth noting that directed dreams are

not always easy to achieve, and they require consistent practice and dedication. However, with the right techniques and mindset, it is possible to enhance your ability to direct your dreams and harness their potential for personal growth and transformation. Additionally, when it comes to interpreting directed dreams, you have more details about this technique in the next chapter, it is essential to bear in mind the question you wrote in your dream journal to induce that dream.

RANDOM DREAMS

These are non-directed dreams. For instance, you wake up one day and you remember that you had a dream the night before, without intentionally asking for one. Messages in all dreams are important. Random dreams are like surprise packages from the subconscious. They show up uninvited, often catching us off guard when we least expect it. It is as if our inner storyteller takes the stage without us consciously pulling the strings. These dreams can cover a wide range of scenarios—from fantastical adventures in distant lands to mundane interactions with familiar faces. While they may seem haphazard, they carry valuable messages woven into their fabric. Paying attention to the emotions, symbols, and events within these random dreams can offer unexpected

insights into our thoughts, feelings, and even hidden desires. They remind us that the subconscious mind is always active, and its whispers can provide subtle guidance, even when we have not consciously asked for it.

Despite not being intentionally summoned, random dreams often hold significance. The seemingly insignificant details, the fleeting sensations, and the people who wander through these dreamscapes are all part of a subconscious tapestry waiting to be deciphered. By keeping a dream journal and jotting down the fragments of these unsolicited dreams, we can start to uncover patterns, connections, and recurring themes. Over time, this recording process can lead to a deeper understanding of our inner selves, helping us unlock the mysteries of our subconscious.

Embracing the beauty of random dreams allows us to explore uncharted territories of our mind. They remind us that our subconscious is a wellspring of creativity and insight, offering gifts wrapped in enigmatic symbols and emotions. As we honor these spontaneous dream experiences, we develop a richer relationship with our inner world, and we become more attuned to the subtle messages that weave through the fabric of our dreamscapes, whether we intentionally beckon them. The best practice is to write those dreams in your journal, and as you

learn how to interpret your own dream language, you can refer to them and decipher their message. At such times, it is essential to write down a line or two describing what was happening in your "real life" at the time, or what was on your mind that week. Often, random dreams relate to current events, worries or experiences that you are going through. Additionally, current stimuli, such as watching a movie or current world events act as a trigger for your subconscious mind to deal and integrate previous unprocessed feelings or experiences.

SEX & MARRIAGE DREAMS

Dreams about having sex or marrying a person, of the same or opposite sex, are common. They represent integrating with qualities of that gender or person. They can have various interpretations depending on the context and details of the dream and whether it was a directed dream or a random one. When it comes to interpreting dreams of having sex with someone of the same or opposite gender, it is important to look beyond the literal meaning of the act itself and explore the emotional and psychological aspects of the dream. For example, if you dream of having sex with someone of the same gender and you identify as heterosexual, it could signify merging with the

qualities you admire about that person or associate them with.

Similarly, if you dream of getting married to someone of the same or opposite gender, it could be a symbol of merging with the qualities of that person or the gender they represent. For instance, if you dream of marrying a successful businesswoman, it could be a sign that you need to develop or express more assertive and ambitious qualities in yourself to achieve your goals. On the other hand, if you dream of marrying a kind and nurturing man, it could represent the need to cultivate more empathy and compassion in your own personality.

Generally, dreams about sex and marriage can be interpreted as a call to integrate certain qualities or traits that are associated with the gender or person you dreamt about;

or integrating dual aspects within oneself. The female/male aspects are seen as complimenting qualities to create a functional balanced and harmonious being where male/masculine aspect represent drive and the ability to achieve, and female/feminine aspect represents reflective, creative, and nurturing aspect. In a dream, a gender can represent an aspect that you need to activate or assert within yourself. A woman who dreams that she has a penis, for example, indicates asserting the Yang, or the go-get-it male aspect within herself.

Moreover, dreams can offer valuable insights into our unconscious mind, and the imagery and symbols that arise in our dreams can often reflect deeper aspects of our personality or psyche. For example, if a man dreams that he has breasts, it can indicate a need for him to tap into his more nurturing and empathetic qualities. This dream could suggest that he needs to be more in tune with his emotional side, and perhaps rely less on logical thinking or decision-making. On the other hand, if a woman dreams that she has a penis, it can represent a need for her to be more assertive and confident in pursuing her goals and desires. This dream may suggest that she needs to tap into more traditionally masculine qualities such as assertiveness, strength, and confidence, to achieve her objectives. This does not

necessarily mean that she needs to adopt a more masculine identity, but rather that she needs to balance and integrate these qualities into her overall sense of self.

By exploring the emotions and themes that arise in these dreams, you can gain valuable insights into your own psyche and take steps towards personal growth and development. However, try to maintain a personal or subjective interpretation to your dreams. Keep asking your mind what does this symbolize, or represent to me? What do I think of this symbol or person. Ultimately it is up to you to determine their meaning in the context of your own life. While certain symbols and imagery may have general meanings or associations, it is ultimately up to the individual to determine what these symbols mean to them in the context of their own life, experiences, and personal dream language.

PREGNANCY

Another intriguing type of dream involves the imagery of pregnancy, a symbol rich with metaphorical possibilities. Remarkably, this dream theme transcends gender, as both men and women can find themselves dreaming of being pregnant. Such dreams often carry a powerful message, hinting at the potential for creativity, growth, and the

birth of new ideas or projects. It is as if the dreamer is nurturing a concept, gestating it within the depths of their psyche, waiting for the right moment to bring it into the world. This can be particularly relevant during pivotal life transitions, such as recovering from the loss of a partner, the dissolution of a partnership, or the start of a new career. The symbolism extends beyond just external events; it can signify the beginning of a personal transformation, where the dreamer is reborn into a new phase of life, carrying with them the seeds of fresh beginnings.

Historically, dreams have played a pivotal role in shaping the course of human events. Famous examples abound, such as the renowned chemist August Kekulé, who discovered the structure of the benzene molecule through a dream in which he envisioned a snake biting its own tail, suggesting the cyclic nature of the benzene ring. The renowned scientist Albert Einstein also credited some of his ground-breaking insights to dreams. These instances highlight the incredible potential that lies within the dream realm, where the subconscious mind weaves intricate stories, often reflecting the dreamer's innermost desires and aspirations.

Moreover, dreams of giving birth carry their own profound significance. In such dreams, the act of bringing forth new life represents the completion of a creative process, a manifestation of something novel, or the emergence of a previously undiscovered aspect of oneself. This dream imagery can serve as a powerful reminder to release old ways of being, to let go of the past, and to fully embrace the exciting prospects of a new chapter in life. The birth metaphor resonates with the idea that within each of us lies the potential for continual growth and transformation, birthing new versions of ourselves as we evolve through life's dynamic journey.

It is crucial, however, to recognize that dream interpretations are not set in stone. They are fluid, deeply influenced by the dreamer's unique experiences and personal associations. Thus, it is essential to embark on a journey of introspection, reflecting on one's own thoughts, feelings, and life circumstances to unravel the distinct message encoded within the dream. By attentively observing our dreams and engaging in the practice of self-reflection, we open the door to valuable insights into our inner workings. This process not only enhances our self-awareness but also paves the way for intentional personal growth, and consciously weaving the wisdom into the fabric of our waking lives.

CHAPTER 4

DREAM INTERPRETATION

Every dream, like a fingerprint, is an intricate expression unique to its creator - the dreamer. In the realm of dreams, you construct your personal lexicon of symbols, a special language through which your mind communicates invaluable insights to you. These dreams are indeed your own compositions, the product of your mind, tailored specifically to reach your conscious self.

Dreams serve as a deeply personal and subjective voyage, where the symbols and meanings woven into each dream are as distinct as the individual experiencing them. Each one of us holds a personalized "dictionary" of dream symbols, derived from our life's tapestry of experiences, our emotions, and the beliefs that shape us. These symbols, vividly etched in your dreams, emerge as a communication from your unconscious mind, presented in a language that resonates with you. This personalized language ensures that the messages encoded in your dreams are crystal clear, a testament to the deep connection between your dreamscapes and your lived reality.

Consider your dreams as the handwritten notes of your unconscious mind, delivering insights, advice, and reflections to your conscious awareness. By delving into the symbols and meanings embedded in these dreams, you embark on a journey of self-discovery, gaining profound insights into the depths of your thoughts, emotions, and the subtle workings of your unconscious. It is crucial to acknowledge that the meaning of a dream is far from static. Rather, it is a dynamic tapestry that invites interpretation. Each dreamer brings their unique perspective, and as a result, the significance of a dream may vary, reflecting the distinctive lens through which it is viewed.

In essence, your dreams are a personal mirror, reflecting the intricacies of your inner world, a mirror that you alone can interpret, comprehend, and extract wisdom from. By engaging with your dreams, you unlock the door to a richer understanding of yourself, a treasure trove of insights that empowers you to navigate life's journey with heightened self-awareness and a deeper connection to the subtleties of your own psyche.

The Book of Dream Craft is dedicated to guiding you in crafting your unique dream interpretation approach, empowering you to harness the potential of your dream time as a valuable resource for personal growth.

UNIVERSAL DREAM LANGUAGE

Dream interpretation involves recognizing and understanding universal symbols that have been prevalent in dreams across cultures, both in ancient times and in our modern era. These symbols transcend cultural boundaries and reveal insights into our shared human experiences. As our culture evolves, so do the symbols that emerge in our dreams. While ancient civilizations had their own set of common dream symbols, our contemporary society has shaped a fresh set of symbols that reflect the changes and advancements of our time. By familiarizing ourselves with these universal symbols, we can tap into a broader understanding of our dreams and glean insights that resonate with the collective human experience, bridging the gap between the ancient and the contemporary while unraveling the mysteries of our nightly visions.

In ancient cultures, the interpretation of dreams was a multifaceted endeavor shaped by several factors. Contextual elements, like historical and cultural background, societal beliefs, and the individual experiences of the dreamer, all played crucial roles in assigning meaning to dreams. Dreams held profound significance in the civilizations of the past, extending back through the pages of time. In these cultures, dreams were often considered as messages, attributed to gods, nature, animals, or other supernatural forces. This belief led to the emergence of distinct dream languages tailored to decode the symbolism within each society. Interestingly, this collective legacy, or a 'universal dream symbology,' still subtly influences our individual dreams today, as it imprints upon our shared human consciousness.

Ancient Egyptians, for example, crafted a sophisticated system of dream interpretation

documented in the "Dream Book of Thoth." This comprehensive compendium listed various symbols and their meanings, creating a valuable resource for interpreting dreams. The significance of dreams in ancient Egypt went beyond mere curiosity, intertwining with religious and spiritual life, viewing dreams as sacred channels of divine communication. Similar reverence for dreams can be found in ancient Greece, where dreams were seen as messages from the gods. The Greek *Oneirocritica* by Artemidorus, a literary work, provided insights into the meanings of symbols and objects that appeared in dreams, offering a guide to decipher the divine messages inherent within these nocturnal visions.

These historical instances highlight the significant part dreams played in ancient societies, serving as a conduit bridging mortals with the divine and unveiling glimpses into the human journey. Our exploration of this rich historical fabric unveils a profound admiration for our forebearers' nuanced approach to dreams, wherein they valued these nocturnal visions not solely as individual experiences but as wellsprings of spiritual counsel and communal comprehension.

These represent just a few instances how dream interpretation's collective consciousness took shape across diverse civilizations and cultures in ancient times. Over the centuries, dream interpretation has continued its evolutionary journey, with various cultures fashioning their own systems and methodologies to decipher the intricate messages concealed within dreams.

ANCIENT DREAM
INTERPRETATIONS

In ancient China, dreams held a sacred position as messengers from the spirit realm, intricately woven into the fabric of Chinese culture and spirituality. This ancient civilization boasted a rich tradition of dream interpretation, firmly rooted in the notion that the dreamer's subconscious served as a bridge to the spirit world, facilitating the reception of significant messages. This sophisticated system of dream interpretation was deeply influenced by principles from both Taoism and Confucianism, shaping a distinct framework for comprehending the intricate language of dreams.

Within the realm of ancient Chinese dream interpretation, symbols and dream imagery possessed specific meanings, unlocking profound insights into messages from the spiritual realm. This complex tapestry integrated animals, objects, and colors, each representing unique facets of the

dreamer's life and personality. For example, the color red, symbolizing good fortune, happiness, and success, served as a prime illustration of this concept. In dreams, red embodied these positive qualities, signifying promising events on the horizon, akin to a beacon guiding towards optimism and potential.

Additionally, various animals, objects, and colors held symbolic significance, representing diverse aspects of the dreamer's life and personality. Red, often linked to good fortune, happiness, and success, was thought to symbolize these positive qualities, acting as a harbinger of favorable outcomes. Conversely, black was associated with negativity, serving as a warning sign for potential troubles or misfortunes. In contrast, white epitomized purity, innocence, and peace in dreams, signifying spiritual growth and enlightenment. Furthermore, yellow,

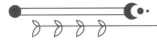

symbolizing authority and power, was interpreted as a sign of success and accomplishment. These symbols provided a form of divination, guiding crucial decisions and offering solutions to problems. The Chinese also believed dreams could diagnose and treat physical and mental ailments, revealing the root causes of illness, leading to specific remedies based on dream imagery.

Alongside the interpretation of symbols and imagery, the Chinese placed significant emphasis on understanding the emotions and experiences of the dreamer. These elements were believed to provide essential insights into the dreamer's subconscious mind and their relationship with the spirit world. Like many cultures and civilizations throughout history, the Chinese held a profound belief in the interpretative power of dreams, viewing them as sources of guidance, wisdom, and unique insights into the inner workings of the universe.

ANCIENT DREAMING HERITAGE

Ancient cultures held a deep respect and reverence for dreams, seeing them as a source of spiritual guidance and wisdom. The following are key points that summarize our ancient dream interpretation heritage:

Spiritual guidance
Different cultures had their own beliefs and interpretations of dreams, each forming a universal dream language.

Sanctity of dreams
Dreams were considered a significant time to connect with a higher power.

Purpose of dreams
Dreams provided guidance for worldly affairs as well healing or cures to physical, emotional, and mental ailments.

Spiritual awareness
Only wise and experienced individuals, such as priests, were trusted to interpret dreams.

Wisdom beyond time
Dreams revealed wisdom from the past, present, and future.

Soul travel
The dreamer's soul traveled to the "lands of the gods" to seek answers.

Importance of dreams

Having answers revealed in a dream was highly valued.

Dream rituals

Each culture had its own prayers or methods to induce and interpret dreams.

Personal awareness

Guidance through dreams was dependent on the level of personal awareness and purity of heart. The ancient belief was that life while awake continued in dream time as well as in the afterlife. They saw a connection between one's actions in their waking life and their experiences in their dreams and in the afterlife. They believed that if a person lived a pure life and had good intentions, they would be rewarded in their afterlife, and this idea was reflected in their dreams.

Life as a dream

The ancients believed that life and the afterlife continued in dream time.

Powerful intentions

A pure heart and good deeds were necessary to receive meaningful dreams.

Transience of life

The ancients believed that worldly life was temporary, and dreams provided a glimpse into the afterlife.

Dream travel

Dreams were seen as a means of astral travel to explore other realms and gain personal growth and spiritual exploration.

Essentially, it becomes clear as you explore ancient dream heritage that they believed that life while awake, continued in dream time, as well as in the afterlife.

The following quote from Neferhotep's tomb in ancient Egypt, highlights the sanctity of dreams and the idea that they provide a connection to the divine and the afterlife. Neferhotep was an ancient Egyptian noble during the reign of King Horemheb, and Divine Father (God father) of Amun-Ra (18th Dynasty 1550-1292 BC). The inscription on his tomb (identified as TT50) became known as 'The Harpist Song':

"There occurs no lingering in the land of
  Egypt,
There is none that does not approach it.
As for the span of earthly affairs
It is the manner of a dream ..."

 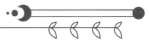
The phrase serves as a reminder of the transience of worldly life and the belief that our experiences while awake continue in dream time and the afterlife. The ancients saw dreams to catch a glimpse into the wisdom and guidance available to the soul, and to make use of this guidance in the material world.

Moreover, the ancients held a unique perspective on the concept of dreaming. To them, dreams were seen as a form of travel to a different realm, where the past, present, and future could be revealed. This idea aligns with modern-day understandings within the body, mind, spirit community, where it is believed that the soul or consciousness can separate from the physical body during dream time and explore other realms and experiences. Astral travel, whether it occurs spontaneously in dreams or through intentional practices, is considered a valuable tool for personal growth and spiritual development.

ANCIENT STORIES EXERCISE

Take a moment to reflect on the stories or ancient myths that have left a lasting impression on you. These narratives often hold clues to your personal symbolism and can offer valuable insights into your dream world. Jot down a brief mention of these impactful stories in your dream journal. By acknowledging their significance, you are embarking on a journey to uncover the hidden layers of your subconscious mind and the symbols that resonate deeply with you. This practice can pave the way for a richer understanding of your dreams and their meanings.

MODERN UNIVERSAL SYMBOLOGY

In modern or contemporary psychology, Sigmund Freud and Carl Jung are two of the most influential psychologists in the field of dream interpretation. While both Freud and Jung believed in the importance of dreams and their ability to shed light on unconscious thoughts and emotions, they had different approaches to interpreting dreams. Freud believed that dreams were the manifestation of unconscious desires, often sexual in nature. He saw dreams as a form of wish fulfillment, where the unconscious mind expresses repressed desires using symbols. According to Freud, the symbols in dreams were often disguised or censored, and it was the job of the analyst to uncover the hidden meaning behind these symbols. He believed that sexual desires and impulses were a common theme in many dreams and that these desires often found expression through symbols in the dream.

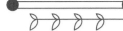

On the other hand, Jung saw dreams as a way for the unconscious to communicate with the conscious mind. He believed that the symbols in dreams were not necessarily representative of repressed desires but were instead a way for the unconscious to communicate important information to the dreamer. Jung saw dreams as having both a personal and collective significance, with symbols reflecting both the dreamer's personal experiences and the collective unconscious shared by all people. Additionally, Freud did not give much importance to the idea of a shared unconscious, or "collective unconscious" among individuals. He believed that each person had their own unique unconscious mind, shaped by their personal experiences and desires. On the other hand, Jung saw the idea of a collective unconscious as an integral part of his psychological theory. He believed that in addition to a personal unconscious, there was also a collective unconscious shared by all individuals. According to Jung, the collective unconscious was made up of archetypes, which were universal symbols and images that were present in the unconscious minds of all people.

These archetypes included symbols such as the mother, the father, the hero, and the shadow, among others. Essentially, Jung saw dreams as having both personal and collective significance, reflecting both the personal experiences and the collective unconscious shared by all individuals. Even though Freud and Jung who both recognized the importance of dreams and their ability to reveal unconscious thoughts and emotions; both had different interpretations of the symbols and meanings in dreams. Freud saw dreams as a manifestation of repressed desires, while Jung saw them as a form of communication from the unconscious to the conscious mind. Having said that, The Book of Dream Craft suggests that you keep an open mind, work with your own dreams, and allow yourself to reach your own conclusions about your dream symbols, to enrich your own self-awareness journey. In this way, you will not miss out on any new self-discoveries!

DREAM ANIMALS EXERCISE

Before delving into the realm of archetypes, let us take a moment to engage in some self-reflection. Consider the animals that have made their presence known in your dreams. Perhaps there are animals that evoke fear, animals you feel a strong affinity for, or animals you simply love. By dedicating a few minutes to this exercise, you are embarking on a journey to uncover the deeper layers of symbolism within your dreams.

Take a moment to jot down a brief description of what each of these animals signifies to you (see figure 10). These descriptions can be a single sentence that captures the essence of their symbolism in your mind. This practice serves as a stepping stone, helping you unearth the symbols that hold significant meaning in your subconscious. Now, challenge yourself to identify your top five animals in this regard. As you do so, you are priming your mind to recognize patterns and symbols that can provide valuable insights into your dreams and their messages.

ANIMAL	TO ME, THIS ANIMAL REPRESENTS	WHY I LOVE/FEAR IT

Figure 9—animal as archetypal symbols

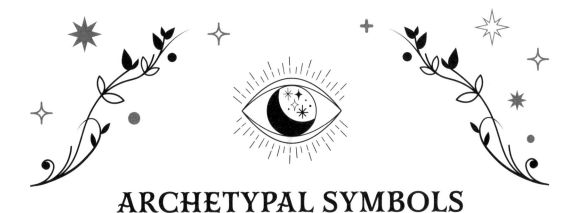

ARCHETYPAL SYMBOLS

Dreams are often rich with archetypes, which are universal symbols or patterns of behavior that are present in the collective unconscious. These archetypes can appear in our dreams in a variety of forms, including animals, objects, people, and settings.

The relationship between animals and humans, and how they have been perceived throughout human history has inevitably formed a collective consciousness that the relatively modern field of psychology refers to as "archetypes". Animals have come to represent something in our minds as a human family—collectively. This is not entirely surprising, since the dawn of human history our ancestors were connected to nature, animals, and the "cosmos". They perceived animals as the embodiment of certain qualities and powers. Additionally, animals were often considered to be divine beings and were worshiped as gods, or means and avenues to reaching higher power, The

Divine Intelligence, to resolve a problem, or even to sustain their daily livelihood.

People believed that animals had special powers and could bring good fortune or misfortune. For example, in ancient Egyptian mythology, the cat was revered as a symbol of beauty and grace and was believed to have the power to protect the dead. In ancient Greek mythology, the horse was associated with speed and strength, and was depicted in many myths and legends. You can say that Animals have always had a special place in the hearts and minds of humans. They evoke a range of emotions in us, from love and affection to fear and revulsion. This is why animals have been depicted in art, literature, and mythology for centuries. They are often seen as symbols of power, freedom, and grace, and are used to represent qualities that human beings admire.

In modern times, our relationship with animals has become more complex. On the

consciousness and will continue to shape our perceptions and beliefs for generations to come.

When it comes to dreaming, the connection between animals and humans is particularly strong. Animals in dreams often symbolize aspects of our personalities and emotions and can reveal a lot about our deepest fears and desires. For example, if you dream about a lion, it may symbolize power and assertiveness, and suggest that you are feeling confident and in control. On the other hand, if you dream about a snake, it may symbolize a fear of the unknown, or a fear of being vulnerable. The presence of animals in our dreams can also reflect our instinctual survival instincts. For example, if you dream about a bear, it may symbolize a fear of being attacked or of being overpowered. This fear is rooted in our primal reflexes, which are wired into our brains to protect us and ensure our survival.

Whether we dream about animals as power animals or as symbols of our deepest fears, they play a powerful role in shaping our subconscious thoughts and beliefs. They help us process our experiences and emotions and offer us a window into the depths of our own psyches. So, next time you have a dream about an animal, try to reflect on what it might be trying to tell you about yourself and your emotions.

one hand, we have domesticated animals and use them for food, transportation, and companionship. On the other hand, we have also come to fear and mistrust some animals, such as snakes and spiders, due to their dangerous and potentially harmful qualities. Regardless of how we feel about them, animals continue to play an important role in our lives and our culture. They inspire us, challenge us, and help us understand our place in the world. Whether we are admiring their beauty, fearing their power, or simply enjoying their companionship, animals are an integral part of our collective

SHADOW ANIMALS

Archetypes can have positive and negative associations in your mind. However, negative associations can change as your attitude changes when you reflect on your dreams and explore what the message is. Animals that trigger a "negative" association as referred to as shadow animals. Just like "power animals" have come to represent our protectors and inspiration, shadow animals represent our deepest fears and phobias.

The concept of shadow animals refers to the unconscious aspects of our personalities that we try to repress or ignore. These are often negative traits, such as anger, fear, guilt, or shame, that we find difficult to acknowledge or accept. In psychology, the shadow is often depicted as the dark side of our personalities, representing the parts of ourselves that we would rather not see. For example, if you have a fear of spiders, you may dream about spiders as shadow animals, representing your fear of the unknown and the dark parts of yourself. By working with these shadow animals in your dreams, you can gain a deeper understanding of your fears and phobias and find ways to overcome them.

Even when you experience a "nightmare" where you are attacked by an animal, there is a strong message for you to address and work through that emotion triggered in your dream. In a sense, our link with the animal kingdom continues as they help us to explore our unconscious beliefs and emotions through our dreams. In the next section, we will explore a few common shadow animals that may pop up in our dreams. These are also examples of universal symbols formed by our collective consciousness.

Spiders

Shadow animals can also represent our deepest fears and phobias. Working with information in our dreams helps us to understand and work through our fears and insecurities. For example, if you dream about a shadow animal that represents your anger, it may be a sign that you need to confront this emotion and find a way to express it in a healthy and constructive way. Take spiders, as an example. You may dream about spiders as shadow animals, representing your fear of the unknown and the dark parts of yourself. You may assume that your dream foretells a "sting" where someone is going to stab you in the back. However, by working with these shadow animals in your dreams, you can gain a deeper understanding of your fears and phobias and find ways to overcome them. Moreover, acknowledging and accepting the parts of ourselves that we may have been trying to hide, we can gain a deeper understanding of our own psychology and learn to integrate these aspects of ourselves

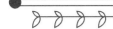

in a positive way as we build our own dream dictionary.

Although spiders are a "common" symbol in many of our dreams, they can also represent something positive for others. For example, spiders are known for weaving webs, which can symbolize protection, safety, and organization or dedicated work and diligence. If you watch a spider weaving its web and reflect on their labor, it is a marvel to behold. Another thing spiders do, is "crawl" out of nowhere, or dangle down a line of silk just in front of where you are. How many times have you experienced this? In some cultures, spiders and their webs are even seen as symbols of good fortune and prosperity. One notable example is the story of Prophet Mohammed at the beginning of spreading his message of Islam when a spider's web

protected him and his companion when they were both hiding in a cave fearing for their lives. However, his adversaries passed by the cave, overlooking Mohammed and his companion; believing that no one had been there since the spider's web was left undisturbed. They both went unnoticed, and unharmed.

This story is often interpreted as a symbol of the power of protection and the strength of the spider's web, God's divine intervention and protection. In this context, the spider and its web become symbols of resilience and security, representing the idea that we are always protected and held in a safe place, even in the darkest of times. Even though spiders in dreams may initially evoke feelings of fear, they can also represent positive aspects of our personalities, such as strength, resilience, and protection. Moreover, no matter how much you fear the outcome of a situation, trusting that a situation may be to our highest good can bring relief. "Divine intervention" can take place, when we explore the message that the spider represents in our dream, releasing us from our worries.

By exploring these themes and possible interpretations of power and shadow animals or archetypes, in your dreams you may be able to gain a deeper understanding of your own subconscious thoughts and emotions. Moreover, viewing the shadow

universal symbols in this manner, may help you to find new ways to channel these positive aspects of a "negative" dream. It may change how you view an animal or a situation in your dream, helping to cope with your "real life" situation.

Snakes

Snakes are a prevalent presence in dreams, and their symbolism takes on different meanings based on the aspect that is relevant in the given context. As a power animal, snakes embody transformation—a profound metamorphosis that goes beyond mere change and holds significant spiritual connotations. This transformation is symbolically tied to self-growth, represented by their unique ability to shed their skin. This shedding signifies personal growth and the embracing of change. Moreover, their connection to medicine and healing arises from the use of their venom in medicinal practices.

However, it is significant to note that the symbolism's scope is not confined to positive interpretations only. Snakes also bear a shadow aspect, signifying fear due to their swift strikes and the potential fatality of their venom. Their rapid bite can lead to grave consequences. Consequently, snakes embody paradoxical symbolism. They represent both healing and transformation, and fear and death. In a dream, a snake might signify an ongoing personal transformation or the necessity to release former patterns of behavior to nurture growth and healing. Furthermore, in numerous ancient cultures, snakes were esteemed greatly and held a special position in religious and spiritual beliefs. Often, they were viewed as potent symbols of renewal. They are associated with wisdom, sovereignty, and the divine.

For instance, the ancient Greeks revered the god Aesculapius, linked to healing and medicine, often depicted with a staff entwined by a snake. The intertwining snakes represented balancing of the dual aspects of illness and cure. The ancient Egyptians too held snakes in reverence, perceiving them as symbols of royalty and power depicting mastering the dual aspects of nature, thus wisdom. Moreover, they were depicted as protective deities safeguarding

pharaohs and the afterlife. Many still regard snakes as symbols of wisdom, rejuvenation, and healing. Depending on dream context, snakes embody impending, inescapable transformation. In the end snakes symbolize the necessity for change.

Furthermore, as a shadow animal, snakes symbolize fear, peril, the unknown, and unforeseen abrupt events. Due to their swift predatory strikes and venomous bite, they frequently intertwine with adverse sentiments. They epitomize vulnerability and can symbolize our profound fears and insecurities regarding sudden upheavals, even mortality. Here, dreaming about snakes may signal the imperative to confront and liberate these fears, thereby effecting life transformation and positive advancement.

In ancient healing practices, snakes also embody wisdom and Kundalini energy. Kundalini, often represented as a coiled snake at the base of the spine, is a concept in yogic philosophy. It signifies latent spiritual energy that, when awakened, leads to transformative experiences and heightened consciousness. This process involves the uncoiling of the "snake," metaphorically representing the ascent of spiritual energy through the chakras. Kundalini awakening is seen as a profound spiritual transformation, resulting in enlightenment, self-realization, and a deep connection to the divine. Just as a snake sheds its skin, this awakening shed old limitations and opens the path to spiritual evolution.

In dreaming of snakes, both aspects of the snake may come into the interpretation of a dream. The latter depends on the context of the dream. Ultimately, perhaps inevitable "transformation" is at the crux of the interpretation.

There are other common universal symbols that involve the animal kingdom and symbolize unconscious fears in dreams. These can include rats, bats, and dark or menacing creatures like wolves or lions. These symbols can indicate deep-seated fears and anxieties that are affecting your waking life. Like with snakes and spiders, these symbols can also have a positive interpretation when viewed as power animals. For example, spiders can symbolize protection, creativity, and resourcefulness, while bats can symbolize intuition, communication with the unconscious, and the ability to navigate the unknown (when it is "dark"). When viewed as shadow animals, universal symbols can indicate the need to confront and release fear. Fear can be released either through facing our emotions directly, or through inner work to understand and overcome the underlying emotional or psychological cause of the fear. In either case, whether as a symbol of power or fear, the appearance of such symbols in a dream holds the potential to serve as potent indicators of the role that fear, and intense emotions play in our life. These emotions often have deep roots, ingrained in the human psyche throughout the course of evolution. Whenever they emerge within your dream, they are beckoning you to confront and address profound fear with you. These fears or anxiety might even be irrational.

However, they reside within your mind, and it is urging you to release them.

ARCHETYPAL PERSONALITIES

Other examples of archetypes can appear in dreams as a personality. They represent universal dream symbols. These archetypal personalities are formed due to what Carl Jung referred to as our collective consciousness. Collective consciousness refers to the shared beliefs, values, ideas, symbols, and experiences that are held by a group or society. If you like, they are the collective pool of knowledge, memories, and cultural elements that individuals within a community or culture draw from. Swiss psychologist Carl Jung developed this idea, later expanded by sociologist Émile Durkheim. It suggests that people are influenced by and contribute to a broader collective awareness. This shapes how they perceive, behave, and understand the world. Essentially, it explains that our thoughts and actions are not just individual. Rather, they are linked to, and are affected are the larger social context.

The Hero

The archetype of the hero is a powerful and enduring symbol that transcends time and culture, representing the universal human desire for courage, resilience, and triumph

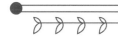

over adversity. This iconic figure is often characterized by their unwavering determination, willingness to face formidable challenges, and a deep sense of purpose. Heroes inspire us with their ability to rise above their limitations, making them a significant presence not only in mythology but also in our dreams, where they appear as a beacon of hope and transformation.

In ancient Greek mythology, for example, the hero archetype was vividly illustrated through the legendary figure of Achilles. Achilles, a central character in Homer's "The Iliad," personified the virtues of heroism. His unparalleled strength and unyielding dedication to honor rendered him the quintessential hero of his age. His tale, replete with both triumphs and tragedies, has etched an enduring imprint on Western culture. He symbolizes courage and the pursuit of greatness, yet this portrayal is juxtaposed with a sense of vulnerability. This vulnerability stemmed from his famous heel, the only point of weakness on his otherwise invulnerable body. Achilles' story illustrates that even the mightiest can possess a vulnerability that, when exposed, can lead to their downfall.

The hero archetype extends beyond the boundaries of ancient Greece, finding resonance in diverse civilizations and cultural narratives. Across history, cultures have celebrated their own heroic figures, each

representing unique qualities and virtues. These figures, whether historical or legendary, often mirror the qualities we admire and aspire to possess. From the valiant knights of medieval Europe to the legendary samurai of feudal Japan, the hero archetype takes on different forms while embodying the timeless values of bravery, selflessness, and the relentless pursuit of justice.

However, symbols in dreams can often represent dual aspects, depending on

the context of the dream. These symbols possess a unique duality, capable of conveying contrasting meanings based on the circumstances that envelop the dream. This underscores the dynamic nature of symbolism within dreams, wherein a single symbol can encapsulate both positive and negative connotations. It can even embody both meanings simultaneously. The interpretation of any symbol within a dream, hinges on the interplay between their inherent representation and the narrative of the dream in which they appear. This intricate interplay of dual aspects adds depth and complexity to dream analysis. It challenges us to unravel the layers of meaning woven into each symbol. Often, pointing to what we need to reflect on or heal.

In modern culture, the hero archetype remains popular. Characters like Luke Skywalker from "Star Wars" and Harry Potter from J.K. Rowling's series capture audiences. These heroes confront immense challenges and embrace their destinies with courage. Their journeys entertain and deeply connect with our aspirations and struggles.

Let us say you had a dream in which you discover yourself within a challenging and adventurous landscape. The backdrop is brimming with obstacles and trials. Within this dream, you exemplify the remarkable qualities of a hero. Someone who displays extraordinary bravery, strength, and determination. As you make your way through this dreamscape, you come across a variety of tests that demand your courage and resilience, reminiscent of the hero archetype. Moreover, in this dream, you find yourself confronting formidable adversaries, or surmounting intimidating obstacles. You might even be driven by a distinct goal or mission, whether it involves rescuing someone in distress, retrieving a valuable artifact, or directly facing a potent adversary.

Your actions within the dream mirror the archetype of the hero. Yet, your emotions in the dream influence your waking state. You may wake up feeling empowered, for example. This feeling lingers beyond the dream, fueling your ability to manage any real-life anxieties effectively. The dream's setting often mirrors the heroic quest, whether it is a mystical realm, a fantastical city, or a treacherous wilderness. Interpreting such a dream, involves considering the heroic qualities that are coming to the forefront in your life. Are you facing a significant challenge or embarking on a new endeavor? The dream may symbolize your inner courage, resilience, and the belief that you can overcome any obstacle. It might also reflect a desire for adventure, personal growth, or a need to step into a leadership role.

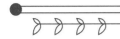

Having such dreams is often a prompt to recognize our own inner strength and the potential for growth and transformation. It encourages us to confront challenges, seize opportunities, and tap into our innate resilience. Often, these dreams remind us that we have the capacity to heroically overcome any adverse situations in real life, much like the heroes we admire in stories and myths.

The Wise man/woman (the sage)

Another prominent archetype you may encounter in dreams, is the wise old man or woman. They symbolize the older and wiser self, representing knowledge, guidance, and wisdom. This archetype has deep roots in various cultures and mythologies. In ancient Greek mythology, the wise centaur Chiron was renowned for his wisdom and mentorship, impacting the lives of many legendary figures. Similarly, in Native American traditions, the wise elder or sage often appears as a revered figure, offering valuable insights and spiritual guidance to the dreamer.

In modern literature and media, the wise old archetype can be found in iconic characters like Gandalf from J.R.R. Tolkien's "The Lord of the Rings" or Yoda from the "Star Wars" franchise. These characters embody wisdom gained through age and experience, and they often serve as mentors to the main protagonists, providing crucial guidance on their heroic journeys. Furthermore, in The Tarot this archetype personality is represented by The Hermit. Encountering the wise old archetype can represent the dreamer's quest for wisdom, the need for guidance in facing life's challenges, or a desire to tap into their own inner source of knowledge. This archetype serves as a reminder from your unconscious mind, that wisdom is gained through experience and introspection.

Having such a dream can illuminate your path forward.

Dreaming of being in a library can symbolize the presence of the sage archetype, representing wisdom and guidance. This dream scenario might reflect your subconscious search for insights or answers, especially when facing challenges or seeking a higher perspective in waking life. Moreover, this dream encourages you to tap into your own inner wisdom and intuition, reminding you that you possess the ability to access profound insights and understanding. It may also suggest the importance of seeking knowledge, whether through learning, meditation, or seeking advice from those with greater experience. In modern times, the sage can appear as a grandparent, or an older person. Someone whose advise you can trust or would seek in real life.

The Mother

The Mother archetype, a universal and deeply symbolic figure. It encompasses the nurturing, protective, and comforting aspects that often represent the essence of motherhood (The Empress in The Tarot). This archetype carries a profound presence in our dreams, drawing from the wellspring of human experience and cultural mythology. In ancient cultures, the mother archetype found embodiment in revered goddesses like Demeter in Greek mythology, who symbolized the fertile nurturing of the earth and the cycle of life, and Isis in Egyptian mythology, embodying maternal protection and regenerative power.

In modern popular culture, the mother archetype continues to resonate through beloved characters, leaving an indelible mark on our collective consciousness. Molly Weasley from the "Harry Potter" series embodies the essence of maternal love and strength, a steadfast protector of her family, offering warmth and care in the face of adversity. Likewise, Marmee from "Little Women" showcases the motherly wisdom and guidance that nurtures her daughters as they navigate life's challenges, showcasing the archetype's role in shaping character and providing emotional support.

For instance, if in your dream you find yourself in a warm, nurturing environment. You may be surrounded by a sense of comfort and protection; where you encounter a maternal figure, radiating unconditional love and care. This figure embodies the

essence of the mother archetype, symbolizing not only nurturing qualities but also a deep connection to the feminine, intuitive aspects of our being.

In a dream, the mother archetype may take the form of a wise and gentle nurturing and caring woman, much like Molly Weasley from "Harry Potter" or Marmee from "Little Women." She may offer soothing words, a loving embrace, or guidance in a soothing, maternal manner. Her presence provides a sense of security, reminding you that you are supported and loved, much like a mother's embrace. In this instance, the dream is not directly about your mother, but rather represents an image that is imprinted in your mind of what represent a "mother" figure. For example, this can be a friend's mother who stands for such attributes in your mind.

Moreover, your friend's mother can also represent your nurturing aspect, so it is not literally about your friend's mother. Additionally, the dream's setting, often cozy and embracing, reflects the qualities associated with the mother archetype. It may be a serene family home, a beautiful garden, or a haven that evokes a feeling of being nurtured. The dream's atmosphere encourages you to tap into your own inner wellspring of nurturing and compassion, perhaps reminding you to care for yourself or others in a more tender and understanding way.

Interpreting this archetype personality in a dream, also involves considering your relationship with yourself - the nurturing, emotional support, and feminine aspects of your personality. Reflect on whether you have been giving or receiving care. And, whether you may need to embrace those nurturing qualities more in your real life. Moreover, the dream may also suggest a need for emotional healing, or a desire to connect with your own inner motherly instincts. Dreams featuring the mother archetype often invite us to explore the balance between nurturing others and taking care of ourselves. They can remind us to seek emotional comfort, create a loving space for ourselves, or connect with the maternal aspects of our own personality. Just as the mother archetype represents a wellspring of love and protection, these dreams encourage us to open our hearts to compassion, both for ourselves and those around us.

The shadow

Another essential archetype that we encounter in our dreams is the Shadow. It represents the concealed, darker aspects of our psyche that we may be avoiding or suppressing. This archetype delves into the depths of our unconscious, holding profound potential for self-discovery and growth. In ancient mythology, we can find traces of the Shadow

in tales like the Greek myth of Orpheus and Eurydice, where the shadowy underworld symbolizes the realm of the unconscious and the mysteries of death. If you like, it symbolizes the worst version of yourself - depicted in the Tarot by The Devil.

In modern popular culture, characters like Voldemort from "Harry Potter", Ursula from "The Little Mermaid", and The Joker from Batman series; serve as embodiments of the shadow archetype, casting a powerful presence that challenges the protagonists to confront their innermost fears and vulnerabilities. The shadow archetype serves as a mirror, reflecting the hidden aspects we may be reluctant to acknowledge, inviting us to integrate and transcend these

aspects to achieve greater self-awareness and wholeness.

Moreover, dreaming about the Shadow self often involves encountering aspects of yourself that you may be unaware of, denying, or struggling to accept. These dreams can be quite intense. They may present unsettling scenarios or characters that reflect the hidden, less desirable, aspects of your personality or past experiences. For example, if in your dream, you find yourself walking through a dense, eerie forest cloaked in darkness. The air feels heavy, and a sense of foreboding hangs in the atmosphere. As you venture deeper, you notice a figure lurking within the shadows. It takes on the form of a dark, enigmatic presence, stirring a blend of fear and curiosity. Although not directly revealing itself, its presence registers on the periphery of your senses. Within this dream, the dark forest and the enigmatic figure symbolize the shadow archetype. The dream serves as a direct encounter with facets of your unconscious mind that you may be evading in your waking life. The dream extends a symbolic invitation to explore and confront these shadow aspects. By facing the shadow within the dream, you initiate a dialogue with these suppressed elements, seeking comprehension and integration.

So, reflect on your emotions upon waking from a dream. Make sure to write a few

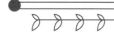 
sentences down in your journal. Consider any recent experiences in your real life that may have triggered that dream. Willingness to explore the deeper layers of your psyche with a compassionate attitude toward the hidden parts of yourself, is essential part of dream craft. Dreams about the shadow archetype can, therefore, be transformative, providing insights into areas where personal growth and healing are needed. They remind us that embracing the entirety of our being, including the less visible aspects, is a crucial step toward self-awareness and a more balanced, authentic life.

In our dreams, archetypes personalities emerge as significant symbols, offering valuable insights into our inner landscape. The Mother archetype may bring comfort and guidance, while the Shadow archetype might reveal areas of unresolved conflict or hidden potential. Do you recall the previous example of the woman sneering at me? She represented my shadow aspect of myself. The part that was not comfortable with being a professional psychic. Archetypal energies in a dream invite self-exploration. They help us unlock the profound layers of our subconscious, gaining a deeper understanding of the intricate interplay between light and darkness within our own psyche.

The Father

This archetype represents authority, stability, and wisdom. In ancient cultures, the father archetype was often personified as a god, such as the Greek god Zeus or the Norse god Odin. In popular culture, the father archetype is embodied in characters like Mufasa from "The Lion King" and Gandalf from "The Lord of the Rings". It represents male guidance, someone who helps us to nurture our logical, assertive side. In the Tarot, this archetype is represented by The Emperor. Dreaming about the father archetype can offer deep insights into our connection with authority, stability, and wisdom. Imagine a dream where you're on a vast mountainside, feeling respect and strength from the landscape. While exploring, you encounter a fatherly figure radiating guidance and security. This figure embodies the father archetype, symbolizing leadership, structure, and rational aspects of our mind.

In this dream, the mountainside represents life's challenges and opportunities, like the support we seek from a fatherly presence during uncertainty. The father figure brings reassurance and a strong foundation in the dream, akin to ancient gods of wisdom and authority. This figure acts as a guiding light and mentor, embodying those timeless qualities.

This dream serves as a prompt to connect with our inner father archetype, nurturing the development of our logical and assertive aspects. It encourages us to embrace leadership and stability within ourselves, akin to the way Mufasa in "The Lion King" and Gandalf in "The Lord of the Rings" exemplify these virtues. The Tarot's Emperor card aligns with this archetype, depicting a figure in command, representing authority, structure, practicality, and the ability to take charge of one's life. In your journal, reflect on whether you are seeking more structure and leadership in your life. Or, if you are being called upon to embody these qualities for others. Reflect on any challenges or decisions you might be facing and how embracing the father archetype's attributes could empower you to tackle them with confidence.

Dreams featuring the father archetype often urge us to integrate these qualities into our daily lives, reminding us that both the paternal and maternal aspects within us are essential for growth and balance. By engaging with the father archetype in our dreams, we tap into a wellspring for nurturing our logical, assertive side and aligning with the stable, authoritative force that resides within us. This archetype in our dreams serves as a reminder that embracing such attributes contributes to our personal development and the fulfillment of our potential.

The Child

This archetype represents innocence, creativity, and potential. The child archetype is often associated with the beginning of life and can symbolize a new beginning or a return to a more innocent state (such as The Fool in the Tarot). In popular culture, the child archetype is embodied in characters like Alice from "Alice in Wonderland" and Scout from "To Kill a Mockingbird." Scout who represents innocence, creativity, and potential, is an inquisitive young girl who is still learning about the world around her. Through her experiences and observations, she begins to understand the complexities of human nature and the injustices of society.

In this sense, Scout represents the child archetype because she symbolizes the beginning of life and the potential for growth and change. Her innocence and open-mindedness serve as a reminder of the value of seeing the world through a fresh perspective

and the importance of retaining a sense of wonder and innocence even as we grow older. Scout's journey in *To Kill a Mockingbird* mirrors our own journey through life, and her character serves as an inspiration for us to remain curious, compassionate, and true to ourselves.

Dreaming about the child archetype can offer profound insights into our innocence, creativity, and the aspects of ourselves that are eager to learn and explore. For instance, if in your dream you find yourself in a lively playground, surrounded by laughter. You meet a child filled with curiosity. This young figure symbolizes not just enthusiasm and openness, but also potential for growth and imagination. The dream's playground mirrors the limitless creativity of the child archetype. Just as a child explores with wonder, this dream prompts you to embrace curiosity for a more open mindset. The child's presence brings innocence and pure intentions, urging you to reconnect with unspoiled aspects of yourself.

In popular culture, characters like Peter Pan from "Peter Pan" and Matilda from Roald Dahl's book carry the essence of the child archetype. They represent the qualities of wonder, resilience, and the ability to see magic in everyday experiences. These characters inspire us to maintain our sense of wonder, even as we grow older. Interpreting this dream involves exploring your relationship with creativity, spontaneity, and the desire to learn and grow. Reflect on whether you have been embracing new experiences. Or have you been feeling stagnant in certain aspects of your life? Consider whether the child figure is trying to convey a message about embracing a more open-hearted and free-spirited approach to life's challenges.

The child archetype in a dream often invites us to nurture our own creativity, spontaneity, and playfulness. They remind us of the importance of maintaining a fresh perspective, even in the face of responsibilities and adulthood. By connecting with the child archetype in our dreams, we unlock a wellspring of imagination, curiosity, and a sense of wonder that can enrich our lives and help us find joy in the simplest moments. As you wake from a dream with the child archetype, consider how you can infuse your waking life with more childlike enthusiasm. Embrace new opportunities, allow yourself to be curious, and explore your creativity without judgment. Just as the child archetype represents the pure potential within us, these dreams encourage us to approach life with open arms and a heart full of wonder.

The Trickster

The trickster archetype embodies mischief, humor, and a challenge to the status quo. In ancient cultures, it was often personified as a god or spirit, such as the Native American Coyote or the Norse god Loki. Similarly, in popular culture, characters like Bugs Bunny from "Looney Tunes" and The Joker from "Batman" embody this archetype.

Norse mythology portrays Loki as a trickster archetype due to his mischievous and cunning nature. He played pranks on other gods, creating chaos through his wit and deception. However, his actions were also essential for keeping the gods alert and preventing complacency. Similarly, The Joker, a trickster archetype in popular culture, uses his wit to challenge authority and disrupt the established order. Both Loki and The Joker challenge the status quo to bring about change. Their mischievous behavior encourages society to question assumptions and evolve.

Dreaming about the trickster archetype can be thought-provoking. Picture a dream in a bustling city where a figure exudes mischievousness and unpredictability. This character represents the trickster archetype, challenging the ordinary and disrupting the mundane. In this dream, the cityscape symbolizes routine, while the trickster figure injects chaos and humor. Just as the Native American Coyote or Norse god Loki embodied this archetype, the dream's trickster encourages breaking free from the ordinary and embracing the unconventional.

The trickster's presence in the dream acts as a catalyst for change, reminding that a touch of mischief can lead to growth. Loki, in Norse mythology, was known for his pranks, stirring chaos while keeping the gods vigilant. Similarly, The Joker, a trickster archetype in popular culture, challenges authority and order, symbolizing a force of change that pushes society to re-evaluate its assumptions.

The trickster's archetype is playful yet challenging energy. Reflect on where you might be stuck in routines and hesitant to challenge the ordinary. Consider how introducing a bit of unpredictability could lead to positive transformation. The trickster archetype in your dream serves as a reminder

that embracing change, even with a touch of chaos, can foster growth, innovation, and a fresh perspective on life's possibilities.

The Lover

This archetype represents passion, intimacy, and connection. The lover archetype can symbolize our desire for romantic love or our search for deeper connections with others. In popular culture, the lover archetype is embodied in characters like Romeo from "Romeo and Juliet" and Jack from "Titanic." In the movie, Jack is depicted as a brave, selfless, and charismatic young man who is determined to protect those he loves and to help others in need. Despite facing many challenges and obstacles, Jack remains optimistic and resourceful, always finding a way to overcome adversity. Furthermore, Jack's relationship with Rose, the film's protagonist, also showcases the lover archetype as he is her protector and helps her to find the strength to overcome her own obstacles.

The lover archetype, often personifying passion, connection, and deep emotions is a powerful presence in both dreams and waking life. Imagine a dream where you find yourself in a serene garden, surrounded by lush flowers and vibrant colors. Amidst this beauty, you encounter a captivating figure, radiating an intense yet gentle energy—a symbol of the lover archetype. This figure embodies not just romantic love but a profound connection to life, creativity, and a genuine appreciation of the world's richness. In this dream, the garden represents the fertile ground of emotions, desires, and the human heart. The lover's presence evokes feelings of warmth, intimacy, and a heightened sense of connection, stirring your deepest passions. Just as lovers are often portrayed in literature and art, this dream's archetype encourages you to explore the depth of your emotions, not only in romantic relationships but also in your connection to the world around you.

The lover archetype in this dream serves as a reminder of the importance of passion, affection, and meaningful connections. It urges you to embrace the richness of life, fully engaging with the people, experiences, and creative pursuits that stir your heart. Much like famous lover archetypes such as Romeo and Juliet or the characters in the works of Shakespeare, this dream's figure symbolizes the intensity of feeling and the desire for a genuine, heartfelt experience. Interpreting this dream involves exploring your emotional landscape and relationships. Reflect on how you connect with others, the passions that ignite your spirit, and the things that bring joy and fulfillment to your life. The lover archetype in your dream reminds you of the beauty of

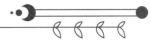

pursue love in its various forms, whether it's a romantic partnership, deep friendships, or a profound appreciation for the world's wonders. Embracing the lover within you can lead to a more vibrant and enriching life, nurturing not only your own heart but also the hearts of those around you.

Dream archetypes are, therefore, not just limited to ancient history and mythology but can also be found as symbols of modern values and beliefs. They are part of our collective heritage if you like. For example, the

hero archetype is still a common symbol in modern popular culture, appearing in films, TV shows, and books as a symbol of courage, bravery, and determination. This archetype can take many different forms in modern culture, from the traditional, strong, and stoic hero, to the flawed, anti-hero, who challenges traditional ideas of what a hero should be.

Similarly, the trickster archetype can also be found in modern popular culture. This archetype is often portrayed as a mischievous character who uses wit, cunning, and humor to challenge the status quo and to bring about change. Characters like Bugs Bunny, The Simpsons' Bart Simpson, and the Marvel Comics character, Deadpool, are all examples of the trickster archetype in contemporary culture. Furthermore, the mother figure archetype, which is often associated with nurturing, protection, and guidance, is also a common symbol. Characters like Mama Bear from the television show, We Bare Bears, and Marge Simpson from The Simpsons are both examples of the mother figure archetype in contemporary culture.

These are just a few examples of the many universal archetypes that can appear in our dreams. Furthermore, archetypes continue to be a powerful tool for representing universal themes and values that are relevant to contemporary audiences. Whether we

encounter heroes, mothers, shadows, or any other archetypes in your dreams, these symbols can offer valuable insight into our unconscious minds and help us better understand our deepest fears, desires, and aspirations and meaning to the interpretation of the dream. Such representations can appear at any time in our dreams. They symbolize a quality within you, rather than the personality or character itself.

ARCHETYPES EXERCISE

To delve further into the intricate web of archetypes that reside within your psyche, spare a few moments for introspection. Consider the characters and personalities that consistently capture your attention or evoke an aversion within you. Take the time to compile a list, noting down the top five archetypes that stand out most prominently in your mind or hold a particular significance for you. By engaging in this exercise, you are opening a doorway to unraveling the hidden layers of your dreams and the motivations that shape your conscious thoughts and actions.

As you identify and list these archetypes, your journey of self-discovery begins. These archetypal patterns can reveal the underlying currents of emotion and desire that flow through your dreams, influencing your perceptions and steering your decisions. So, pause for a moment and ask yourself: What are the top five archetypes that leave their mark on your psyche? This exploration is a vital step towards deciphering the intricate tapestry of your dreams and understanding the profound impact of archetypes on your life's narrative (see figure 11).

Finally, working with shadow and universal archetype symbols consciously, through journaling your dreams, is a powerful and safe tool for personal growth and self-discovery. It changes our perspective too, by releasing any repressed aspects of our personalities, fears, and insecurities. Just imagine how wonderful it would be when the "nightmares" stop, and we can begin to enjoy real life as well as dream time!

ARCHETYPES EXERCISE

ARCHETYPE	REPRESENTED BY (NAME A PERSON/CHARACTER)
The Hero	
The Mother	
The Father	
The Child	
The Trickster	
The Lover	
(Other: the victim, the mentor, the wanderer)	

UNIVERSAL DREAM THEMES

Universal themes in dreams are common subject matters that often appear across cultures. They are symbols that seep through to our minds and get embedded in our culture. They may not necessarily be archetypes, but they are recurring symbols that can have similar meanings and interpretations in our modern collective unconsciousness. They can reveal deep-seated fears, desires, and anxieties that are shared by many people, as well as common aspects of life that we all go through regardless of where we come from, such as birth, death, teeth falling, and many more. Here are some of the common symbols that often appear in dreams and carry a universal interpretation. These symbols may have different personal significance for everyone but have an underlying overarching meaning.

BIRTH

Dreams of births and new-born babies often hold a universal symbolism of new beginnings and fresh starts. The image of a birth in a dream can reflect various aspects of our lives, such as embarking on a new phase, undergoing a significant transition, or entering a new cycle. Just as a birth signifies the arrival of something new and transformative in waking life, this dream symbolizes a shift or a reawakening within us.

Furthermore, the act of giving birth in a dream can mirror our subconscious desire for growth, change, and the opportunity to start afresh. It is as if our inner selves are yearning for a blank canvas upon which we can paint the next chapter of our journey. Moreover, dreaming of giving birth to a baby girl might symbolize embracing your feminine qualities, tapping into your intuitive and nurturing side; or embarking on a new phase of self-discovery and emotional growth. On the other hand, dreaming of a baby boy's birth could represent your connection with your assertive and masculine traits, signaling a time of assertiveness and assertive action in your life.

Furthermore, the sex of the baby in your dream can offer insights into the aspects of yourself that are currently in the process of renewal. Just as the baby represents new beginnings, the gender can reflect the qualities you are nurturing within you. For instance, if you dream of giving birth to a baby girl and you are a man, it might signify a newfound connection with your emotional side, encouraging you to embrace vulnerability and empathy. Alternatively, if you are a woman and dream of a baby boy's birth, it could point to a phase of assertiveness and external action that's unfolding within you. These dreams remind us that our inner landscape is dynamic and ever evolving, offering us the chance to explore and integrate various facets of ourselves as we navigate the journey of life.

Additionally, the ease or difficulty of birth portrayed in dreams can offer further layers of insight into the process of embracing new beginnings. Just as the physical act of giving birth can range from effortless to challenging, the symbolism in dreams can mirror the ease or struggle associated with embarking

on a new phase or transition in our lives. Imagine dreaming of a smooth and painless birth, where the baby comes into the world with minimal effort. This scenario might signify that you are entering a new chapter with grace and ease, where opportunities align seamlessly, and the path forward is clear. It reflects a sense of readiness and confidence in embracing change.

On the other hand, dreaming of labor pains and a difficult birth can symbolize the challenges and resistance that often accompany transitions and new beginnings. These dreams might point to the obstacles or emotional hurdles you are encountering as you venture into uncharted territory. Just as labor pains represent the intense effort and discomfort of bringing forth new life, the dream signifies the effort and perseverance required to establish the changes you seek. For instance, envision a dream where you experience prolonged and challenging labor pains before finally giving birth. This could reflect the struggles and setbacks you are facing in your pursuit of a new endeavor. However, this dream also highlights your determination and willingness to push through difficulties, ultimately leading to the birth of a transformed phase in your life.

These dreams remind us that while some changes may come effortlessly, others might demand resilience and perseverance. The

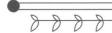
symbolism of ease or difficulty in birth underscores the diverse range of experiences we encounter when embracing new beginnings. Just as real-life labor pains eventually give way to the joy of new life, these dreams indicate that challenges can lead to growth and transformation, ultimately paving the way for a fresh chapter to unfold.

CELEBRITIES OR LEADERS

Dreams involving celebrities or leaders can be fascinating because they often represent aspects of ourselves, or qualities imprinted in our psyche, that we admire or want to emulate. For example, if you dream about a celebrity that you admire for their confidence and charisma, it might symbolize your own desire to be more confident in your waking life. This could be especially true if you find yourself in a situation in the dream where you are interacting with the celebrity and feel envious of their confidence. On the other hand, if you dream about a leader that you disagree with, it could represent your own inner conflict and feelings of opposition towards certain ideas or values. Additionally, dreaming about a celebrity or leader could also be a manifestation of our collective cultural beliefs and values. For instance, a popular leader may symbolize the collective hopes and aspirations of a community, while a celebrity known for their controversy may symbolize a cultural fear or unease about certain societal issues.

It is also important to note that the specific celebrity or leader in a dream can be significant as well. For example, dreaming about a historical figure like Martin Luther King Jr. may symbolize a desire for social justice and equality, while dreaming about a celebrity known for their beauty and style might symbolize our own desires to be more attractive or stylish.

Moreover, dreams involving celebrities or leaders offer a unique perspective on our psyche, sometimes revealing a strong ego or an inner drive for recognition and fame. Such dreams could manifest as a reflection of our desire to stand out and be acknowledged in the same way these prominent figures are. For instance, envision dreaming about being in the spotlight alongside a celebrity, sharing their limelight. This dream might signify a longing for recognition and validation, potentially indicating a need to explore what truly fuels our self-worth and whether external validation aligns with our core values.

Similarly, if you find yourself assuming a leadership role in a dream, commanding attention and admiration, it could suggest a burgeoning desire to be in a position of influence. However, it is essential to consider

whether this ambition aligns with your authentic self or if it's merely a projection of societal ideals. These dreams can prompt us to reflect on the motivations behind our ambitions, urging us to discern between pursuing acclaim for genuine fulfillment versus pursuing it for the sake of appeasing our ego.

In such cases, the dream serves as an invitation to delve into our core values and what truly resonates with our innermost desires. It encourages us to examine whether the pursuit of fame aligns with our authenticity or if it's driven by external pressures. Celebrity and leader dreams can reveal a lot about our personal desires and values, as well as our collective cultural beliefs and values. These dreams can offer insight into what we aspire to become and what we fear and can help us better understand ourselves and

our place in the world. By dissecting these dreams and their underlying messages, we can gain a clearer understanding of what we genuinely yearn for and whether our aspirations are in harmony with our true selves.

COMMUNICATION DEVICES

Dreams involving communication methods like telephone calls offer a fascinating glimpse into our subconscious desires for connection and interaction. For instance, dreaming about engaging in a lively conversation over the phone with a close friend. This dream might symbolize a longing for meaningful connections and the need to communicate openly with people who matter to you. On the other hand, a dream of being unable to dial a number or encountering technical issues with the phone could point to challenges in expressing yourself or difficulties in reaching out to others.

Additionally, a dream of receiving a text message, could signify the anticipation of receiving important news or information in your waking life. For example, if you dream of anxiously checking your phone for a text message from a potential employer, it could reflect your eagerness to hear about a job offer or interview opportunity. Similarly, a dream where you find yourself texting a romantic interest might reflect your desire to establish a closer connection with that person. These dreams encourage introspection into whether you're seizing the chances for connection that come your way.

Moreover, the mode of communication itself can offer clues about the timing and significance of the information being conveyed. For instance, a dream of reading an old-fashioned letter or newspaper might indicate the retrieval of memories or insights. Dreaming about reading a faded newspaper article, for example, about a historical event could suggest a need to reflect on your personal history or explore a situation from the past. On the other hand, digital communication methods like emails or online newspapers might foreshadow future news or events. A dream where you receive an email from a colleague about a meeting could symbolize upcoming discussions or collaborations in your professional life.

Dreams of receiving news through a telephone call could suggest current matters, while the urgency of mobile calls implies immediate communication. For example, envision dreaming of receiving an unexpected mobile call from a family member who lives abroad, informing you of an imminent visit. This dream could reflect your excitement about the upcoming reunion and the anticipation of connecting with your family member in person. Furthermore, the

dream's chosen communication medium offers valuable insights into its timing and urgency, assisting in the interpretation of its relevance to your waking life.

DEATH

Death in a dream can hold profound symbolic meanings that extend beyond the literal concept of physical mortality. In the realm of dream interpretation, death often signifies the endings. For example, ending of a chapter, the completion of a cycle, and the initiation of new beginnings. It is, therefore, important to remember that these dreams rarely foretell actual demise; rather, they speak to the transitions and transformations we experience in various aspects of our lives.

For instance, dreaming of witnessing a funeral, where people gather to bid farewell to a loved one. This could symbolize the closure of a certain phase or situation in your life. Just as a funeral mark the end of someone's earthly journey, this dream might reflect your acknowledgment of a significant ending in your waking life. It could be a representation of leaving behind outdated beliefs, letting go of unhelpful habits, or concluding a significant project.

Similarly, dreaming about walking through a dark tunnel, a passage that eventually leads to a bright, sunny landscape.

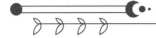
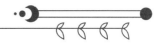

This dream scenario can mirror the concept of death symbolizing the transition from one phase to another. The tunnel signifies the passage between the old and the new, the unfamiliar and the known. In this dream, the journey through the tunnel represents the process of navigating the changes that life presents. Just as the tunnel's darkness eventually gives way to light, your dream underscores that even in moments of transition, positivity and renewal are attainable.

Moreover, consider a dream where you encounter a withered tree, its leaves falling as if in the throes of autumn. This imagery is reminiscent of the changing seasons, where the shedding of leaves signifies the natural progression from one phase to another. Similarly, in the context of the dream, the image of the withered ding of one cycle or

phase, and the necessity of beginning of another. It may symbolize the passing of a particular stage, making way for a new and rejuvenated phase. This dream encourages you to embrace change and understand that every ending paves the way for a fresh start; much like the Death card in the Tarot. Death dreams reflect our psyche's recognition of closure and new beginnings. By viewing these dreams through the lens of symbolism rather than the literal notion of death, we can gain insight into the ebb and flow of life's cycles, ultimately guiding us toward personal development and embracing the opportunities that transitions bring.

EDUCATION: SCHOOL/COLLEGE/UNIVERSITY

Dreams featuring educational institutions offer a rich tapestry of symbolism, encompassing various facets of our personal and professional evolution. Just as these institutions serve as hubs of learning in the waking world, their presence in our dreams unveils a realm of desires for knowledge and understanding. If in your dream you find yourself back in a classroom setting; it reflects the need to learn a lesson in life depending on what is currently going on in your life. Such dreams may arise when you are feeling uncertain or perhaps require a refresher on fundamental aspects of your life or a specific situation you are navigating.

Furthermore, dreaming about enrolling in a college or university encapsulates not only the yearning for intellectual advancement and personal growth; but also, that your level of awareness is now higher- as opposed to going back to lower school as in the previous example. It is as if your subconscious is urging you to embrace novel ideas, forge new connections, and embark on uncharted experiences that foster your journey; signaling a period of further personal growth that you are undergoing. The way your interactions and experiences unfold within this dream's educational setting can offer additional insights into aspects of your life that might be posing challenges, causing stress, or triggering a desire for deeper understanding. Moreover, the specific academic domain you engage with in the dream, be it science, literature, or art, adds an additional level of meaning, shedding light on your current frame of mind or an aspect to explore in your life currently.

Additionally, dreams involving educational settings also offer a glimpse into the past. As you navigate through familiar hallways that evoke memories of school days, these dreams encourage you to confront emotions and recollections woven into your personal history—lessons from the past which are still not learned! They provide a means to process and integrate past experiences into your current reality. If your dream takes you back to an elementary or primary school, it nudges you to approach your present circumstances with the innocence and openness of a child. As a student, you are prompted to absorb and learn before progressing to a deeper understanding.

Educational institutions within dreams go beyond their physical presence; they morph into powerful symbols of personal journeys. These dreams serve as reminders to stay open to lifelong learning, to embrace personal growth, and to reflect on how past experiences influence present decisions. By interpreting these dreams considering your unique life path and aspirations, you unlock a path to self-awareness, allowing your subconscious to shed light on your ongoing voyage of self-discovery. House/Home/Sofa

A house in dreams carries profound

meanings, often evoking a sense of security, stability, and familiarity—like a refuge we call our own. Its interpretation can have diverse implications, yet a common thread weaves through them all: the notion of home, emotions, and personal growth. The house stands as a representation of your inner sanctum, your emotional landscape, and your current state of mind. For instance, a dream featuring a cluttered or disorderly house might mirror feelings of chaos or uncertainty. On the other hand, an image of a serene and tidy house may mirror your inner sense of peace and equilibrium. Furthermore, this symbol extends its reach to encompass your personal evolution, as it mirrors your inner self—the very dwelling place of your soul.

Consider the dimensions of the house within your dream. A home is more than a structure. It is like a canvas painted with intricate nuances. A grand, expansive house may mirror your aspirations for growth and broadening horizons. Conversely, a small, cramped dwelling might echo sentiments of being confined or limited in your current circumstances. The absence of a roof may signify a sense of insecurity, particularly following a jarring experience. Dreams featuring crowded households—bustling with family members—can reflect a yearning for acknowledgment within a group, or

conversely, a feeling of being overwhelmed by the desire to "fit in." Such dreams might also underscore a sense of responsibility towards the well-being of those in your close circles.

Yet, the essence of a house within dreams is not confined to the present moment. It represents a repository of memories, both pleasant and challenging. A childhood home that emerges in a dream might summon long-forgotten emotions and recollections from that period of life, opening a gateway to the past. As you decipher the symbolism of houses in your dreams, remember that it reflects your deepest self, your emotional terrain, and the ever-unfolding journey of personal growth too.

LOCATIONS: UNKNOWN VS. FAMILIAR

Dreams featuring unfamiliar locations might initially puzzle you, yet they often mirror a sense of bewilderment or uncertainty experienced in your waking life. If you find yourself in a dream where a familiar place appears in an entirely unfamiliar setting, it may symbolize an alarm bell—signaling a shift in your reality or a wavering of your foundations. This transformation might usher in positivity or negativity. However, what is certain is that your unconscious mind is attracting your attention (so you can

remember it when waking up). The dream will stand out in your mind, disrupting your routine and the familiarity you have come to rely upon.

A familiar backdrop transplanted into an unfamiliar terrain can also carry the whisper of exploration. This dream signifies your readiness to embrace new changes in your life or take the plunge into uncharted waters. It may reflect your itch for fresh experiences or yearning to venture beyond your comfort zone. Conversely, it could hint at a longing for the comforting embrace of the known when confronted with the unfamiliar. Moreover, the contrast again may allow you to remember and therefore pay attention to the message of the dream. Specifically, that it is not about the familiar, but that there is a twist to what you are familiar with. Essentially, dreaming of unfamiliar landscapes can serve as a mirror reflecting the hidden aspects of your subconscious. Within these dreams, emotions and memories that you may not have addressed in your conscious state can surface, unveiling the uncharted regions of your inner realm. As you dissect the finer details of these dreams, you peel back layers of your psyche that remain unexplored, offering a precious key to unlocking the mysteries of your inner world. Location drams, if you like, shine a light on unexplored facets within yourself or

your life. Whether these journeys through the unknown leave you feeling uplifted or bewildered, it is important to take note of the emotions and particulars they bring to the forefront. These subtle cues act as breadcrumbs, guiding you towards a more profound understanding of your existence and the challenges you encounter.

NATURE'S ELEMENTS

In the world of dream interpretation, we also delve into the intriguing realm of symbolic meanings attached to the elements of nature. Fire, water, wind, and earth in dreams act as powerful symbols that carry messages relating to our emotions, ambitions, challenges, and personal growth. As we explore their

symbolism, we unlock a practical language that offers insights, encourages introspection, and enhances our comprehension of our inner thoughts and life encounters.

Earth

Grounded and steadfast, the earth element in dreams serves as a symbol of stability, foundation, necessary groundwork, and our connection to the physical world. In the tarot, this element is represented by The Pentacles—the result of our endeavors. Dreams featuring earth often reflect our need for security, financial security, a solid footing, and a sense of rootedness. Moreover, a dream of fertile soil may signify the potential for growth and nourishment in our lives, whether in relationships, careers, or personal pursuits. Similarly, tilling the earth in a dream might symbolize the effort we invest in establishing strong foundations for our endeavors.

Dreams of walking on solid ground or feeling the earth beneath our feet can evoke a sense of stability and assurance. Such dreams might occur during times when we seek balance and a reliable base to support us. Conversely, dreams of earthquakes or shifting landscapes might mirror the upheavals or uncertainties we are experiencing in waking life. The earth element's presence in our dreams encourages us to reflect on the solidity of our plans, the strength of our connections, and the need to stay grounded amidst the ever-changing tides of existence. Just as roots anchor a tree, the earth in dreams reminds us to find stability within ourselves even as we navigate the fluctuations of the external world. Is the path to your next life cycle or platform clear? If not, this makes a great question to ask your mind at dreamtime in your dream journal!

Fire

Fire, a symbol of transformation, growth and drive, ignites the landscapes of our dreams with its dynamic power. In dreamscapes, fire represents not only destruction (of the old) and change but also the creative force that propels us forward. A dream featuring a comforting and cozy fire can evoke feelings of security and warmth, representing

feeling good about life presently, or the need for solace and stability. On the other hand, a dream filled with roaring flames might allude to the need for a cathartic release or the urge to let go of the past, making way for new beginnings.

Beyond its destructive potential, fire embodies the essence of passion, drive, and desire. For Tarot enthusiasts, this element is represented by The Wands minor arcana. Just as it consumes and transforms, fire in dreams can symbolize the passion and drive that illuminate our fervent aspirations and yearnings. It serves as a beacon guiding us toward our deepest wishes and innermost longings. Like a phoenix rising from its ashes, fire in dreams signifies the cycle of rebirth and renewal, compelling us to

embrace change, confront challenges, and harness our creative potential to shape our waking reality.

Water

Water, as a powerful elemental force, mirrors the ebb and flow of our emotions in dreams. It serves as a metaphor for our internal emotional landscapes, ranging from tranquility to turmoil. The representation of water can be dualistic, encompassing both serene calmness and tempestuous intensity. A dream of tranquil waters, whether in the form of an expansive ocean, serene lake, or gentle stream, often symbolizes a state of inner peace and emotional equilibrium. Such dreams hint at a harmonious connection with our feelings and a sense of emotional stability.

Conversely, dreams involving turbulent or murky waters reflect emotional unrest, difficult emotive relationships and uncertainty. These dreams may signify unresolved emotions, fear of the unknown, or challenges within relationships. Like ripples in water, our emotional reactions can spread across various aspects of our lives, echoing the complex interplay of feelings both within ourselves and in relation to others. Ultimately, water's symbolism in dreams serves as a mirror that reflects the depths of our emotional journey, inviting us to dive

into the waters of our subconscious to better understand the currents that shape our waking experiences. In the Tarot, the water element is represented by The Cups minor arcana- the vessel hat contains our emotions and feelings of hope.

Wind

The wind, an intangible yet powerful force, dances through our dreams as a symbol of mental expression, movement of thoughts, and the unseen currents that shape our lives. Dreams featuring the wind often carry messages of change, transition, and the need to adapt to shifting circumstances. In the Tarot, the wind element is represented by The Swords minor arcana. Furthermore, a gentle breeze might signify a subtle shift in our lives, nudging us to embrace new opportunities. On the other hand, dreams of a violent storm may reflect inner turmoil or the challenges we face in navigating turbulent times, or lack of mental clarity.

The wind's presence in dreams can also indicate the flow of ideas and information. A dream of wind carrying whispers or messages might suggest the need to pay attention to subtle cues or seek insights from unexpected sources. Just as wind can quickly change direction, dreams of wind can encourage us to remain flexible and open-minded, allowing us to harness the power of change to our advantage. Wind can also be associated with inspiration and quick thinking and decisive action. It urges us to let our thoughts and ideas take flight like leaves carried by a gust. And, to explore uncharted territories and embracing novel perspectives.

The myth of Icarus and his father Daedalus brings some of the elements together. Icarus planned to escape from imprisonment on the island of Crete by crafting wings (wind) made of feathers and wax. Daedalus warned his son not to fly too close to the sun (see the next section on Sun & Moon), or the sea (water); as it would lead to disaster. However, Icarus becomes intoxicated by the thrill of flying and ignores his father's advice. As he soars higher, the sun's heat melts the wax on his wings, causing them to disintegrate. The wind then carries Icarus to his tragic downfall, as he plummets into the sea and drowns.

This story showcases the powerful symbolism of wind in dreams, representing not only the exhilaration of freedom and aspiration but also the potential dangers of recklessness and ignoring caution. Icarus's failure to heed his father's advice serves as a cautionary tale about the consequences of flying too close to the sun (giver of energy), reflecting how the wind's influence can lead to both glorious heights and devastating falls in the realm of dreams.

PEOPLE

Dreaming of people, we know is a common experience. It can be especially confusing when they look different in our dreams. In these cases, it is important to remember that the people in our dreams are not necessarily literal representations of the people themselves, but rather symbols of aspects of ourselves that are connected, symbolized by qualities which describe the person we dream about. These dream symbols can be connected to memories, experiences, character attributes, or emotions that we associate with those people in our waking lives.

For example, if you dream of a friend who looks different, it may symbolize a change in your relationship with that person, or a change in the way you view them; or that person may not be who you think they are. If you dream of a family member who looks different, it may symbolize a change in your relationship with your family, or a change in your understanding of your family history. Similarly, if you dream of a loved one who looks different, it may symbolize a change in the way you feel about that person, or a change in your relationship with them. In these cases, the key to understanding the meaning of the dream is to reflect on what the person represents to you and what changes you are currently experiencing in your life. By exploring these connections, you can gain deeper insight into your unconscious thoughts and emotions.

Sex dreams

Dreams about sex can be a common occurrence and can hold a variety of interpretations, as mentioned earlier. In general, sexual dreams symbolize our desires, needs, and inner motivations. They can also represent our search for intimacy and connection with others. Repressed sexual desires or suppressed emotions can sometimes manifest in sexual dreams, indicating an inner conflict about one's sexual identity or desires.

On the other hand, sexual dreams can symbolize the need for physical and emotional fulfillment in one's waking life, especially for those who feel lonely or unsatisfied in their relationships. Interpretations of sexual dreams can vary greatly based on personal experiences, cultural background, and beliefs. The dreamer should approach these dreams with openness and self-reflection, taking the time to consider what they might mean for them personally (also, see previous chapter).

Generally, dreaming of having sex with a specific person can symbolize a desire to embody the qualities or attributes that person represents—metaphorically intertwining with their attributes or qualities. For example, dreaming of having sex with someone confident and strong may indicate

a desire for self-assurance and courage, while dreaming of having sex with someone insecure may represent a fear of vulnerability. The sexual act symbolizes the fusion of these qualities, helping the dreamer feel more complete or satisfied in their waking life as they work to integrate these traits into their personality.

Dreams about having the sex organs of the opposite gender can symbolize a desire to embody the traits and qualities associated with that gender. For example, a man dreaming about having a vagina may indicate a desire to be more receptive and in touch with his emotions, while a woman dreaming about having a penis may signify a desire to be more assertive and confident. This can reflect an attempt to reconcile gender identity with suppressed aspects of the personality and to balance the masculine and feminine aspects within oneself. In some cases, these dreams may also reflect the dreamer's curiosity about the experiences and perceptions of the opposite gender, leading to a deeper sense of empathy and connection.

Furthermore, this can be interpreted as the dreamer's unconscious mind attempting to reconcile their own gender identity with the various aspects of their personality that they may feel are suppressed or not fully expressed. It can also symbolize a desire to balance the masculine and feminine aspects within themselves, allowing for a more harmonious and integrated sense of self. In some cases, these dreams may also reflect the dreamer's curiosity about the experiences and perceptions of the opposite gender. It can be seen as a way for the dreamer to explore and understand different perspectives, leading to a deeper sense of empathy and connection with others.

SUN & MOON

The sun and the moon carry significant symbolism in dreams. Often, they represent the interplay between light and darkness, life and death, and birth and renewal. Moreover, the dual aspect in nature which balance, and harmony necessitates. These celestial bodies can also mirror the dual nature of our conscious and unconscious minds, serving as symbols of harmony and balance or struggles between opposing forces within us.

For instance, envision a dream where the sun radiates its brilliance, casting its warm

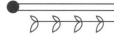

light upon everything. This can symbolize clarity, hope, and a positive outlook, possibly indicating that you are gaining insight or finding a sense of direction in your waking life. Conversely, dreaming of the moon hidden in shadow can evoke feelings of uncertainty, fear, or even a lack of guidance. This might signify a situation in which you are grappling with doubts or facing unknown challenges.

Remember that these celestial bodies are interconnected rather than at odds with each other. The moon often follows the sun in a rhythmic cycle, embodying a natural progression. In the realm of dreams, the sun's radiance can signify the call to act with confidence and clarity, like the decisive rays of the morning sun prompting growth and advancement. On the other hand, the moon's phases, transitioning from darkness to illumination, can reflect a need for patience, trust, and the gradual unveiling of insights.

As an example, dreaming of the moon might encourage you to listen to your intuition and proceed cautiously, acknowledging that some information may be hidden from view. The moon's invitation

to explore the unknown and trust in the timing of events can offer solace, just as the sun's vibrant presence urges you to act based on clear logic and tangible factors. In this way, dreams involving the sun and the moon offer guidance on how to navigate the intricate dance of light and shadow within ourselves, ultimately aiding us in finding equilibrium and understanding in our waking lives.

Furthermore, dreams involving the sun and the moon have left their mark in various cultural and historical contexts. One of the most notable examples comes from the biblical story of Joseph. In his dream, he saw the sun, the moon, and eleven stars bowing down to him. This vivid imagery from Joseph's dream in the book of Genesis illustrates how celestial symbols can be potent carriers of meaning. In this dream, the sun and the moon are interpreted as representations of his parents, while the eleven stars symbolize his brothers. The dream foreshadows Joseph's rise to power signifying leadership and a prominent destiny (in contrast to his brother's). This biblical narrative serves as a timeless example of how the sun and the moon in dreams can hold profound significance, offering insights into personal relationships, growth, and destiny.

DREAM BACKDROP EXERCISE

As you jot down your reflections in your journal, reflect on the predominant aspect that your dreams seem to gravitate towards. Consider whether the backdrop of your dream story is shrouded in darkness or bathed in the illumination of sunlight. Additionally, take note of recurring elements, such as the moon or the sun, that frequently make their appearance in your dreamscapes. This observation can unveil an unspoken theme that your dreams are whispering to you, offering insight into the balance and harmony your psyche may be seeking.

Delve deeper into this analysis by contemplating how you can bridge the gap between these seemingly opposing forces within your dreams. Just like the yin and yang, there is often a hidden wisdom in seeking the equilibrium between these elements. For instance, if your dreams often showcase fervent activity and constant motion, consider if introducing moments of stillness and introspection could bring about a harmonious blend. On the other hand, if your dreams frequently dance around contemplative moments, perhaps a dash of action and decisive steps could infuse a sense of balance.

So, let your introspection guide you towards these realizations. Are you leaning too heavily towards one aspect, neglecting its counterpart? Are you overindulging in action when a pause is essential, or hesitating when action beckons? Your dreams can serve as insightful mirrors, reflecting your conscious and subconscious inclinations. By unearthing these patterns and seeking equilibrium, you set forth on a journey of self-discovery and personal growth, gradually aligning the harmonious dance of your inner forces.

TEETH

Dreams about falling teeth are quite common and can hold various interpretations that resonate with change and transformation. One prevalent explanation is that these dreams often reflect feelings of vulnerability or a sense of powerlessness in the face of life changes. Just as teeth are essential for communication and eating, their loss in a dream can symbolize a fear of losing one's ability to effectively navigate life's challenges or express oneself. For instance, if you are going through a significant life transition such as starting a new job or moving to a different city, a dream about falling teeth might represent the apprehension or uncertainties associated with these changes.

Additionally, these dreams might indicate a need to let go of something in your life that has been holding you back. Just as teeth naturally fall out to make way for new ones, dreaming of falling teeth could be a subconscious message to release old habits, beliefs, or situations that no longer serve your growth. For example, if you dream about losing your teeth while trying to speak in front of a large audience, it could signify a fear of being misunderstood or judged in your waking life. The dream might be encouraging you to shed self-doubt and embrace a new, confident way of expressing yourself.

Another interpretation is that falling teeth dreams can relate to feelings of aging or the passage of time. Teeth are associated with youth and vitality, so their loss in a dream might signify concerns about aging or the passage of time. However, this does not necessarily indicate a negative connotation; it can also symbolize a readiness to embrace new phases in life with wisdom and grace. For example, if you are approaching a milestone birthday or reflecting on your life journey, a dream about falling teeth could represent your thoughts and emotions related to the aging process and the changes it brings.

Falling teeth dreams offer an opportunity to reflect on the changes and transitions happening in your life. By considering the specific context and emotions within the dream, you can gain insights into areas where you may be experiencing vulnerability, letting go of the old, or contemplating the passage of time. These dreams serve as a reminder that change is a natural part of life's journey, and they encourage you to navigate these shifts with a sense of awareness and adaptability.

TRANSPORT

Transportation symbols in dreams can represent our movement through life, our sense

of direction and control, and our ability to get from one place to another. Additionally, they can represent moving from one cycle or phase of life into another, as well as the speed with which changes are to come about. In other words, this represents our progress, ability to reach goals, and drive. Timing can be an added layer of interpretation depending on the mode of transport. Different modes of transportation can carry different meanings and interpretations. In general, vehicles in a dream often represent movement and progression, and the speed at which we progress.

Cars are often seen as symbols of personal power, independence, and drive, representing the ability to take control of our own lives and make our own decisions. A dream of driving a car can symbolize a sense of confidence and direction, while a dream of being a passenger in a car can symbolize a sense of dependence or being along for the ride. Note who in your dream is doing the driving and who is in the passenger seat. Moreover, the choice of taking a taxi in a dream, could represent a decision to let someone else, like a guide or authority figure, lead the way; or the need to ask for help an assistance in the matter. Alternatively, the dreamer taking control of the taxi could symbolize their own desire to be in control of their life's journey and direction. The speed, condition, and style of the taxi (or any vehicle) in the dream can also carry additional meaning and offer more insight into the dreamer's current state of mind and situation.

Additionally, dreaming of taking a flight, or planes can symbolize a sense of escape or the desire to soar above our everyday problems. It symbolizes a sense of desiring freedom and liberation speedily. A dream of flying on a plane can symbolize a desire to break free from the constraints of everyday life, while a dream of a crashing plane can symbolize fears or anxieties about losing control. Rockets, on the other hand can symbolize a sense of adventure and excitement, as well as a desire for exploration and discovery. A dream of launching into space can symbolize a desire to reach new heights and explore uncharted territory, while a dream of a malfunctioning rocket can symbolize fears or anxieties about taking risks and venturing into unknown territory.

Furthermore, bikes can represent a sense of freedom and independence, while buses can symbolize a sense of community and shared experience, or the desire to share an experience with the support of others. Boats can represent a journey through life, and the ups and downs that come with it but particularity an 'emotional' journey (water) to do with our relationship to others. Each mode of transportation in a dream can have

a unique interpretation, shaped by the individual's personal experiences and memories, as well as the specific context of the dream. But overall, transportation symbols can offer insight into our feelings about movement, direction, and control in our lives, as well as the speed of change or direction in life.

As we have explored together, 'universal' symbols can provide insight into the unconscious desires and needs of the dreamer. They can help us to better understand ourselves and our place in the world. Think of them as collective themes, or examples that highlight the idea that dreams are influenced by our collective unconscious. They are, if you like, a form of universal dream dictionary or

DREAM SYMBOLS EXERCISE

Take a practical approach by focusing on the images that frequently recur in your dreams. These images act as messengers from your subconscious, carrying unique meanings that hold personal significance. Take a moment to describe each image in a paragraph, exploring its relevance in your life and emotional landscape. What memories and personal associations do you have with each? For instance, if you often dream of flying, consider what freedom or liberation means to you.

If you encounter water frequently in your dreams, think about how it mirrors your emotions or current state of mind. By translating your thoughts into words, you begin to unravel the puzzle of your dream language, revealing the hidden insights that shape your inner story. This exercise acts as a valuable tool for deciphering your dreams, providing a glimpse into the intricate map of your mind, and untangling the messages it wants to communicate. Use Figure 12 to write your thoughts on what these symbols mean for you.

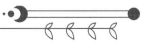

language where the symbols are universally dreamt about, despite cultural or personal differences.

Furthermore, the interpretation of these symbols in a dream are greatly influenced by our own personal experiences, cultural background, and emotions, making the meaning of each dream unique to the individual dreamer as you unravel additional layers of interpreting the dream story.

DREAM SYMBOLS EXERCISE

CHAPTER 5

DIRECTING
YOUR
DREAMS

Directing your dreams involves a deliberate focus on a specific topic or question before going to bed, with the aim of generating a dream that revolves around that subject. This technique finds its roots in dream incubation, an approach practiced by ancient civilizations. In this method, people in antiquity sought divine guidance during sleep to address specific challenges. The objective was to shape the dream's content in a way that would provide insights and solutions to real-world issues.

Throughout history, dream incubation was widely embraced by cultures like the Egyptians, Greeks, and Romans. These societies believed that sleeping in sacred locations, such as temples, would bring them closer to deities and increase the likelihood of receiving profound dreams. By intentionally inviting dreams in these sacred spaces, people anticipated messages of divine wisdom, guidance, and even healing. The interpretation of the dream's narrative and symbols was often aided by priests, facilitating the extraction of meaningful insights.

Although the practice of dream incubation has waned over time, the concept of intentionally inviting dreams for guidance persists within various spiritual and religious traditions. In contemporary terms, we might refer to it as directing dreams or intentional dreaming. The method involves a conscious effort to shape the dream landscape and narrative to explore specific issues, gain insights, or seek solutions through the dream experience. By intentionally focusing on a particular subject before sleep, individuals in modern times continue to harness the power of dreams as a source of guidance and inner exploration.

Directing your dreams is a practical tool for diving into personal matters. The idea behind intentional dreaming is rooted in the belief that your subconscious mind is receptive to suggestions and can be guided to produce dreams that hold significance and aid. Intentional dreaming, therefore, aids in gaining problem-solving insights, and even sparking creative ideas for projects. Start by formulating a question, or an intention. If you are uncertain how to phrase a question, simply jot down *"please give me a dream on this issue (name it)."* Next, jot down the date in your dream journal along with a brief note about your current real-life circumstances. This link between your dream's meaning and your waking world can help build your own personal dream dictionary, facilitating better understanding over time.

Writing down your intention essentially hones your focus and conveys a clear message to your subconscious mind. Alternatively, you can meditate on your intention or repeat the intention as an affirmation to yourself as

ENGAGING WITH YOUR DREAM INTENTION

Find a quiet and comfortable space, close your eyes, and focus on your intention. Breathe deeply and slowly, letting go of any distractions. As you do this, repeat your intention to yourself like a mantra. For instance, if your intention is to gain clarity on a career decision, you might repeat to yourself, *"I will receive clear guidance about my career path in my dream tonight."* Allow the intention to sink into your mind as you continue to breathe and focus. Once you feel calm and cantered, you can let go and allow yourself to drift off to sleep.

Another technique is to turn your intention into a positive **affirmation**. As you lie in bed ready to sleep, repeat your intention as an affirmation to yourself. For example, if you are seeking insight into a relationship issue, you could say, *"I am open to receiving valuable insights about my relationship in my dream tonight."* Repeat this affirmation several times, allowing it to become a part of your mental landscape as you start to relax and fall asleep.

Additionally, **visualization** can be a powerful tool. As you lay down, close your eyes, and imagine yourself in a dream scenario where you are receiving the answers you seek. Visualize the details—the surroundings, the people, and the emotions you would feel. Let yourself fully experience this dream scene in your mind, as if it is happening right now. This can create a strong connection between your conscious and subconscious mind, increasing the likelihood of your dream addressing your intention.

The power of **feeling the relief** and excitement of receiving an answer or solving a problem in your dreams cannot be overstated. To your brain, the emotions you experience, and the actual occurrence of events are closely linked. When you

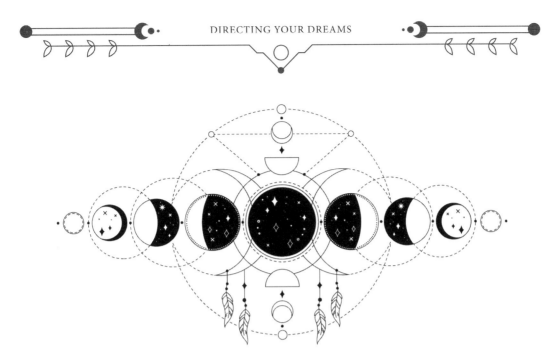

genuinely feel the relief and joy of having found a solution or gaining insight, your brain interprets this as a real experience. It treats the emotional response as evidence that the issue has been resolved. This emotional connection serves as a signal to your subconscious mind that the matter is significant and deserves attention.

The more vividly and intensely you can evoke the feeling of relief and excitement, the more likely your brain is to generate dreams that align with those emotions. It is like sending a clear message to your subconscious that you are ready and open to receiving guidance. This emotional trigger helps set the stage for dreams that offer insights, solutions, or revelations related to your intention. Focus on the result rather than the details of how this relief could come

about. Let your mind direct you on that. Your dreams have the potential to offer you alternatives and even direct guidance on the issues you have in mind. By immersing yourself in the positive emotions associated with resolution or understanding, you create a fertile ground for your dreams to respond in kind. Moreover, dreams have a unique way of presenting situations and options that might not be immediately apparent in your waking life. They can shed light on creative possibilities, overlooked aspects, or even present you with a symbolic representation that holds the key to understanding your situation better.

As you reflect on your dreams, you may find that the symbols, interactions, and events hold valuable insights that can guide you towards making informed decisions or gaining a fresh perspective on your challenges. By incorporating these methods into your bedtime routine, you are actively directing your focus towards your intention, increasing the chances of your dreams aligning with your desires. Furthermore, approach dream direction practice with an open mind, and without rigid expectations. Understand that the dream you receive might not directly mirror your intention, or it might require interpretation to grasp its meaning. Overthinking the process might hinder rather than enhance dream recall. Simply trust that your mind is absorbing your requests and will respond accordingly.

The practice of dream direction enables you a deeper connection with your inner self. By consistently directing your dreams, you might notice your dream experiences becoming more vivid and meaningful over time, providing deeper insights into your psyche. When venturing into dream direction, clarity of intent and concentration on the desired outcome are crucial. Setting a clear intention before bed steers your subconscious towards crafting dream content that aligns with your focus. Additionally, patience is vital, as immediate results are not guaranteed. Mastering dream direction takes practice and perseverance. Yet, the valuable insights and guidance that directed dreams yield make the effort well worth it.

So, becoming adept at dream direction requires consistent practice and determination. Like any skill, it is about refining your ability to set clear intentions and guide your dreams toward specific themes. Keep in mind that progress might not be immediate. Patience is, therefore, crucial. The more you work on directing your dreams, the more you will notice subtle changes in their content. Preserving will help you understand the unique language of your subconscious mind. With consistent commitment, your dreams become more responsive to your intentions. This can be self-empowering as you learn to call in a dream and be able to understand its meaning. With practice, you will get better at directing your dreams. Your dreams will become your tools for self-discovery and self-guidance. You will literally be able to "sleep on it" and guide yourself to coping with any issue you might face.

RESTORATIVE DREAMS

Remember, not all dreams necessitate interpretation. Some might simply reflect daily experiences or thoughts, serving as a mental release valve, which we refer to in The Book of Dream Craft as healing dreams. Others are healing by providing fun and creativity you might need. Furthermore, just as our minds process and organize information during sleep, some dreams help us make sense of the events and thoughts that occupy our waking hours. This is because dreams often mirror our routine activities, conversations, or concerns, providing a safe space for our minds to unwind and process. While these dreams may not hold profound symbolic meanings, they play a vital role in maintaining mental balance and well-being. By distinguishing between dreams that are simply processing daily stimuli and those that carry deeper symbolic significance, you can focus your efforts on interpreting dreams that offer insights, guidance, or revelations. This

discernment allows you to make the most of your dream analysis journey and cultivate a deeper understanding of your inner world.

However, while delving into dream interpretation can be enlightening and introspective, it is essential to remember that dreams can also be delightful, entertaining and are simply fun. Just like our conscious lives, our dream world offers a space for exploration, enjoyment, and even playfulness. As part of a holistic approach to dream work, consider designating some weekends for what you might call a "healing dream." These are dreams that you simply let unfold without the need for interpretation, allowing yourself to enjoy the experience fully.

During these healing dream nights, you might consciously set the intention to have enjoyable, uplifting dreams that provide a sense of relaxation and joy. For example, you could imagine yourself on a dream vacation, exploring exotic landscapes, or engaging in exciting adventures. Alternatively, you could embrace dreams that awaken your sensuality, such as having a romantic encounter or even experiencing a sex dream.

Speaking of sex dreams, it is worth noting that they can serve as a creative outlet within the realm of dreams. Just as dreams can be symbolic and metaphorical, they can also be a canvas for the uninhibited expression of your desires and imagination. Engaging in sex dreams can tap into your innate creativity, allowing you to explore aspects of yourself and your emotions in a unique

and liberating way. In a sense, these dreams offer a space where you can let go of societal norms and expectations, tapping into a realm of pleasure, connection, and personal discovery.

Additionally, you can also ask for a love dream, for instance. Bobby Darin, the American singer, songwriter, and actor who gained popularity in the 1950s and 1960s had a famous song entitled "Dream Lover". It captured the sentiment of yearning for companionship, and connection even within the realm of dreams: "I want a dream lover,

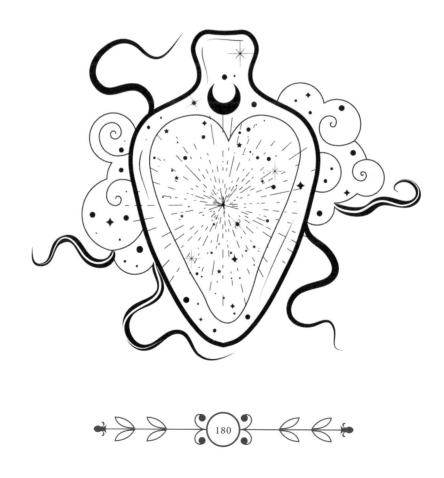

so I do not have to dream alone." It reflects the desire to find solace and company in dreams, embracing the notion that dreams can provide a sanctuary for companionship and fulfillment. If this is one of your indentions, here is a Dream Lover Meditation that might help!

DREAM MEDITATIONS

Dream Lover Meditation

Find a comfortable and quiet space where you can relax and let go of any distractions. Take a few deep breaths, inhaling positivity and exhaling any tension. Close your eyes and imagine yourself in a serene landscape—a place where your dreams can take flight.

Picture a soft, warm light surrounding you, creating a cocoon of safety and comfort. As you embrace this soothing ambiance, imagine that you are inviting in a dream lover—a presence that embodies your deepest desires and supports your creative journey.

Visualize your dream lover standing before you, radiating a gentle energy that resonates with your heart's desires. Feel their loving presence enveloping you, offering a sense of companionship and understanding. Allow

yourself to bask in this feeling, knowing that your dream lover is here to nurture and inspire you.

Now, express your intentions to your dream lover. Share your creative aspirations, your desires for personal growth, or simply your wish to enjoy a dream adventure together. As you speak, notice how your dream lover listens attentively, their eyes reflecting encouragement and support.

Feel a connection growing between you and your dream lover, a bond that transcends the ordinary boundaries of reality. Let yourself be open to the guidance and inspiration they offer. You might even ask a question or seek insight—trusting that their responses will come to you in the form of dreams.

As you feel a deeper connection, express gratitude to your dream lover for their presence and the connection you have shared. Allow yourself to drift to sleep, feeling the gentle rhythm of your breath and the loving sensation that surrounds you. Remember, your dream lover is always here to accompany you on your creative and introspective journey, whenever you seek their companionship. With each dream, you invite them into your inner world, where creativity and insight flourish, and where you are never alone.

Feel free to personalize this meditation to your liking. You can record it with your own voice, and play is back to yourself as you fall asleep.

Healing Dream Meditation

Whenever you find yourself facing a road-block in life, an emotional hurdle, or a sense of emotional or mental stagnation, you can turn to this healing dream meditation to release your block and start dreaming (again). Whether it is a current block, or a past trauma, a persistent fear, or a negative thought pattern; this meditation offers a pathway to harnessing the healing power of your dreams. By focusing your intention of letting go of the block you are facing, you create a space within your subconscious mind for healing to take place. This will allow your mind to balance and form a dream that can answer your questions afterwards.

The following meditation serves as a conduit to invite the transformative energy of your dreams, enabling you to experience a profound sense of relief, renewal, and emotional release. Through this practice, you give yourself the opportunity to engage in deep healing without the need for interpreting your dream, as the dream itself becomes the vessel of transformation:

Find a quiet and comfortable place to sit or lie down. Close your eyes and take a few deep breaths, allowing your body to relax with each exhale.

As you continue to breathe deeply, imagine yourself surrounded by a warm and soothing light. This light represents healing energy. It is here to support you on your journey.

Now, focus your attention on your intention the question you have: "What issue do I need to heal now in my life that helps me release the block I am facing?" Repeat this question in your mind a few times, allowing it to sink in.

Visualize yourself standing at the entrance of a beautiful garden. This garden symbolizes your inner world, a place where you can explore and find answers. As you walk through the garden, notice the vibrant colors, the calming scents, and the gentle breeze.

As you continue your walk, imagine coming across a serene pond. This pond reflects the pool of your subconscious mind, holding insights and healing wisdom. Gently kneel by the edge of the pond and ask your question aloud: "I desire a healing dream to help me release the emotional/mental/financial (chose one) block I am facing now in my life?"

As you speak the words, visualize ripples forming on the surface of the pond. These

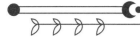 
ripples represent the energy of your question, spreading through the water and connecting with the depths of your subconscious.

Now, watch as an image or symbol representing a key begins to emerge from the depths of the pond. This key unlocks the issue you need to heal. Trust your intuition and let your key emerge to you naturally.

Once you can sense the key, or its symbol fully, take a moment to observe and understand it.

Now, with gratitude, gently release the key back into the water. Know that it will remain within your subconscious, guiding you even after this meditation.

Imagine that you now slowly stand up, and begin to walk back through your ideal garden, feeling a sense of peace and clarity. Allow yourself to drift to sleep, knowing that your mind now holds the key to healing your current block.

Take a few deep breaths and reflect on the image or key symbol you saw. Feel the relief you experience knowing that you have begun to release the block bringing healing into your life.

Remember, this meditation is a tool for self-discovery and healing. You can revisit it whenever you feel the need to explore your inner world and heal whatever is blocking your dreamtime.

TWENTY TIPS FOR ENHANCING YOUR DREAMCRAFT

Here are some techniques that can help you induce an intentional dream and remember it too:

1. KEEP A DREAM JOURNAL

Keeping a dream journal is a great way to increase your dream recall, direction, and gain insights into your subconscious mind. By writing down your dreams as soon as you wake up, you can capture important details that may otherwise be forgotten. Over time, you may notice patterns, symbols, or themes in your dreams that can provide you with valuable information about your thoughts, emotions, and behaviors. When you wake up, take a few moments to write down any dream, or part of a dream, you may remember, however insignificant it may seem. Over

time, you may start noticing patterns or recurring themes in your dreams that can give you valuable information about your thoughts, emotions, and behaviors. Writing down your dreams also helps you to remember them more vividly and can increase your motivation to continue your dream work. More details on how to journal are coming up in chapter seven.

2. RELAX BEFORE BED

Participating in soothing activities before going to bed can have a positive impact on both the quality of your sleep and your dream recall. Stress and anxiety can disrupt sleep patterns and hinder dream remembrance. Engaging in calming practices like reading a book, taking a warm bath, or

practicing meditation can be effective in quieting the mind and alleviating stress. By incorporating these activities into your evening routine, you establish a gentle transition from wakefulness to rest, signaling to your body and mind that it's time to unwind (more about this in the following section on Mindful Dream Direction).

Meditation can be a powerful tool to prepare your mind for sleep and enhance dream recall. Utilizing techniques such as deep breathing, visualization, or mindfulness meditation can help clear your thoughts and create a more peaceful mental state. The Dream Lover, or Healing Dream meditations mentioned earlier can also be beneficial in setting intentions for healing or enhancing dream experiences. These techniques guide your subconscious mind toward specific dream content while promoting a calm and receptive mental environment.

In addition to relaxation techniques and meditation, keeping a consistent sleep schedule and ensuring a comfortable sleep environment can further promote quality sleep and dream recall. A quiet, dark, and comfortable room can enhance your sleep experience and increase the likelihood of vivid dream recollection. By fostering a holistic approach that combines relaxation practices, intention-setting through meditation, and a sleep-conducive environment, you will create an optimal foundation for deep sleep and memorable dream experiences.

3. SET AN INTENTION

Setting an intention before bed is a powerful way to focus your mind on your dreams and increase your dream recall. This practice involves deliberately channeling your mental energy towards your dream experiences, opening the door for potential insights and revelations. Intention-setting before sleep can take various forms—perhaps you aim to remember your dreams more vividly, seek a particular theme, or hope to gain valuable guidance. Repetition is a key element in this process. As you drift into sleep, gently repeat your intention in your mind. This repetition strengthens your connection with your subconscious, fostering a receptive space where your dreams can unfold. Visualize yourself upon awakening with a crystal-clear memory of the dream you intend to experience. By

actively engaging your imagination in this manner, you create a pathway for your subconscious to align with your intention.

As you continue this practice over time, know that you will be forging a bridge between your conscious desires and the messages in your dreams. Your subconscious becomes a collaborator in your personal growth journey, offering insights that can empower you in your waking life. The simple act of setting an intention before sleep, cultivates a more profound relationship with your inner wisdom. It helps you to tap into a wellspring of knowledge that can enrich your understanding of yourself and the world around you.

4. GET ENOUGH SLEEP

Securing sufficient sleep is not just about feeling rested. It significantly influences your capacity to remember dreams. Aim for a solid 7-9 hours of slumber every night. This ample time allows your brain to traverse through the various sleep cycles, particularly the REM (Rapid Eye Movement) phase when dreams often unfold. Skimping on sleep can result in weariness, mental haziness, and a dip in dream recall. Therefore, dedicating time to quality sleep ought to be a cornerstone of your self-care regime.

During REM sleep, your brain is active, weaving together images, emotions, and narratives, creating the rich tapestry of dreams. Adequate sleep bolsters these processes, enhancing your ability to recall these night time journeys upon waking. As you wake up, you feel alert and in tune with your experiences from the night. Your dream memories are vivid, and you can easily jot down the details in your dream journal. In contrast, a night of insufficient sleep might leave you feeling groggy and disconnected from your dreams, struggling to grasp the fleeting fragments of your night-time escapades. Remember, sleep is more than just a period of rest. Good sleep is a foundation for your mental and emotional well-being, including your dream recall abilities.

5. USE PROMPTS

Using prompts such as dream catchers, crystals, or special pillow sprays can be a wonderful way to create a dedicated and supportive environment for your dream exploration. These tools act as tangible reminders and aids, helping you maintain focus on your dream practice and enhancing your ability to remember and engage with your dreams. Experiment with different prompts to find what works best for you. Here are a few suggestions:

symbolically reminding yourself to be attentive to your dreams. When you wake up, the sight of the dream catcher can trigger a moment of reflection and prompt you to recall the dream experiences from the night. This visual connection can serve as a powerful trigger for bringing your dreams into conscious awareness.

Crystals: Amplifying intention and energy

Crystals have long been associated with various energies and intentions. Choosing a crystal that aligns with your dream work, such as amethyst or moonstone, can help amplify your commitment to understanding your dreams. Placing the crystal on your nightstand or under your pillow infuses your dream space with its unique energy. As you go to bed, you can hold the crystal and set the intention to remember your dreams. This practice can create a subtle yet influential connection between your conscious mind and the realm of dreams.

Dream Catchers: capturing dreams and awareness

Imagine a dream catcher hanging near your sleeping space. This traditional item has roots in various Indigenous cultures and is believed to "catch" dreams as they drift through the night. By placing a dream catcher within your view, you are

Special Pillow Sprays: ritualizing your dream routine

Pillow sprays infused with essential oils like lavender, chamomile, or sandalwood can be soothing and comforting. Incorporating these sprays into your bedtime routine not only promotes relaxation but also establishes

a ritual around your dream practice. This routine can signal to your mind that it is time to transition into a more receptive state for dreaming. As you spray your pillow, take a moment to set the intention to have vivid dreams and remember them upon waking.

The effectiveness of these prompts can vary from person to person. The key is to experiment and discover what resonates best with you. You might find that a combination of these prompts works even better. Pay attention to how these tools influence your dream recall, overall dream experiences, and your mindset towards engaging with your dreams.

Incorporating these prompts into your dream practice not only enhances your

ability to remember dreams but also encourages a deeper connection with your inner self. Remember that these tools serve as companions on your journey of self-discovery through dreams. Each time you interact with them, you are affirming your commitment to exploring the fascinating realm of your subconscious mind.

6. BE AWARE

Being aware of your dreams and paying attention to them as they happen. This is key to increasing dream recall and gaining insights into your subconscious mind. One way to increase your awareness is to practice lucid dreaming, where you become conscious within your dream and can direct the action. To become more aware, you can ask yourself throughout the day if you are dreaming and do reality checks, such as looking at your hands or a clock. By developing a habit of checking in with yourself, you can train your mind to be more alert and focused on your dreams.

7. SEEK DREAM SUPPORT

If you are having trouble remembering your dreams or interpreting their meaning, consider one of the following suggestions:

their dreams and help each other make sense of them. It is a chance to share your drams and hear others' perspectives, which often leads to interesting insights. Being part of a dream group means you are not only sharing but also learning from others. You might discover techniques that work for them in remembering dreams or uncovering their meanings. It's like having a supportive team in your quest to understand your dreams better.

Starting Your Own Dream Group

If you cannot find a dream group that suits you, why not create one yourself? Gather a few friends, family members, or anyone who is curious about dreams. Together, you can embark on this dream-exploration journey and decode the mysteries of your night time adventures. Creating your own dream group is an opportunity to connect with like-minded individuals and build a community around the fascination of dreams. It is a shared journey that can lead to a deeper understanding of your own mind and experiences.

Working with a Dream Therapist

If remembering your dreams, or figuring out what they mean, is a challenge; reaching out to a dream analysis therapist could be a great step. Such professionals are experts in decoding dreams, and they can offer you helpful guidance. They can share techniques to improve your dream recall, like doing exercises that focus on dreams. They will also help you understand the symbols and themes in your dreams and translate the language of your subconscious mind.

Joining a dream Group or Community

For those who enjoy a collaborative approach, joining a dream group or community could be beneficial. Think of it as a club where people come together to discuss

8. PRACTICE MINDFUL DREAM DIRECTION

Mindfully directing your dreams is a powerful way to gain insights into your

subconscious mind and set intentions for your waking life. When you write down a question or intention in your dream journal before going to bed, you are essentially initiating a direct conversation with your subconscious. It is important to understand that your subconscious mind is always active, processing thoughts, emotions, and experiences. This happens even when you are not consciously aware of it. However, when you make a deliberate effort to communicate your desires by writing down your intention, or question, your unconscious starts paying attention. Remember that everything that goes into the unconscious, gets there consciously—while you are aware.

Writing sends a clear signal to your subconscious. Moreover, as you start shifting into a more relaxed or altered state of mind before falling asleep, your brain becomes highly receptive to suggestions. It is as if you are handing over a message to your subconscious, saying, *"This is important; pay attention."* If you like, your subconscious as a silent, attentive assistant waiting for your instructions. Your written question or intention becomes the

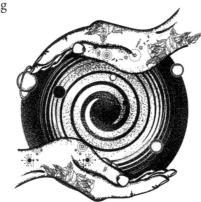

task at hand. Your subconscious mind now begins to focus its resources and energy on understanding and responding to this query.

Throughout the night, as you progress through different stages of sleep, your subconscious continues processing and seeking answers to your question or intention. It can trigger dreams, symbols, or scenarios that hold relevance to the subject you have brought forward. These dream experiences serve as a form of communication between your conscious and subconscious minds. And that is why when you wake up, your dream journal becomes a valuable record of this dialogue. It is not just a collection of dreams. Your dream journal is a conversation with your inner self. By reviewing and reflecting on these dreams, you can uncover insights, patterns, and solutions that might have eluded your conscious awareness.

Furthermore, dream direction is a profound exercise in self-discovery and personal growth. It allows you to tap into the vast reservoir of wisdom within your subconscious, helping you set intentions, overcome challenges, and navigate your waking life with greater clarity and

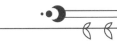
purpose. For example, you might write *"What do I need to know about my career?"* or *"Help me find a solution to my relationship problem."* By getting into the habit of intentional dreaming, you are directing your subconscious mind to unravel; revealing vital information by generating a dream related to your question. Upon waking up, get into the habit of integrating this communication into waking life. Begin by writing down anything that you remember, such as symbols, feelings, your state of mind, make a drawing, or color that you remember. All these fragments will help enhance your dream recollection and decipher the answer to the dream that answers your question.

To get you started, here are suggested prompts to consider in your dream journal:

"What can I learn from my current challenges?"

"How can I enhance my self-confidence?"

"What steps should I take to improve my well-being?"

"Give me a dream that guides me on understanding/improving my relationships better."

DREAM CYCLE EXERCISE

List below questions that are important for you during the next week (remember, direct your dreams for 5 days and plan on two-day fun dreams that you do not journal or attempt to interpret):

1. _____

2. _____

3. _____

4. _____

5. _____

6. Fun Dream: (example holiday)

_____

7. Fun Dream: (example: love dream)

_____

"Show me how to tap into my inner creativity."

"What is the next step in my personal growth?"

Dream direction is about engaging with your dreams as a source of guidance. Each night holds the potential for new insights, and with consistent practice, you can uncover valuable lessons that contribute to your personal and spiritual growth. However, give yourself a break! Remember to add to your intentions a fun component Ask for a fun dream, or a love dream, a healing one, or a sex dream.

9. PRACTICE REALITY CHECKS

Reality checks are a technique used to help you become more aware of when you are dreaming. The goal is to create a habit of mindful observation and engagement with your surroundings. By regularly checking to see if you are in a dream state, you can become more attuned to the dream state and improve your dream recall. For example, you might try to push your finger through your palm or look at a clock and then look away and look back again. If you are in a dream, these checks will often fail, which can trigger lucidity and improve dream recall (refer to the lucid dreaming section).

Furthermore, practicing reality checks is like training your mind to question reality. Throughout your waking hours, pause and genuinely ask yourself if you are awake or in a dream. Engage in a specific action that blurs the line between the two states. By doing so, you cultivate a habit of critical self-awareness that can naturally extend into your dream experiences. These checks act as reality anchors, offering you a means to distinguish between your daily reality and the surreal landscape of your dreams. Integrating reality checks into your routine does not demand constant effort. It is about infusing your daily activities with a touch of curiosity. Whenever you glance at a clock, glance away, then look back. Observe whether the time remains consistent or takes an otherworldly leap. Attempt to read a sentence twice to see if the words change their arrangement. Gradually, these habits blend seamlessly into your subconscious, and when they reappear in your dreams, they become triggers for realization.

The power of reality checks lies not only in their potential for inducing lucidity but also in enhancing dream recall. The act of questioning your reality fosters a profound connection with your dream experiences. As you build the habit of inquiry, you are likely to find yourself questioning your surroundings within dreams as well. This, in turn, can

lead to moments of lucidity where you grasp the dream state, opening avenues for active participation and, consequently, a richer recollection of dream content upon waking.

10. USE AFFIRMATIONS

Affirmations can be a powerful tool for improving dream recall as they help to reprogram your subconscious mind to remember your dreams. By repeating positive affirmations about your dream recall, you are essentially rewiring your brain to focus on and remember your dreams. To use affirmations for improving dream recall, choose a positive statement that reflects your goal, such as *"I remember my dreams with ease and clarity every morning."* Repeat this affirmation to yourself throughout the day, especially before bed, and visualize yourself remembering your dreams in detail.

You may also choose to write your affirmation down and place it somewhere visible, such as on your nightstand or bathroom mirror, as a reminder to focus on your dream recall. It is important to note that affirmations may not work overnight and may require consistent repetition over time. But with practice and patience, affirmations can become a powerful tool for improving dream recall and helping to promote a deeper understanding of your inner self. So

next time you are struggling to remember your dreams, try incorporating affirmations into your daily routine and see how they can enhance your dream recall.

11. KEEP A REGULAR SLEEP SCHEDULE

Maintaining a consistent sleep schedule can help regulate your body's natural sleep-wake cycle, making it easier to fall asleep and improving the quality of your sleep. This can lead to more restful and vivid dreams that are easier to remember. To establish a regular sleep schedule, try to go to bed and wake up at the same time each day, even on weekends. In addition to a steady sleep schedule, certain

bedtime rituals can promote better sleep and contribute to more memorable dreams. Consider incorporating calming herbal teas into your evening routine. Chamomile, lavender, or valerian root teas have relaxing properties that can help soothe your mind and prepare you for a peaceful night's rest. The gentle warmth and comforting aroma of these teas create a serene environment conducive to vivid dreaming.

Additionally, engaging in regular physical activity can also positively impact your dream experiences. Exercise not only promotes better sleep but can also lead to more dynamic dreams. Taking a walk during the evening hours can be particularly effective. The cool, fresh air and rhythmic movement provide an opportunity for your mind to unwind and your body to relax, setting the stage for imaginative and memorable dreams. Moreover, sometimes, a short nap during the day can work wonders for your dream life. A well-timed nap, around 10 to 20 minutes in duration, can provide a quick reset and an invigorating boost. Surprisingly, these brief moments of shut eye can yield some of the most vivid and captivating dreams. While the nap itself might be short, the dream experience can feel incredibly vivid and rich, as if you have journeyed through hours of dream exploration within just a few minutes.

Nurturing a regular sleep schedule, using relaxation techniques like herbal teas and evening walks, and occasionally incorporating short, rejuvenating naps; helps you to set the stage for a dream-rich sleep experience. These mindful choices not only foster better sleep but also invite you to embark on imaginative journeys in the world of dreams.

12. CREATE A DREAM-FRIENDLY ENVIRONMENT

The environment in which you sleep can have a significant impact on your dream recall. Creating a dream-friendly environment involves making changes to your sleeping space to make it more conducive to dreaming. This can include keeping your bedroom cool and quiet, minimizing external noise and light, and using comfortable bedding. Another way to create a dream-friendly environment is to incorporate scents and sounds that promote relaxation and deep sleep. This can include using essential oils, such as lavender or chamomile, in a diffuser or playing calming music or nature sounds.

Enhancing a dream-friendly environment can also involve embracing scents and sounds that foster relaxation and deep slumber. Using essential oils, such as lavender or chamomile, in a diffuser can yield remarkable results. These gentle fragrances

permeate the air, creating an atmosphere that gently lulls your senses and guides you into tranquil sleep. Similarly, immersing yourself in the soft embrace of calming music or the soothing symphony of nature sounds can orchestrate an environment conducive to dream exploration.

Moreover, consider establishing your sleep haven as a technology-free zone to amplify its dream-friendly qualities. The artificial illumination emitted by screens from devices such as phones, tablets, and computers can interfere with your body's production of melatonin—the hormone governing your sleep patterns. By detaching from screens at least an hour before bedtime, you extend an invitation to your body to gradually unwind and transition into a state primed for immersive dream experiences. Experimentation is key to determining what suits you best. For instance, if you find that sleeping in a dark room enhances your dream experiences, draw the curtains to eliminate external light sources. Tailoring your sleep environment to your preferences can make a significant difference in the quality of your dreams.

13. PRACTICE DREAM INCUBATION

Dream incubation goes beyond intention alone; it encompasses the practice of creating a focused ritual to enhance your dream experiences. This method involves immersing yourself in a deliberate process before bedtime, allowing your mind to marinate in the essence of dreaming. Through such rituals, you can deeply connect with the act of dreaming and guide your subconscious toward your desired dreamscape. Crafting your dream incubation ritual is akin to creating an immersive experience that engages all your senses.

Start by choosing a calm and solitary space where silence becomes your ally, fostering a space of inner reflection and openness. To enhance this process, consider activities that induce relaxation, like enjoying a tranquil bath infused with calming essential oils. As you step into this sensory haven, immerse yourself in the pre-sleep ritual, turning it into a multi-sensory journey of intention. Dedicate time to formulate a question or select a symbol that encapsulates the dream theme, or an issue, you are drawn to explore. With a clear focus in mind, jot down your question. Additionally, sketch a meaningful image or symbols that resonates with your goals. In doing so, you are infusing your thoughts with the very essence of your desired dream scenario.

The act of crafting and sketching these symbols becomes a form of meditation, immersing you deeply in the intention of your dream. It is about imprinting your

subconscious with a clear directive. This quiet ritual serves as your personal invitation to the dream realm, setting the stage for your mind's journey into the world of dreams. As you transition from this immersive ritual to sleep, you carry your intentions with you. Your senses have been engaged, your thoughts aligned, and your dreamscape prepared. The other tips given here also help in creating your own dream ritual.

14. USE LUCID DREAMING TECHNIQUES

Lucid dreaming is the ability to become aware that you are dreaming and potentially control the outcome of your dreams. Using lucid dreaming techniques can help increase the likelihood of lucid dreaming and improve dream recall. To practice lucid dreaming, begin by keeping a dream journal and regularly performing reality checks throughout the day. Reality checks involve questioning whether you are awake or dreaming by checking your surroundings, such as looking at a clock or trying to push your finger through your palm. These reality checks can help train your mind to become more aware of when you are dreaming, leading to more frequent lucid dreams and improved dream recall (refer to chapter three for more information).

15. STAY HYDRATED

Dehydration can significantly impact your sleep quality and, consequently, your ability to remember dreams. When our bodies lack proper hydration, they become more prone to fatigue and may experience shallower sleep cycles, leading to fewer and less vivid dreams. Ensuring you are well-hydrated is

like providing your body with the essential fuel it needs for optimal functioning, much like a well-maintained battery. Moreover, hydration plays a critical role in supporting various bodily functions, including maintaining a steady heart rhythm, nourishing brain activities, and promoting restful sleep. However, finding the right balance is not a one-size-fits-all approach. It involves considering factors such as your body weight, height, weather conditions, and immediate surroundings to tailor your fluid intake to your individual needs. This personalized approach sets the stage for well-hydrated bodies that are better equipped for restorative sleep and improved dream recall.

To ensure your hydration is on track, prioritize drinking water consistently throughout the day, especially in the hours leading up to bedtime. This practice creates a foundation for your body to enter a state of restorative sleep, potentially enhancing your dream experiences. Additionally, be mindful of your beverage choices. This

simple yet essential practice can contribute to an improved overall sleep experience and potentially unlock richer dreamscapes during your nightly slumber. By keeping your body well-hydrated, you are providing it with the support it needs for better sleep and more vibrant dreams.

16. AVOID ALCOHOL AND DRUGS

Caffeine, alcohol and drugs can have a dehydrating effect, potentially impacting your sleep quality and dream recall. Alcohol and drugs can have a negative impact on your sleep quality and dream recall. These substances can disrupt the natural sleep-wake cycle, leading to shallow sleep and fewer vivid dreams. If you are struggling with chronic sleep issues or are experiencing frequent nightmares, it may be helpful to avoid alcohol, caffeine, and drugs altogether. If you do choose to consume these substances, use your commons sense. Try to limit your intake of caffeine and alcohol and avoid consuming them in the hours leading up to bedtime.

Additionally, illicit drugs or certain prescription medications can also lead to intense and often bewildering dream scenarios. If you find that substances are affecting your dreams in distressing or unwanted ways, seeking professional help, whether

from a medical doctor or a mental health professional, can provide valuable insights and guidance. Open communication and expert advice can aid in understanding the connection between substances and dreams, allowing for informed decisions that prioritize your well-being and dream experiences.

17. SEEK PROFESSIONAL HELP

If you are experiencing chronic sleep issues or frequent nightmares, seeking the help of a mental health professional may be beneficial. A therapist can provide guidance and support in managing these issues and improving your dream. Dealing with prolonged sleep disruptions or recurring distressing dreams can be a daunting experience. When chronic sleep issues or persistent nightmares disrupt your nightly rest, the guidance of a mental health professional can provide a fresh perspective.

Moreover, the presence of a mental health professional can offer a safe space for open dialogue about your dreams and any emotional turbulence they might stir. They can help you unravel the threads of recurring nightmares, guiding you towards understanding their origins and potential meanings. Through this exploration, you may uncover deep-seated concerns that your subconscious mind is trying to communicate through the language of dreams.

Working with a mental health professional isn't a mere quest for a good night's sleep; it's a holistic journey towards nurturing your mental and emotional well-being. With their assistance, you can cultivate resilience in the face of sleep challenges and develop effective coping mechanisms. As you gradually restore balance to your sleep patterns and dream experiences, you pave the way for a more harmonious relationship between your conscious and unconscious mind.

18. USE TAROT OR ORACLE CARDS

Another technique that can be used to induce, remember, or interpret dreams is the use of tarot or oracle cards. Tarot and oracle cards contain symbolic imagery that can act as a trigger for the subconscious mind, helping to bring forth images and insights from the dream world. To use tarot or oracle cards for dream work, select a card that resonates with you or your question before going to bed.

Begin by selecting a card that resonates with you or symbolizes your inquiry before drifting into sleep. Take a few moments to absorb the image, allowing it to stir emotions, trigger feelings, or rekindle memories. You may choose to write few lines in your dream journal about this symbols and what

WHEEL OF FORTUNE

your dream world. As you awaken, capturing any fragments of dreams that linger in your consciousness, pay particular attention to symbols or themes that may resonate with the card you selected. Write a few lines describing your insights. These connections between your dreams and the card can offer valuable clues and insights to decode.

Jot down any remembered dream fragments, then turn your attention to the card once again. Allow its imagery to intertwine with your dream recollections, a canvas upon which to paint interpretations and reflections. Delve into the symbolism. Reflect on how your card, your dream, and real life can be interwoven. This can lead you to profound realizations, offering glimpses into the depths of your subconscious mind.

Enriching your dream practice with tarot or oracle cards offers a pathway into your intuition to uncover valuable insights. Regardless of whether you are aiming to spark dream experiences, strengthen dream recollection, or untangle the significance of your dreams; the synergy between these cards and your subconscious mind can prove immensely valuable. As you explore the landscapes of dreams and symbolism, your favorite tarot, or oracle, cards become trusted companions, quietly revealing hidden revelations that build bridges between your conscious and unconscious mind.

thoughts, emotions, or memories it has evoked with you. This deliberate engagement invites the card's symbolism to intermingle with your thoughts, potentially weaving its influence into your dreamscape.

Place your chosen card underneath your pillow, or next to your bed as you sleep. This proximity serves as a subtle yet potent reminder of your intention, creating a bridge between the card's energy and

19. CHANGE YOUR DREAM ATTITUDE

(See pages 68–71.)

20. FASTING

Fasting has been used for centuries as a tool to induce vivid and meaningful dreams. Many cultures have incorporated fasting into their spiritual practices to gain insight and guidance from the dream world. It is believed to enhance the clarity and intensity of dreams, allowing for a deeper connection to the subconscious mind.

Fasting can take many forms, from complete abstinence from food and drink to more moderate restrictions such as eliminating certain foods or reducing the number of meals per day. Regardless of the specific

method, the act of fasting creates a physical and mental shift that can trigger powerful dream experiences.

One example of fasting being used to induce dreams comes from the ancient Greek tradition of the "Dream Incubation" ritual. This involved fasting and sleeping in a temple dedicated to the god of dreams, with the intention of receiving a divine message or prophetic vision. Similar practices can be found in other cultures, such as the Native American vision quest or the Hindu practice of tapas, which involves various forms of self-discipline including fasting.

Incorporating such techniques into your dream routine, can increase the likelihood of remembering your dreams and gaining insights. Remember to be patient with yourself, as improving dream recall can take time and practice. Additionally, the lunar cycle is a powerful tool for generating dreams that can help realize and manifest your desires. By aligning your intentions with the moon's phases, you can tap into its energy and manifest your desires more effectively.

In the following chapter, we will explore how to use your dream journal to ask the right questions during the four phases of the moon to help you obtain dreams from your subconscious mind to give you guidance, direction and help you realize what you seek.

CHAPTER 6

LUNAR DREAMING

"They ask you, (O Muhammad), about the new moons. Say, 'They are measurements of time for the people'."

Surah Al-Baqarah, Ayat 189

For those who dare to look skyward and dream, the moon offers its guidance. It whispers secrets in the language of the night, painting the canvas of our dreams with the brushstrokes of the cosmos. In the dance between our dreams and the moon's phases, we find not only our own reflection but a reflection of the universe itself. It is a reminder that we are part of something greater, connected to the grand tapestry of existence, and that the wisdom of the cosmos is always there for those who seek it.

Furthermore, the moon has long been associated with magic and mystery. For centuries, people have looked to the moon for guidance and inspiration, and it has played a significant role in many spiritual and religious practices. From the earliest moments of human history, our ancestors looked up at the night sky and found themselves drawn to the moon. Its silvery glow against the backdrop of the celestial canvas was a source of both mystery and wonder. The moon's

constant cycle of transformation, from the shadowy New Moon to the radiant Full Moon and back again, was a reminder that change is an inherent part of existence.

Moreover, the moon's influence transcended geographical and cultural boundaries. Ancient civilizations worldwide recognized the profound impact of lunar rhythms on various aspects of human existence. For instance, in ancient Egypt, the moon was linked to the goddess Isis, symbolizing fertility and the natural cycles of life. In Chinese culture, the lunar calendar played a crucial role in determining festivals and agricultural practices, aligning life with the moon's ebbs and flows. They revered the moon's cycles, believing them to hold profound significance in their lives.

Given the moon's enduring presence and its association with transformation, it is no surprise that those on the path of self-discovery and wisdom have turned to lunar rhythms as a potent guide. The moon's

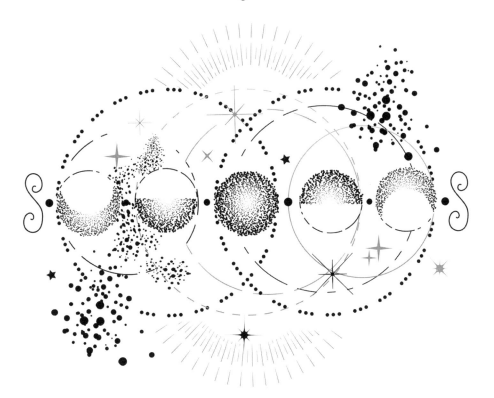

phases serve as a mirror of our own inner states, reflecting the cyclical nature of our lives. Dreamers have recognized the intimate connection between the moon and the world of dreams. The moon's waxing and waning correspond to the ebb and flow of our sub-conscious realms. Just as the moon shifts from darkness to radiance, our dreams tran-sition from shadowy mysteries to moments of profound insight.

Incorporating lunar rhythms into dream craft is akin to a sacred dance with the cosmos, a way of aligning with the timeless wisdom that has guided humanity for gener-ations. It's an invitation to step into the river of universal energies that flow through the ages, connecting us to the dreams and aspi-rations of countless souls who have gazed upon the same celestial canvas.

As we embark on this cosmic journey, we become like cosmic archaeologists, excavat-ing the rich tapestry of our dreams and the moon's phases. During Lunar dreaming, we unearth a treasure trove of insight, like gems hidden in the depths of the earth, waiting to be discovered. In the quiet moments of the night, when the moon casts its gentle glow upon our slumbering world, we find illumination. Our dreams become beacons of understanding, shedding light on the mysteries of our inner selves. The moon, in all its celestial glory, stands as a symbol of our shared human journey—a reminder that we are all stardust travelers on a path of discovery.

To enhance Lunar Dreaming, in modern times, people have used fasting to explore their own subconscious mind and gain insight into their personal lives. For example, one person might fast for a period and then record their dreams in a journal, looking for patterns or symbols that could provide guidance or clarity on a particular issue. Others might use fasting as a tool for lucid dreaming, intentionally inducing a state where they can become aware of and control their dream experience.

While fasting can be a powerful tool for inducing vivid dreams, it is important to approach it with caution and respect. Fasting can have physical and psychological effects that should be carefully considered, and it

may not be appropriate for everyone. As with any practice involving altered states of consciousness, it is recommended to seek guidance from a qualified practitioner or mentor before embarking on a fasting journey.

Moreover, fasting from food or speaking, can be a deep spiritual practice to clarify the mind and soul. It is deeply rooted in historical lunar calendars and carries both spiritual and practical significance. It expresses the rich interplay between culture, spirituality, and the natural world. Understanding this connection can provide valuable insights for your work, particularly when discussing the cultural and spiritual dimensions of self-awareness and self-empowerment. Fasting in any form, can serve as a gateway to heightened sensory perception. Your dreams may become more vivid and memorable.

HISTORICAL LUNAR CALENDARS

In essence, the connection between lunar months and fasting is a cross-cultural phenomenon that transcends borders and belief systems. The link between fasting and a lunar month, as seen in traditions like Ramadan

in Islam, and Lent in Christianity; is rooted in the lunar calendar that many ancient cultures used to track time.

In antiquity, various civilizations used lunar calendars to organize their timekeeping. Unlike the Gregorian calendar, which is solar-based and follows the Earth's orbit around the sun, lunar calendars are based on the phases of the moon. This lunar connection influenced the practice of fasting in several ways:

Lunar Months

The concept of lunar months and their association with fasting is not limited to one specific culture or religion; it has been a recurring theme in various societies throughout history. Lunar months, roughly 29.5 days long, align closely with the moon's cycle from one new moon to the next. This natural division of time became significant in cultures that followed lunar calendars, providing a framework for various fasting practices.

Observing the Moon

Across diverse cultures, the moon's phases, especially the crescent moon marking the start of a new lunar month, were observable celestial events. People in ancient civilizations looked to the night sky to gauge the passage of time. This lunar observation served as a reliable method of marking months and seasons, and it often held spiritual or cultural significance.

Spiritual Significance

The connection between lunar months and fasting frequently carried spiritual or religious significance in different cultures. For example, in Islam, Ramadan, the ninth month of the Islamic lunar calendar, is a sacred time of fasting and reflection. Similarly, in Hinduism, fasting during specific lunar phases, such as Ekadashi, is a common practice aimed at spiritual purification and self-discipline. Ramadan is the fasting lunar month in Islam. It has immense importance. It commemorates the month during which the Qur'an, the holy book of Islam, is believed to have been revealed to the Prophet Muhammad. It is a time of heightened spirituality, self-reflection,

and increased devotion to prayer and good deeds. Similarly, the Christian tradition of Lent holds profound religious and spiritual significance within the lunar calendar. Lent, spanning 40 days leading up to Easter Sunday, commences with Ash Wednesday and culminates with the celebration of Jesus Christ's resurrection. This observance coincides with the lunar cycle, starting on a specific date and concluding with Easter, which varies annually in alignment with lunar phases.

Lent is deeply rooted in the Christian faith and serves as a period of reflection and preparation. Just as with other forms of lunar fasting, it encompasses more than mere abstention from certain foods or practices. Lent invites believers to embark on a spiritual journey that involves self-examination, repentance, and personal growth. It symbolizes the 40 days Jesus spent fasting in the wilderness, emphasizing the importance of inner contemplation and renewal.

Throughout Lent, Christians often choose to fast from specific foods or luxuries, engaging in acts of self-denial to draw closer to their faith. This period of introspection is marked by increased devotion, prayer, and a heightened commitment to living in accordance with Christian values. Lenten fasting, within the lunar calendar, signifies a profound connection between the individual's inner world

and the rhythms of the cosmos, mirroring the principles of self-awareness and self-empowerment found in your holistic approach. The practice of Lent underscores the universal theme of using lunar cycles as a time for inner reflection, spiritual devotion, and personal growth. In many ways, Lent and Ramadan align with the broader concept of lunar fasting from food.

Lunar Cycles and Agriculture

In addition to their spiritual connotations, lunar months were often linked to agricultural practices in certain societies. Fasting during lunar phases might have been associated with agricultural cycles, such as crop planting or harvesting. The lunar calendar, with its close ties to natural phenomena,

influenced not only spiritual practices but also the rhythms of daily life and sustenance.

Variability and Anticipation

One notable characteristic of the lunar calendar is its variability compared to the solar calendar, such as the Gregorian calendar. Lunar months shift in relation to the solar year, creating anticipation and adding spiritual significance to fasting during specific lunar months. This variability can be seen as a reflection of life's cyclical nature, emphasizing the ebb and flow of time and the opportunities for personal growth and reflection that each lunar cycle offers. Because the lunar calendar does not align precisely with the solar calendar, fasting during lunar months can occur in different seasons, leading to variations in fasting durations and experiences. Additionally, the sighting of the crescent moon marks the start of a new lunar month and the beginning of fasting. This tradition is still followed in some cultures and adds an element of community involvement. Moreover, Lunar calendars allow for flexibility in religious observances, as they are not tied to a fixed date on the Gregorian calendar. This flexibility can be seen to adapt religious practices to the changing natural world.

In the context of this Dream Craft, Lunar dreaming is inspired from the practice of

lunar fasting. Using the cycle of the Moon as a guide, expresses your commitment to deepening the connection with yourself. It serves you as a tool to the Moon your ally in gaining deeper insights and guidance through your dreams.

SILENT FASTING

Fasting from speaking aligns with the idea of mindfulness and self-awareness, which are integral to your holistic approach. It is a valuable practice that resonates deeply with the principles of mindfulness and self-awareness in your holistic approach. It encourages individuals to become more conscious of their communication, emotions, and thoughts, fostering personal growth and empowerment. Silent fasting can help you tune into and listen to your voice.

Silent fasting and dreaming is a fascinating intersection of practices that can lead to profound insights and self-awareness. In your holistic approach, which emphasizes the integration of dreams and the unconscious into conscious life, exploring this topic is highly relevant. The flexibility of choosing to fast from speaking for varying durations, whether it is a week, two to three days, or the entire lunar month, can assist in forming questions for your unconscious mind to answer in a dream.

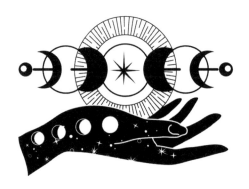

SILENT FASTING AND DREAMING: A HOLISTIC JOURNEY

Silent fasting and dreaming are both powerful tools for self-awareness and self-empowerment. When combined, they can create a unique and transformative experience. For instance, you might experience its effect in a variety of ways:

Heightened Sensitivity

Fasting from speaking and certain foods during a silent fasting period can enhance your sensory perception. This heightened sensitivity can spill over into your dream world, making dreams more vivid and memorable. The absence of verbal communication sharpens their attention to non-verbal cues, such as body language, facial expressions, and environmental sounds. This heightened awareness extends to the dream world.

Increased Mindfulness

As you practice silence and mindfulness during your fasting period, you become more attuned to your thoughts and emotions. With the mind less occupied by conversation and the consumption of certain foods, attention naturally shifts to the senses you may notice subtleties in taste, smell, touch, and sight that often go unnoticed in your daily life. This heightened awareness can allow you to observe and reflect on your dreams with greater clarity. It is as though observe your thoughts without the distraction of verbal expression; like turning the spotlight of awareness onto the inner workings of your mind.

Dream Journaling

During silent fasting, maintaining a dream journal can be particularly insightful.

Recording your dreams upon waking and reflecting on them throughout the fasting period can help you uncover hidden messages, symbols, and emotions in your dreams. The heightened sensory experiences in dreams can also manifest as symbolism. For example, an individual who has been fasting from certain foods might dream of a feast, which could symbolize their relationship with consumption or desires. These symbolic elements can offer valuable insights into one's inner world.

Emotional Release

Fasting can sometimes trigger emotional release as you confront feelings or experiences that were previously suppressed. By practicing silence, you can become more attuned to your emotions. Instead of reacting immediately through speech, you can begin to recognize and understand your feelings before expressing them. These emotions may manifest in your dreams, offering a safe space for processing and healing. It may provide an opportunity to delve into emotional awareness and understanding.

Spiritual Connection

Both silent fasting and dreaming have spiritual connotations in various cultures. Combining these practices can deepen your spiritual connection, providing opportunities for inner exploration and guidance from the unconscious mind.

Memorability

Dreams may become more vivid, lifelike, and sensorially rich. Vivid dreams tend to be more memorable. People often wake up with a stronger recollection of the sights, sounds, and emotions experienced in their dreams. This can be especially valuable for dream analysis and personal growth. The clarity and vividness of your dreams can facilitate introspection and self-reflection, helping you gain insights into your thought patterns and beliefs. Symbolism in dreams often reflects an individual's belief system. Analyzing these symbols can lead to a deeper understanding of one's core beliefs and values.

Paradoxically, practicing silence can also enhance one's ability to communicate when they do choose to speak. With a clearer mind and better understanding of their emotions, they can express themselves more effectively and authentically.

IMPLEMENTING SILENCE MINDFULLY

To incorporate silence into one's daily routine for the purpose of mental clarity, here are some practical steps:

1. Set Aside Quiet Time

Allocate specific periods during the day for silence. This could be in the morning for meditation, during a daily walk, or before bedtime. Allocating specific periods during the day for silence is a practice that can have profound effects on self-awareness

and mental clarity. In the morning, as the world awakens, it is an ideal time for meditation. The stillness of dawn provides a tranquil backdrop for turning inward and connecting with one's thoughts and emotions. Daily walks, especially in natural settings, offer a moving meditation. The rhythmic pace of each step can synchronize with your breath, grounding you in the present moment. Finally, before bedtime, silent reflection allows you to review the events of the day, process emotions, and set intentions for the night's rest. This dedicated quiet time provides a consistent framework for self-discovery and growth.

2. Mindful Breathing

Combine silence with mindful breathing. Focus on your breath to anchor your awareness to the present moment. Combining silence with mindful breathing is a practice that fosters deep introspection. The act of focusing on your breath serves as an anchor to the present moment. It is a simple yet powerful technique that can be practiced anywhere, whether seated in silence or engaged in daily activities. As you inhale and exhale deliberately, you become attuned to the rhythm of your breath, quieting mental chatter. This mindful breathing cultivates a sense of inner peace and clarity, allowing you to observe your thoughts and emotions

with greater objectivity. Breathing is a tool you can carry with you throughout the day, transforming even routine tasks into opportunities for mindfulness and self-awareness.

3. Journaling

Use this silent time for journaling thoughts and feelings. Writing them down can be as powerful as saying them aloud. Utilizing silent time for journaling is akin to opening a window to your inner world. When you put pen to paper or type your thoughts, you give voice to your inner dialogue. This process allows you to articulate your feelings, ideas, and questions with clarity. Journaling during silent moments enables a deep dive into your psyche, facilitating self-exploration and self-expression. The written word carries a unique potency; it captures your thoughts in a tangible form, making them more tangible and comprehensible. Whether you choose to record your daily experiences, explore your dreams, or ponder life's questions, journaling is a transformative practice that aligns seamlessly with your holistic approach.

4. Digital Detox

Extend the concept of silence to your digital life. Take breaks from screens and notifications to declutter your mental space. Extending the concept of silence to your digital life is a modern-day necessity for

mental well-being. The incessant notifications, social media, and digital distractions can drown out the stillness needed for self-awareness. By consciously taking breaks from screens and technology, you declutter your mental space. These moments of digital silence create an opportunity for introspection, allowing you to connect with your thoughts and emotions without external influence. It's a chance to reclaim your time and attention, fostering a more profound understanding of yourself and your relationship with the digital world. Digital detoxes are essential for maintaining a balanced, self-aware lifestyle in today's hyperconnected society.

5. Silent Activities

Engage in activities that encourage silence, such as reading, art, or simply enjoying nature. Engaging in activities that encourage silence is a deliberate choice to immerse oneself in the present moment. Reading, for instance, is a silent activity that transports you to different worlds and perspectives. As you lose yourself in a book, you simultaneously gain insights into your own thoughts and beliefs. Art, whether it's painting, drawing, or any creative pursuit, is another silent avenue for self-expression and self-discovery. The act of creation can be meditative, unveiling hidden aspects of your

inner self. Finally, simply enjoying nature in silence can be a profound experience. The beauty of the natural world invites contemplation and connection, serving as a gentle reminder of your place within the grand tapestry of existence. These silent activities offer diverse pathways to self-awareness and are valuable tools within your holistic methodology.

PRACTICAL TIPS FOR SILENT FASTING AND DREAMING

If you are interested in incorporating silent fasting and dreaming into your holistic approach, here are some practical steps:

1. Set an Intention

Begin your silent fasting period with a clear intention related to your dreams. What

insights or guidance are you seeking? Setting intentions can help focus your mind.

Commencing your silent fasting period with a clear intention related to your dreams is akin to charting a course for self-exploration. What are you seeking to uncover in the depths of your subconscious? Perhaps you yearn for insights into a personal challenge, guidance on a decision, or simply a deeper understanding of yourself. Setting intentions sharpens your focus and directs the subconscious mind toward the specific areas you wish to explore during your fasting-induced dream state. This intention acts as a guiding star, allowing you to navigate the dream world with purpose.

As you set your intention, contemplate the questions you aim to address in your dreams. For example, if you seek clarity on a career choice, your intention might be to dream of a path illuminated by your inner wisdom. Or if you're on a journey of emotional healing, your intention could be to uncover symbols or narratives in your dreams that relate to your healing process. This intentional approach ensures that your silent fasting period becomes a meaningful quest into the realms of your unconscious mind.

2. Dream Journal

Keep a dedicated dream journal during the fasting period. Note the date your fasting starts and reflect on the type and quality of your dreams during that period. You may elect to continue using your current dream journal or starting a new one when fasting. Whatever you decide on, remember to record your dreams immediately upon waking, even if they seem fragmented or unclear.

A dedicated dream journal is your faithful companion during the silent fasting journey. The moment your fasting period begins, note the date and time. Each morning upon waking, record your dreams, no matter how fragmented or unclear they may seem. The act of writing them down immediately preserves the details and emotions associated with your dreams, preventing them from fading into the recesses of your memory. Your dream journal becomes a sacred space where you document the landscapes of your inner world. It's a canvas upon which you paint the narratives, symbols, and emotions that emerge from your dreams. Over the course of your silent fasting period, this journal becomes a treasure trove of insights and revelations. It allows you to observe patterns, recurring symbols, and shifts in emotional states, all of which are valuable clues to your inner self.

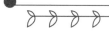 

relate to your waking life or personal growth journey? This phase of reflection bridges the gap between the dream world and your conscious awareness.

Engaging in dream reflection is an art that invites you to become an interpreter of your own subconscious language. Reflection is an act of self-discovery where you explore the rich tapestry of your dreams and extract meaning from their intricate threads. As you decode the symbols and emotions woven into your dreams, you gain insights into your fears, desires, unresolved issues, and potential paths of growth. This reflective practice deepens your understanding of the messages your unconscious mind is conveying, helping you unearth hidden truths about yourself and your life's journey.

4. Meditation and Visualization

Incorporate meditation and visualization practices into your fasting routine. These can facilitate a deeper connection with your dreams and inner self.

This integration between meditation and visualization practices into your silent fasting routine serves as a bridge between your waking consciousness and the dream world. As you enter meditative states, you create a receptive space for dream exploration. Begin your meditation by focusing on your intention for the fasting period,

3. Reflect and Interpret

Take time to reflect on your dream entries. After diligently recording your dreams, take time to reflect and interpret their significance. What symbols or emotions stand out? Are there recurring themes that beckon your attention? How might these dream elements allowing it to permeate your mind and spirit. Visualize yourself embarking on a journey into the realm of dreams, where the answers to your questions and the guidance you seek await. During your meditation, you can also practice visualization techniques that invite specific dream scenarios. For instance, if you wish to gain insight into a particular challenge, visualize yourself encountering symbols or situations in your dreams that provide clarity and solutions. These visualizations can influence the content of your dreams, aligning them with your intentions and desires.

Meditation and visualization are tools that deepen your connection with your inner self and enhance the receptivity of your subconscious mind. They amplify the potency of your silent fasting journey, facilitating profound dream experiences that offer guidance, healing, and self-awareness.

Including these practices into your silent fasting routine transforms it into a purposeful and transformative journey. Setting intentions, maintaining a dedicated dream journal, reflecting on dream entries, and incorporating meditation and visualization all contribute to a holistic exploration of the rich terrain of your unconscious mind. This intentional approach allows you to unlock the potential for self-discovery and personal growth that lies within the realm of dreams.

FASTING FROM FOOD

Fasting a lunar month can also help individuals tap into their subconscious mind and gain greater clarity on our goals and desires. Lunar Dreaming is a powerful tool that can help you focus your unconscious and conscious mind to work together towards your desired goals. By dedicating each lunar month to a specific subject or question, you can bring clarity and direction to your dreams. If you are looking to manifest a project or find the right partner, Lunar Dreaming can be particularly helpful.

During the new moon phase, which is a blank canvas and a time for new beginnings, you can set your intention and ask your dreams to help guide you towards your goal. Your dreams can help bring up any underlying emotions or obstacles that may be holding you back or reveal what steps you need to take to achieve your goal. As the moon waxes, you can continue to focus your intention and act towards your goal, using your dreams as a guide and source of inspiration.

In recent years, there has been a noticeable surge in the interest surrounding the utilization of moon cycles to manifest our dreams. More and more individuals are turning their attention to the waxing and waning of the moon's phases as a guiding force to help them realize their aspirations. Just as the moon's rhythmic dance influences the tides of the oceans, it can also influence the tides of our lives. In a similar vein, we can harness the lunar rhythm to encourage our subconscious minds to weave dreams that serve as guiding stars during the four distinct phases of the moon. The moon, as a celestial timekeeper, can act as a silent partner in our quest for self-discovery and personal growth.

During the New Moon phase, we can invoke the lunar cycle to request dreams that bring clarity to unresolved issues from our past. These dreams become the lanterns illuminating the hidden corners of our psyche, helping us understand and heal past wounds. As the moon waxes and gains luminance, we can direct our dream requests towards guidance in achieving our desired goals or dreams in life. These dreams become the blueprints for our waking hours, offering us insights and strategies to navigate the path ahead.

When the moon reaches its fullness, our dreams can be a source of profound revelation, shedding light on the culmination of our intentions and aspirations. These dreams are like celestial compasses, helping us chart our course in alignment with our true desires. As the moon wanes and retreats into darkness, we can use this phase to request dreams that assist us in letting go of what no longer serves us. These dreams are like gentle winds that clear the path for new beginnings.

The nightly landscape of our dreams becomes a laboratory where we can experiment with ideas, explore possibilities, and develop concrete plans to apply in "real life". By working in harmony with the lunar cycle, we not only gain access to the wisdom of our subconscious mind but also empower ourselves to manifest our dreams in the waking world. In this intricate dance between the moon and our dreams, we discover that the boundaries between the ethereal and the tangible blur, and our lives become a canvas upon which our nocturnal visions paint the path to our aspirations. The moon, as our celestial companion, guides us on this extraordinary journey of self-discovery and dream realization.

PRACTICAL TIPS FOR FOOD FASTING

1. Setting an Intention for Lunar Fasting from Food

Like setting intentions for silent fasting, embarking on a lunar fasting journey from food begins with a clear and purposeful intention. Consider what you wish to achieve or explore through this period of

abstaining from nourishment. Your intention could revolve around spiritual growth, physical detoxification, or simply gaining a deeper understanding of your relationship with food and nourishment. Setting a well-defined intention helps anchor your fasting experience and provides a meaningful context for your lunar fast.

Your intention might be to enhance your spiritual connection during the lunar fasting period, using the heightened state of physical emptiness to draw closer to your inner self and the cosmos. Alternatively, it could revolve around achieving mental clarity and focus, recognizing that fasting can clear mental fog and promote mindfulness. Whatever your intention, it guides your fasting journey and infuses it with purpose and direction, aligning with the self-awareness and self-empowerment principles in your methodology.

2. Recording the Lunar Fasting Journey

Just as with silent fasting, keeping a dedicated journal is a powerful practice during lunar fasting from food. Begin by noting the start date of your fasting period and the specific lunar phase you're observing. Throughout the fasting period, document your physical sensations, emotional states, and any insights or thoughts that arise. Pay attention to the waxing and waning of your hunger, as well as any changes in energy levels or mood. This journal becomes a vital record of your lunar fasting journey.

One unique aspect of lunar fasting from food is the synchronization with the lunar phases. Reflect on how your fasting experience aligns with the moon's cycles. Consider whether certain lunar phases evoke emotions or revelations. For example, during the new moon, you may find yourself drawn to introspection and new beginnings, while the full moon might illuminate areas of your life that require release or transformation. By noting these lunar connections, you deepen your awareness of the interconnectedness of your inner world and the natural world.

3. Reflecting on the Fasting Experience

As your lunar fasting journey unfolds, take time to reflect on the physical, emotional, and mental aspects of the experience. How do you feel physically as your body adapts to the absence of food? What emotions arise during moments of hunger or satisfaction from fasting? How does your mental state change throughout the lunar fasting period? Reflecting on these dimensions allows you to gain a comprehensive understanding of your fasting experience.

Consider also how your lunar fasting journey aligns with your broader self-awareness and self-empowerment goals. Are there patterns or revelations in your fasting experience that resonate with Body, Emotions, Mind, Belief System? For instance, you might notice a heightened sense of mindfulness

and emotional awareness during the fasting period, aligning with your holistic approach. Reflecting on these connections between your fasting experience and your methodology enriches your understanding of the holistic interplay between the physical, emotional, and mental dimensions of self-awareness and empowerment. Lunar fasting from food allows you to explore this unique aspect of your holistic approach. Setting intentions, maintaining a dedicated journal, and reflecting on the fasting experience all contribute to a deepened awareness of the interconnectedness between your inner self and the lunar cycles. This intentional approach elevates lunar fasting from food beyond a physical practice and transforms it into a profound journey of self-discovery and growth.

THE COMPLETE LUNAR DREAMING CYCLE

Lunar dreaming, whether you chose to fast or not, harnesses the power of dream-driven inquiry to dive deeper into self-awareness. By posing specific questions before bedtime, we set a clear intention for our dream journey. These questions act as beacons, guiding our dreams toward our desired outcomes. They serve as bridges between our conscious and subconscious minds, facilitating a profound exploration of our inner world.

As we consistently set these intentions and diligently record our dreams, we establish a profound connection with the depths of our being. This practice of self-communication allows us to gain a greater understanding of ourselves and the intricate tapestry of our lives. Each dream becomes a piece of the puzzle, offering insights, revelations, and a deeper sense of purpose.

During a Lunar Dreaming month, we invite the mysteries of the subconscious to reveal themselves, and each dream becomes a sacred gift, guiding us on our path of self-awareness and empowerment. By experimenting with different questions, we unlock the wisdom of our dreams, uncovering hidden gems within that illuminate our journey and lead us toward our truest selves.

Let us explore the full lunar cycle and how it can relate to lunar dreaming. Lunar Dreaming is a practice that can help you understand your life in a way that is both fun and more meaningful self-discovery. The beauty of Lunar Dreaming lies in its timeless accessibility, for you can engage in this transformative journey in any month, or even extend it over the course of the next twelve months. Moreover, it is a creative way of dream journaling that channels the energy of the moon and its ever-evolving cycle to cast a luminous light upon your mind and to shape your dreams.

Furthermore, as you immerse yourself in Lunar Dreaming, the moon becomes your steadfast ally, illuminating the uncharted recesses of your consciousness. Its phases serve as a celestial guide, if you like, offering you a road map to navigate the terrain of your dreams and aspirations. Moreover, you need not wait for a specific month to begin this enchanting journey. Let the new moon guide you to the start of this journey for you. Whether you choose to dedicate a single month or an entire year, the moon's wisdom remains ever-present, ready to impart its insights. Each lunar cycle carries its unique energy, symbolizing a fresh chapter in your life's story.

Additionally, as you align your dreams with the moon's phases, you will uncover a tapestry of experiences and revelations. Moreover, you will be able to experience the power of intention-setting during the New Moon, the transformative energy of the Full Moon, and the wisdom of reflection during the Last Quarter. The moon's gentle guidance allows you to craft your dreams, translating them into actionable steps in your waking life. So, whether you embark on this journey today or at any point in the coming months, remember that Lunar Dreaming is a timeless practice, always ready to illuminate your path, enrich your understanding of life, and empower you to manifest your dreams. The moon, as your celestial companion, stands ever watchful, inviting you to step into the world of your dreams with purpose and intention.

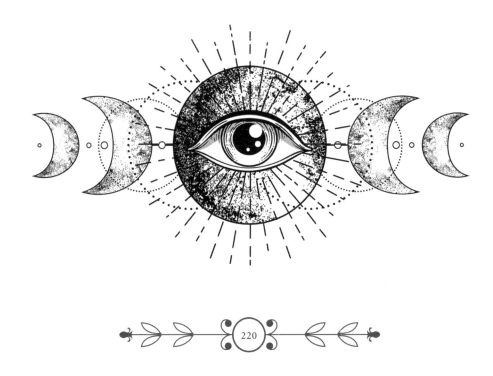

LUNAR PHASES

The Moon completes one orbit around the Earth every approximately 29 days, while the Earth takes 365 days to orbit around the Sun. The appearance of the Moon in the sky, including its different phases, determined by its position relative to the Sun. The illuminated part of the Moon visible to us is determined by the position of the Sun in relation to the Moon (see figure 13). Each phase has its unique energy and represents different aspects of the manifestation process. In between each phase, there are also four intermediate waxing and waning phases.

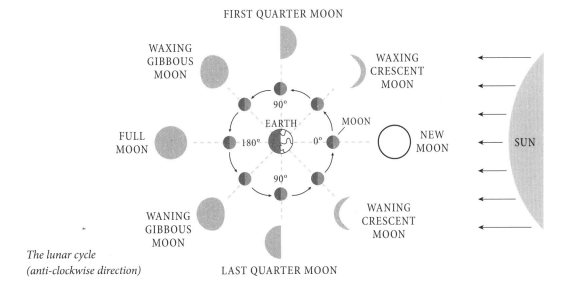

The lunar cycle (anti-clockwise direction)

The lunar dreaming cycle unfolds in harmony with the phases of the moon, creating a structured rhythm for dream exploration and self-awareness. Divided into four weeks for convenience, each week corresponds to a primary lunar phase, providing a framework for understanding and working with the interplay between lunar cycles and dreaming. This intentional connection between your goals and the moon's energy can amplify your dream exploration and personal growth:

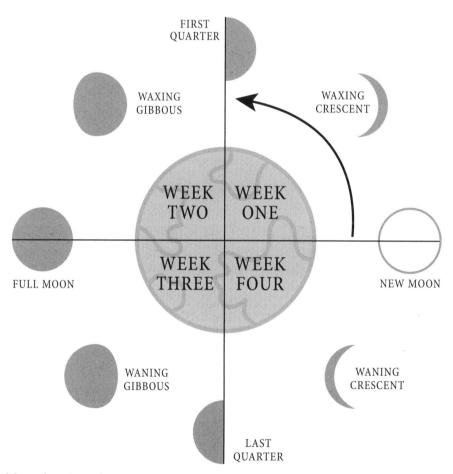

Four week lunar dreaming cycle

WEEK ONE: PLANTING SEEDS

The New Moon. This is a primary phase of the moon followed by Waxing Crescent Moon, which is a secondary lunar phase.

Week one of the lunar dreaming cycle, marked by the New Moon and Waxing Crescent Moon, is a time of fresh beginnings and nurturing the seeds of intention (see figure 14). As the lunar cycle commences with the dark canvas of the New Moon, it offers a blank slate to set our dreams and aspirations. During this week, we plant the seeds of our desires, crafting clear intentions and goals. The Waxing Crescent Moon then gently nurtures these intentions, allowing them to take root and flourish. It's a period of self-reflection and the initiation of a journey into our inner world, where dreams become the fertile soil for the intentions we seek to manifest in the coming weeks.

WEEK TWO: TAKING ACTION

The First Quarter, or Half Moon (primary phase) followed by Waxing Gibbous Moon which is a secondary phase.

Week two of the lunar dreaming cycle, encompassing the First Quarter Moon and Waxing Gibbous Moon, represents a phase of action and refinement. As the moon approaches its first quarter, we find ourselves at the midpoint between the New Moon and the Full Moon. It's a time of heightened dream experiences, where our intentions set during the New Moon begin to materialize and take shape in our dreams. Dreams during this week often provide guidance on practical steps and actions needed to manifest our desires. We refine our goals, paying close attention to the details, as the Waxing Gibbous Moon intensifies our dream experiences. It's a dynamic phase where our dreams become vivid and meaningful, offering valuable insights and a deeper understanding of the path we are embarking on. This week encourages us to be proactive and decisive in aligning our dreams with our chosen journey of self-awareness and empowerment.

WEEK THREE: FULFILLMENT AND GRATITUDE

The Full Moon, a primary lunar phase, followed by Wanning Gibbous Moon (secondary phase).

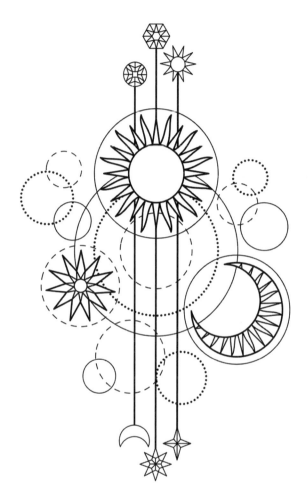

lunar cycle. This phase sheds light on hidden obstacles so we can refine our plans. The Waning Gibbous Moon serves as a mirror, revealing the details that require polishing and adjustment in our journey towards self-awareness and empowerment.

This phase invites us to release what no longer serves us, be it old habits, limiting beliefs, or stagnant energies. This week is an opportunity for gratitude, as we acknowledge the wisdom gained from our dreamscapes and the progress made on our path. Dreams during this week may carry a sense of liberation and clarity, guiding us to let go of what hinders our growth. You are called to express gratitude for the lessons learned and the journey ahead.

WEEK FOUR:
LETTING GO AND RESET

Week four of the lunar dreaming cycle, encompassing the Last Quarter Moon and Waning Crescent Moon, marks a phase of surrender, reset, and rejuvenation. As the moon continues to wane, we find ourselves in a period of profound reflection and inner work. The Last Quarter Moon serves as a pivot point in our dream journey, encouraging us to assess our progress and release what no longer aligns with our path of self-awareness and empowerment.

Week three of the lunar dreaming cycle, characterized by the Waning Gibbous Moon, represents a phase of reflection, release, and gratitude. As the moon begins to wane, we enter a period of introspection and discernment. Dreams during this week prompt us to reflect on the insights gained thus far in the

During this week, we engage in deep introspection, meditating on old habits and patterns that have outworn their purpose. It's a time of letting go, shedding layers of the past to create space for new beginnings. The energy shifts from outward action to inner contemplation, as we turn our gaze inward to reset our inner compass. This phase emphasizes the importance of surrendering and recharging, allowing us to enter the next lunar cycle with clarity and purpose. As the Waning Crescent Moon approaches, our dreams become quieter and more introspective, providing solace, healing, and a sense of release. This week is an opportunity to cleanse and rejuvenate our inner landscape,

preparing us for the upcoming New Moon where we plant fresh intentions and pose new questions in our dream journal. Week four is a transformative phase that ensures we embark on the next leg of our journey with clarity and renewed purpose.

The Eight phases of the Lunar Dreaming in order are:

1. New Moon Initiations and Planting Seeds

The New Moon, with its dark and blank canvas in the night sky, symbolizes new beginnings and fresh starts. It is a time when the moon is aligned with the sun, signifying

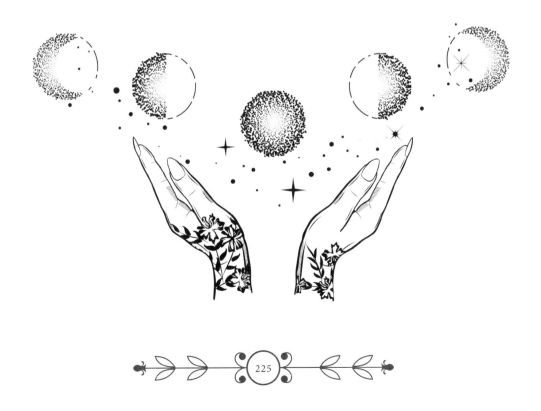

2. Waxing Crescent Moon: Nurturing Growth

With the moon beginning to grow, so does our dream journey. The Waxing Crescent phase nurtures the intentions we've planted, allowing our dreams to take root and expand. It's a time of nurturing and tending to the dreamscape, as they gradually gain strength and significance.

3. First Quarter Moon (primary): Taking Action

Marking the midpoint between the New Moon and Full Moon, the First Quarter Moon is a focal point for action in our dreamwork. Dreams become more vivid and meaningful as our intentions begin to materialize. This phase prompts us to take tangible steps toward manifesting our aspirations, aligning our dreams with our chosen path.

4. Waxing Gibbous Moon: Refinement & Expansion

This phase is about expansion. The Waxing Moon represents growth and expansion. During this phase the moon's illumination increases. This makes it an opportune time for goals cantered on progress and development. Aspirations aligned with the Waxing Moon can include endeavors such as skill acquisition, professional advancement, or

the planting of seeds. To make the most of this phase, consider setting goals that resonate with new beginnings and initial stages of development. These can be aspirations related to starting a new project, adopting healthier habits, or cultivating a budding relationship. The New Moon's energy supports the germination of your intentions and the setting of clear directions.

nurturing relationships to reach new heights. The energy of this phase encourages the nurturing and expansion of your intentions, allowing them to flourish and reach their full potential.

5. Full Moon (primary): Illumination & Clarity

As the moon reaches its full luminance during the Full Moon phase, it offers a profound illumination both in the night sky and within your dreams. Goals aligned with the Full Moon can revolve around gaining clarity and insight. These might include aspirations related to achieving a deeper understanding of a complex situation, making important decisions, or celebrating significant milestones in your journey. The Full Moon's radiant light shines a spotlight on your goals, bringing clarity and revelations to your path.

6. Waning Gibbous: Releasing and Gratitude

During the Waning Moon phases, the moon begins to decrease in illumination, mirroring the process of shedding and letting go. This phase is ideal for setting goals focused on releasing obstacles, breaking free from limiting beliefs, or decluttering your life. Consider aspirations that involve personal growth through the process of release and renewal. Whether it's relinquishing old habits, forgiving past grievances, or simplifying your life, the Waning Moon's energy supports the transformative power of letting go.

7. Last Quarter Moon (primary): Reflection.

Marking the midpoint between the Full Moon and the next New Moon, the Last Quarter Moon serves as a pivot in our dream journey. It's a time to assess progress, release what needs to be let go, and prepare for the next cycle of intentions. Dreams may prompt us to shed old patterns or beliefs.

8. Waning Crescent Moon: Surrender & Release

During the Waning Moon phases, the moon begins to decrease in illumination, mirroring the process of shedding and letting go. This phase is ideal for setting goals focused on releasing obstacles, breaking free from limiting beliefs, or decluttering your life. Consider aspirations that involve personal growth through the process of release and renewal. Whether it's relinquishing old habits, forgiving past grievances, or simplifying your life, the Waning Moon's energy supports the transformative power of letting go.

HARMONIZING WITH THE LUNAR CYCLE

To tailor your goals effectively to the lunar phases, take time to meditate on the specific energy and symbolism associated with each phase. Visualize how your aspirations resonate with the characteristics of that phase. This intentional alignment creates a harmonious synergy between your dreams and the natural rhythms of the moon, enhancing your dreamwork and self-awareness.

Meditate on Lunar Energy

Begin by setting aside moments of quiet contemplation during each lunar phase. As you enter this meditative space, focus your awareness on the specific qualities associated with that phase. For example, during the New Moon, envision the stillness and potential of a blank canvas. During the Full Moon, immerse yourself in the radiant illumination and clarity it offers. This meditation acts as a bridge between your consciousness and the

moon's energy, allowing you to attune your intentions with its natural rhythms.

Through these lunar meditations, you connect with the ancient wisdom embedded in the moon's phases. Feel the ebb and flow of its energy as it mirrors the cycles of life. This practice deepens your self-awareness and intuition, enabling you to navigate life's challenges with grace and purpose. As you meditate on lunar energy, you'll discover a profound connection to the cosmos, forging a path of self-empowerment and spiritual growth.

Visualize Aspirational Resonance

With your goals in mind, visualize how they resonate with the energy of the current lunar phase. Picture your aspirations as seeds taking root during the New Moon, growing steadily with the Waxing Moon, reaching their peak under the Full Moon's brilliance,

releasing what no longer serves during the Waning Moon, and expanding further with the Waxing Moon once again. This mental imagery serves as a powerful tool for aligning your intentions with the moon's phases. Additionally, it deepens your connection to the natural world and your own inner cycles, fostering self-awareness and personal growth. As you engage in this practice of aligning your goals with the lunar phases, embrace the natural ebb and flow of life's rhythms. Just as the moon waxes and wanes, recognize that there are times for action and times for reflection in your own journey. Trust the process and allow yourself to surrender to the cosmic dance of the moon and stars. In doing so, you not only enhance your dreamwork but also cultivate a deeper sense of self-awareness and empowerment.

Intentional Alignment

As you meditate and visualize, you are actively creating an intentional alignment between your inner world and the celestial energies. This alignment fosters a harmonious synergy that infuses your dreamscapes with purpose and direction. Imagine that you are co-creating your dreams with the moon, inviting its influence to guide you toward your aspirations. This intentional collaboration deepens your dreamwork and heightens self-awareness, making your dreams more

potent and insightful. By consciously aligning your intentions with the lunar phases, you become attuned to the ever-changing tapestry of your inner and outer worlds. As you navigate the cycles of growth, release, and transformation, you gain a profound understanding of the interconnectedness of your dreams, your subconscious mind, and the cosmos. This alignment fosters not only personal growth but also a sense of unity with the universe, as you recognize that you are an integral part of the celestial dance. Your dreams become a canvas upon which the moon paints its wisdom, offering guidance and illumination on your journey of self-discovery.

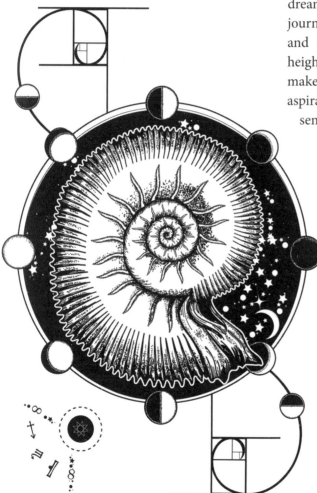

Enhancing Dreamwork and Self-Awareness

By consistently practicing this intentional alignment with the lunar phases, you empower your dream exploration to become a dynamic tool for personal growth. Your dreams evolve into mirrors of your inner journey, reflecting the progress, challenges, and insights related to your goals. This heightened self-awareness allows you to make more informed decisions, refine your aspirations, and navigate life with a greater sense of purpose.

Being mindful of the resonance and symbolism of each phase of the moon during lunar dreaming month, transforms dreaming from a passive experience into an active co-creation with the moon's energies. This can have a profound effect on your dreams your mind generates, not only aligning your dreams with your goals, but also to deepen your understanding of yourself and the intricate connection between your inner world and the cosmos. Moreover, throughout your journey with the eight lunar phases, you will discover a valuable toolkit tailored to enhance your lunar dreaming experience. This comprehensive toolkit includes three essential components: affirmations, journal questions, and herbal oil allies, meticulously crafted to empower and enrich your connection with the moon's energies.

Affirmations

Following each lunar dreaming phase below, you will also find affirmations to inspire your own dreaming. These empowering statements serve as guiding beacons throughout your lunar dreaming journey. The affirmations are designed to align your consciousness with the specific energies of that moment, reinforcing your intentions and aspirations. Feel free to compose your own as per your goals for each lunar phase. As you prepare to embark on each phase of the lunar dream cycle, consider incorporating specific affirmations into your nightly routine before going to bed. These affirmations act as beacons, guiding your subconscious mind toward the themes and intentions that align with each lunar phase. Whether you are entering the tranquil darkness of the New Moon, the delicate illumination of the Waxing Crescent, or the active phase of Taking Actions. Affirmations can set the stage for dreams that are not only vivid but deeply connected to your aspirations and desires.

Journal Questions

Elevating your lunar dreaming experience, these meticulously crafted inquiries serve as powerful tools for self-reflection and personal growth. Immerse yourself in the profound insights and wisdom hidden within your dreams by pondering these thought-provoking questions. Delve deeper into your inner world, desires, and aspirations as you use these inquiries to navigate your lunar journey. Each question is designed to guide you on a transformative path of self-reflection, self-awareness, and self-empowerment, aligning your dreams with the natural rhythms of the moon. Whether you choose from our selection or create your own, these inquiries are gateways to unlock the limitless potential of your lunar dreamscapes, igniting inspiration and enhancing your exploration of self.

HERBAL ESSENTIAL OIL ALLIES

To complement your lunar journey, each phase is paired with a carefully selected herbal oil ally and a suggested flower remedy too. These botanical essences resonate with the unique qualities of the lunar phase, providing aromatic support for your emotional and spiritual well-being. These oils are not just companions but catalysts, amplifying your lunar dreaming experience. Use them

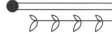

as aromatherapy, by diffusing them. Or any routine as part of your nightly ritual to enhance your connection with the lunar phases and infuse your dreams with their respective energies.

Moreover, Essential oils can play a significant role in enhancing your lunar dreaming practices by influencing your mood, emotions, and overall well-being. To incorporate essential oils into your dream-enhancing ritual, consider diffusing them in your sleeping space, adding a drop or two to a tissue placed beneath your pillow, or diluting them with a carrier oil for a soothing self-massage before bedtime. Each oil carries its own unique energetic signature, allowing you to tailor your selection to the specific intentions and energies of each lunar phase. As you embark on your lunar dreaming journey, let the exquisite scents of essential oils transport you to the realms of the subconscious, where dreams and self-awareness intertwine, guiding you towards a more profound understanding of your inner world and the boundless potential of your lunar dreamscapes. Here are some of the ways that essential oils can help you during Lunar Dreaming:

Emotional and Psychological Support

Essential oils have the power to evoke specific emotions and feelings. When used during your lunar dreaming rituals, they can help create the right emotional atmosphere for relaxation, self-reflection, and dreamwork. For example, calming oils like lavender or chamomile can induce a sense of tranquility, making it easier to enter a meditative or dream-like state. Moreover, certain essential oils, such as frankincense and sandalwood, are known for their ability to deepen spiritual connection and enhance intuition. By incorporating these oils into your lunar dreaming practice, you can tap into your inner wisdom and strengthen your

connection with the dream realm. Whether you seek emotional healing, personal insight, or spiritual growth through your dreams, the carefully chosen use of essential oils can provide invaluable support on your lunar dreaming journey, allowing you to navigate the depths of your subconscious with greater ease and clarity.

Aromatherapy and Relaxation

Aromatherapy, the use of essential oils for therapeutic purposes, can promote relaxation and reduce stress and anxiety. Incorporating essential oils into your pre-sleep routine can help you calm your mind and body, making it easier to transition into a receptive state for dream exploration. In addition to their relaxing properties, essential oils can enhance the sensory experience of your lunar dreaming rituals. The gentle scent of these oils can create a soothing ambiance in your sleep space, providing a sensory cue to your mind that it's time for rest and introspection. This olfactory connection can serve as a signal to your brain, helping it shift from the busyness of the day to the serenity of the night, where dreams can be more vivid and profound. The use of essential oils not only aids in relaxation but also deepens the connection between your waking and dreaming states, enriching your lunar dreaming journey with sensory harmony and tranquility.

Sensory Stimulation

Essential oils are often used as a sensory trigger. Associating a particular scent with your lunar dreaming practice can create a Pavlovian response, where your brain associates the aroma with relaxation and dream awareness. Over time, this can help signal your mind that it's time for focused dreamwork. As you incorporate essential oils into your lunar dreaming routine, consider experimenting with different scents during each phase of the moon. This deliberate choice of oils can further enhance your connection to the lunar energies, allowing you to attune your dreams to the specific qualities of each phase. For example, during the New Moon, you might choose a fresh, invigorating scent to symbolize new beginnings. On the other hand, during the Waning Crescent phase of surrender, opt for a calming and grounding aroma. By aligning the scents with the moon's energy, you deepen the sensory experience of your lunar dreaming, forging a deeper connection between your dreams and the natural rhythms of the cosmos.

Dream Recall

Certain essential oils are believed to enhance dream recall. These oils can stimulate memory and help you remember your dreams more vividly upon waking. Frankincense, clary sage, and rosemary are examples of essential oils that may support this aspect of lunar dreaming. To harness the full potential of essential oils for dream recall, you can create a simple bedtime ritual. Before sleep, apply a diluted blend of your chosen oils to your pulse points or inhale the scent from a diffuser. As you breathe in the aroma, set your intention to remember your dreams clearly and vividly. This olfactory cue serves as a gentle reminder to your subconscious mind, prompting it to prioritize dream memory. Over time, this practice can become a powerful ally in your lunar dreaming journey, helping you unlock the rich tapestry of your dreamscapes and gain deeper insights into your inner world.

Setting Intentions

Before sleep, you can apply essential oils with the intention of enhancing your dreamwork. This act of intention-setting can create a psychological connection between the oil and your lunar dreaming goals. You might use oils associated with clarity, insight, or spiritual connection, such as sandalwood or myrrh, to help set the stage for meaningful dreams. As you apply these oils, take a moment to focus on your lunar dreaming intentions. Visualize the desired outcomes of your dream exploration and how these intentions align with the chosen essential oils. Allow the soothing aroma to envelop you, deepening your connection to your inner self and the moon's energy. This intentional practice can serve as a bridge between the physical and metaphysical realms, guiding you toward transformative dream experiences that resonate with your lunar goals.

Meditation and Visualization

Essential oils can be used during meditation and visualization exercises to help you enter a receptive and focused state. Scents like frankincense, cedarwood, and patchouli are often chosen for their grounding and spiritual properties, which can support your connection to your dreams and inner self. Moreover, allow the fragrance of these essential oils to envelop you. Inhale deeply, letting the aroma penetrate your senses, and visualize your dreamscape unfolding before you. The grounding and spiritual properties of these oils act as anchors, helping you navigate the depths of your consciousness with clarity and purpose. This aromatic synergy between your inner world and the natural world can amplify the effectiveness of your meditation and visualization practices,

in your dreamwork rituals. The scent can act as a bridge, transporting you back to those moments of dream clarity and insight. Through this familiar fragrance, you can tap into the reservoir of wisdom that your dreams hold, enhancing your connection to your inner self and the mysteries of the lunar cycle.

Finally, when using essential oils for lunar dreaming, it is essential to choose high-quality, pure oils, and to dilute them appropriately if you plan to apply them to your skin. You can use oils in various ways, such as diffusing them in your sleep space, adding a few drops to a warm bath before bedtime, or using them in massage or body oils. Ultimately, the scents and sensations created by essential oils can help you create a conducive environment for exploring the depths of your inner world during lunar dreaming. In case you are dealing with medical conditions, always consult your therapist or doctor before using essential oils.

empowering you to tap into the profound wisdom of your dreams.

Personal Associations

Your personal experiences and associations with specific scents can also influence your lunar dreaming. For example, if you have had positive dream experiences while using a particular oil, its scent can trigger a sense of readiness and receptivity for dreamwork. These personal associations can become powerful tools in your lunar dreaming arsenal. If a certain essential oil has accompanied you on memorable dream journeys in the past, keep it as a cherished companion

FLOWER REMEDIES

Flower remedies, such as Bach Flower Remedies or Australian Bush Flower Essences, can be used to support your lunar dreaming practices in several ways. These remedies are natural and vibrational in nature, capturing the energy and essence of

specific flowers. They are typically created through a process of infusing the flower's essence into water, harnessing the healing properties of the plant. This water is then preserved with alcohol and diluted to create the final remedy. The resulting flower essences can be taken orally or applied topically, making them a gentle and non-invasive tool for emotional and spiritual well-being. Each flower essence carries its unique vibrational signature, offering emotional and energetic support that can align with your lunar dreamwork intentions.

Emotional Balance

Flower remedies are known for their ability to address emotional imbalances and promote emotional well-being. By taking the appropriate flower remedy, you can enhance emotional stability and create a harmonious inner environment conducive to dream exploration. For example, if anxiety or fear is hindering your ability to relax and dream, a remedy like Rescue Remedy (a combination of several Bach Flower Remedies) can help restore a sense of calm. These remedies work on the vibrational level, gently nudging your emotional state towards equilibrium, which can be especially beneficial for achieving a peaceful and receptive mind during lunar dreaming.

Self-Reflection

Flower remedies can assist in deepening your self-awareness and self-reflection during lunar dreaming. These remedies work at a subtle level to gently uncover and address underlying emotional issues or patterns that may be affecting your dream experiences. By addressing these emotional blocks, you may find it easier to connect with your dreams and gain valuable insights. This process of self-reflection can be a profound aspect of lunar dreaming, as it allows you to explore the depths of your inner world with greater clarity and understanding.

Setting Intentions

Much like essential oils, flower remedies can be used to set intentions for your lunar dreaming practices. Before sleep, you can take a few drops of a flower remedy that aligns with your specific intention or the energy of the moon phase you are working with. For example, using a remedy associated with clarity and insight during the Full Moon phase can enhance your ability to receive illuminating dream messages.

Dream Recall

Some flower remedies are believed to improve dream recall by enhancing memory and mental clarity. If you struggle with remembering your dreams upon waking, a flower remedy that supports mental acuity, such as Ginkgo Biloba or Clematis (a Bach Flower Remedy), may be beneficial.

Sensory Awareness

Flower remedies can heighten your sensory awareness, making you more attuned to subtle energies and dream symbols. This heightened awareness can deepen your dream experiences and make dream symbols more vivid and meaningful. As you work with flower remedies, you may find that your ability to perceive and interpret the symbolism in your dreams becomes more refined. This sensory awareness can open new doors to self-discovery and insight as you navigate the rich landscape of your dream world.

Chakra Balancing

Some flower remedies are associated with specific chakras or energy centers in the body. Balancing these energy centers through flower remedies can promote a sense of inner harmony and alignment, which can positively influence your dreamwork. For example, the heart chakra, located at the center of the chest, is linked to love, compassion, and emotional balance. Flower remedies that align with the heart chakra can

help release emotional blockages, fostering a greater sense of love and connection in both waking life and within the dream world.

Similarly, the third eye chakra, located in the center of the forehead, is associated with intuition, insight, and psychic abilities. Flower remedies that resonate with the third eye chakra can enhance your ability to access and interpret the intuitive messages and symbols present in your dreams. They can amplify your receptivity to the subtle energies of the dream realm, making your lunar dreaming experiences more profound and enlightening.

Finally, using flower remedies to balance your chakras, you create an internal environment that is receptive, harmonious, and attuned to the energies of the moon and the dream world. This alignment enhances your dreamwork, allowing you to tap into the deeper layers of your consciousness and gain valuable insights through your lunar dreams. To use flower remedies for lunar dreaming, follow these steps:

Select the Appropriate Remedy

Research the various flower remedies available and choose one that aligns with your specific lunar dreaming goals, emotions, or challenges.

Take the Remedy

Most flower remedies come in liquid form and can be taken orally by placing a few drops under your tongue or diluting them in water. Follow the recommended dosage instructions on the product label.

Set Intentions

Before taking the remedy, set a clear intention for your lunar dreaming practice. Focus on what you hope to achieve, explore, or release during your dreamwork.

Repeat as Needed

Depending on the remedy and your specific needs, you may need to take it regularly to experience its full benefits. Consistency is key in flower remedy therapy.

Remember that flower remedies work subtly and gently over time, so be patient with the process. They can be a valuable addition to your lunar dreaming toolkit, helping you create a more supportive emotional and energetic environment for your dream exploration. Together, these three components, affirmations, dream journal questions and herbal allies form a harmonious and potent blend, empowering you to harness the transformative energies of each lunar phase, paving the way for deeper self-awareness, personal growth, and the wisdom that resides within your dreams.

WEEK ONE:
PLANTING SEEDS &
NURTURING GROWTH

During this phase, we plant the seeds of our desires and aspirations through our dreams. This week serves as a powerful time to manifest dreams that provide insight or guidance on our chosen issues. At this point, the Earth, Moon, and Sun are aligned. The moon is positioned closest to the sun with its illuminated side facing away from us, resulting in a New Moon phase that appears dark. During the New Moon, the night sky is veiled in darkness, and it marks a symbolic blank canvas, a cosmic canvas ready to receive our intentions.

New Moon: Planting Seeds with Intention

The New Moon is often associated with new beginnings and is an opportune time to start fresh, set intentions, and establish new goals.

It is a time when we plant the seeds of our desires and aspirations through our dreams. In this lunar phase, our dreams become fertile soil, where our intentions can take root and flourish. This is a time to focus on what you want to achieve and to write down your goals in a dream journal. Intentions involves making a declaration of what you aim to achieve through your actions, and it is a way to commit to your desired journey as you progress on your spiritual path. Moreover, week one (the new moon) can serve as a powerful time to set intentions and manifest a dream that provides insight or guidance on that issue.

During this phase, you can take the time to reflect on your issue and formulate a clear and specific question to ask your subconscious mind in your dream. As you set your intention for your dream, you can repeat a mantra or affirmation, such as *"I will receive guidance and clarity on my issue through my dream,"* to help focus your mind and energy. Your intention becomes a sacred contract between your conscious self and your subconscious, ensuring that your dream journey is purposeful and directed.

YOUR DREAM INTENTION STATEMENT

To begin, find a quiet place and write down what you want to achieve during this cycle. Be specific and clear about your goals and focus on what you truly desire. Ask yourself what you want to manifest in your life and write it down in your dream journal. Take the time to visualize what it would feel like to achieve your goals and use this feeling as motivation to move forward. Writing down your intention in a dream journal is helpful in solidifying your goals and ensuring that you remember the dream once you wake up. Let us refer to this as **Dream Intention statement**.

For example, in your journal you can write a statement about the issue or subject matter you want to explore on the new moon as: "I will have a dream about (state your intention) which I will remember when I wake up." Utilizing the energy and symbolism of

the New Moon phase can be a powerful tool in generating a dream that provides valuable insights and guidance on your issue. Once the seeds are planted, mindfully attend and track your dreams for the next 4 weeks.

Here are some examples of questions you can ask yourself to help you clarify and refine your intentions. During each lunar phase, you can formulate a new question refine it, or phrase it in a slightly different way to activate your unconscious mind. For example, "What do I want to achieve during this lunar cycle?", or "What do I need to focus on creating in my life right now?", "What is my biggest goal or desire currently?", clarify further by asking "What steps do I need to take to get closer to my goals?" If your inquiry is general, try asking your mind "What can I do to improve my physical, emotional, or spiritual well-being?. If your intention is specific around a relationship, "What can I do to improve my relationships or create more fulfilling connections with others?" And if your intention is to rejuvenate your life "What new opportunities do I want to attract into my life?" Crafting the right question can help you induce clearer guidance through your dreams.

Reflecting on the next new moon, what is your intention for the upcoming lunar month? Start by writing one word, then craft your questions around it. When your question is clear, so would the dream you induce. Your one-word theme for the month can, for example, be: Relationships, Abundance, health, Career advancement. Alternatively, if you are starting a new project such as writing a book, or creating a course, etc., craft a specific question for each lunar week of the month around your task.

What is your one-word theme for the next lunar month? Write it below now. My Lunar Cycle Intention is:

_____

Additionally, one way to enhance your dream work is to write down a different question in your dream journal each day of the week. Varying the phrasing of your questions can stimulate your subconscious mind and potentially lead to different dream

experiences from different angles. By the end of the week, you may have a few dreams that relate to your initial intention. Writing down each dream in your journal can help you clarify your intentions and focus your energy on what you truly want. Additionally, interpreting your dreams can provide valuable guidance on how to manifest or heal aspects of your life.

As you sow these seeds of intention, cultivate a sense of mindfulness that extends into the forthcoming 14 days. These seeds are not planted in soil but within the fertile ground of your consciousness. You have invoked the moon's energy to act as a beacon, guiding your inner world towards the dream you seek. During this time, become a vigilant observer of your dreamscapes. Keep a watchful eye on the messages that unfold within your nightly visions. The dreams that

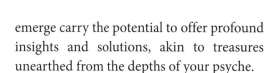
emerge carry the potential to offer profound insights and solutions, akin to treasures unearthed from the depths of your psyche.

New Moon Affirmation

*"I embrace new beginnings
and plant the seeds of my intentions."*

NEW MOON HERBAL ALLIES

Essential Oil: Lavender oil represents the fresh start and new beginnings associated with the New Moon. It has a calming and grounding aroma that helps you plant the seeds of intention in a tranquil and centered state of mind. Lavender promotes clarity and focus, making it an ideal ally for setting your dreams and aspirations during this phase.

Flower Remedy: Walnut (Bach Flower Remedy) or **Macrocarpa** (Australian Bush Flower Essence). Walnut helps you adapt to change and protect your intentions during the vulnerable beginning stages. Macrocarpa connects you with your inner wisdom and supports new beginnings.

WAXING CRESCENT MOON: NURTURING GROWTH

In this intermediatory phase, the moon is moving from New Moon to First Quarter Moon. During the Waxing Moon, the energy is focused on growth and expansion. With the moon beginning to grow, so does your dream journey. The Waxing Crescent phase nurtures the intentions you have planted, allowing your dreams to take root and expand. It is a time of nurturing and tending to the dreamscape, as they gradually gain strength and significance.

As the moon begins its waxing journey, moving away from the shadow of the Sun

it progresses towards complete fullness. With it, our dreams shift in harmony with this growing energy. Just as a tender shoot emerges from the earth, our dreams now focus on nurturing the growth of our intentions. As the energy is focused on growth and expansion, making it the perfect time to act towards your desired outcome. During this week, it is time to explore the steps and actions required to support and cultivate our dreams as they flourish like young plants in the spring. Use this time to refine your plan questions, jot more questions in your dream journal; or perhaps to rephrase them approaching the issue from a different angle.

Reflect on the dreams you already received in week one or form new questions that would clarify the answer and guidance you received in previous dreams. You can for instance ask for a dream that shows you clearly what can motivate you, or what action you could take now that move you a step closer to finding out the answers in your dreams this month. For example, your intention statement might be something like this: "what are of my life could I do to receive more clarity on?" or "give me a dream with insights on the dream(s) I received in week 1 (be specific)." Your dream intention statement can simply be:

"What do I need to grow and expand in my life right now?" Or "What action do I need take (or skill I need to learn), to move forward towards my goal?"

Moreover, you can make drawings of how you feel in your dream journal. Express your feelings in creative colors or symbols. The drawing will reflect your emotions, and your growth when you review them later. The more you engage with the issue you are seeking clarity about, the clearer your dreams will become. Essentially, as the moon approaches its fullness, our dreams become instruments of refinement. They help us discern hidden obstacles, offer insights for fine-tuning our plans, and assist us in preparing for the fullness of manifestation. Our

dreams in this phase serve as mirrors, revealing the details that need polishing.

Therefore, **the waxing crescent moon is about nurturing your growth**. As the moon begins to wax, so does the energy of your intentions. Your dreams during this phase are like tender shoots emerging from the earth. Nurture them by focusing on their growth. Use dreamwork to explore the steps needed to bring your intentions to fruition. During this phase, or week, it is the time to act on your intentions and refine your dream journal questions. When generating a dream during the waxing moon phase, consider how you can explore this expansion in your dream. What aspects do you require more clarification on? Your next dream can provide inspiration and motivation to see your commitments and plans through to completion, both spiritually and in your daily life.

For instance, can you compose more questions around the same issue you wrote about in the previous exercise from a different perspective? For instance, if your first question is "what do I want to achieve during this lunar cycle?", you can reword it the following night to generate another dream clarifying the previous one even further. In this instance, your questions can be something like this: "what am I yearning to accomplish in my life right now?" or "what is my soul's desire this month?" "What am I ready to manifest this month?", and so on.

Use the space below to compose your questions around clarifying your intentions for your Lunar Dreaming Cycle below:

_____

_____

_____

_____

_____

_____

Waxing Crescent Moon Affirmations

These affirmations can help you focus your intentions and energy during the Waxing Crescent Moon phase, nurturing the dreams and goals you've set during the New Moon.

"I lovingly nurture my dreams as they flourish."

"I am nurturing the seeds of my intentions with patience and care."

"Each day, my dreams grow stronger and clearer, aligning with my purpose."

"I trust in the process of growth and transformation as I embrace my lunar journey."

"With each waxing crescent, I become more attuned to the rhythms of the moon, and my dreams reflect this alignment."

Waxing Crescent Moon Herbal Allies

Essential Oil: Rose. Rose oil symbolizes the nurturing and gentle energy of the Waxing Crescent Moon. It encourages the growth of your intentions and dreams, much like the tender sprouting of a new plant. Rose's sweet and comforting fragrance fosters self-love and self-compassion, creating a nurturing environment for your dreams to flourish.

Flower Remedy: Rock Rose (Bach Flower Remedy) or **Dog Rose** (Australian Bush Flower Essence). Rock Rose instills courage and stability as your intentions begin to sprout. Dog Rose encourages trust and gentleness during growth.

Week One Affirmations: Planting Seeds with Intention

The first week is about tending to your intentions. Using affirmations support you in doing just that.

During the New Moon, the night sky is shrouded in darkness, symbolizing fresh beginnings and untapped potential. As the moon begins to wax, your dreams too start to flourish. Affirmations like, *"I am sowing the seeds of my intentions,"* or *"My dreams are fertile ground for new beginnings,"* can help anchor your mind in the realm of possibilities. These affirmations encourage you to set clear intentions for your dreams and allow them to take root in the fertile soil of your subconscious. You can use them during the day, and especially as you fall asleep. Doing this affirms to your mind what you are focusing on during any phase of the moon cycle. Remember, affirmations work best when you repeat them regularly with intention and belief in their power. After affirming, and as you fall asleep repeat the dream journal question you have in your mind and visualize receiving a clear or vivid dream offering the guidance you seek.

Here are a few examples:

"I trust in the power of the universe to bring my intentions to fruition."

"I am open to new beginnings and opportunities in my life.

I trust that the universe will guide me in the right direction."

"I trust in my ability to manifest my intentions and create the life I desire."

"I am creating the life I desire."

"My dreams are growing stronger every night."

"I nurture my aspirations with every dream."

Week One Dream Journal Questions

The following are suggestions of questions you can ask yourself to help generate dreams during the four lunar phases. By pausing to ask yourself these questions and recording them in your dream journal, you can establish a stronger connection between your conscious and subconscious mind. This allows you to interpret the dreams more easily you receive and extract meaningful insights that can help guide you towards your goals. By focusing on specific questions or themes, you can gain a deeper understanding of your inner world and uncover hidden motivations or obstacles that may be holding you back:

"What action steps do I need to take to move closer to my goals?"

"What can I do to overcome obstacles or challenges that may arise?"

"What new skills or knowledge do I need to acquire to achieve my goals?"

"How can I stay motivated and focused on my goals during this phase?"

"What can I do to attract more abundance and prosperity into my life?"

 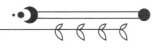
"How can I contribute to the growth and well-being of others during this phase?"

"What inspired action can I take to move closer to my goals?"

"What new habits or behaviors do I need to adopt to support my manifestations?"

"What obstacles do I need to overcome to achieve my desired intention?"

When your dreams reveal the information or requested guidance you asked about, visualize yourself taking these steps and achieving your goals. Use the energy of the Waxing Moon to inspire and motivate you to take this action. When we take inspired action, we signal to the universe that we are ready and willing to receive what we are manifesting. Moreover, the act of journaling also helps to solidify your intentions and keep you focused on your journey.

Furthermore, writing down your dreams and reflecting on their meaning helps you to clarify your goals and priorities, making it easier to take actions that align with your values and aspirations. Through the practice of dream journaling, you can develop a more intimate relationship with your inner self, and cultivate the self-awareness and mindfulness needed to navigate life's challenges

with grace and intention. For example, if your lunar cycle intention is to find true love, or your soul mate, you can break down your intentions into seven steps or questions you need to explore during the first lunar week, in your dreams:

Intention: meeting my soulmate in this lifetime.

Dream Journal Questions:

"What do I value in my ideal relationship?"

"What can I do to express that core value in real life?"

"What is blocking me from expressing this?"

"What would my ideal mate value about me?"

"What qualities do I need to express more of?

"What values do I need to let go of ore resolve for this to happen?"

Finally, nurturing your goals is important because it transforms your intentions into reality. It shows the universe that you are committed to your goals and ready to receive the abundant support and results that are waiting for you.

WEEK TWO:
TAKING ACTION

First Quarter Moon: Action & Decision-Making

Marking the midpoint between the New Moon and Full Moon, the First Quarter Moon emerges as a pivotal juncture in our lunar dream cycle. It serves as a beacon of action and decision-making, where the intentions you have sown during the New Moon begin to take root and flourish in your dreamscapes. Dreams become increasingly vivid and meaningful, guiding us toward practical steps to manifest our aspirations.

Furthermore, during the First Quarter Moon phase, our dreams often act as wise counselors, offering insights into the tangible actions required to align our dreams with our chosen path. These dream-guided actions can range from small, daily adjustments to significant life choices. You are invited to introspect, and self-assess, as you

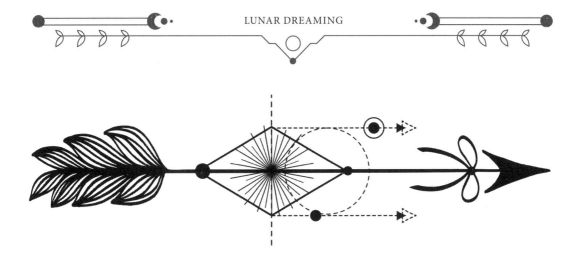

evaluate your progress and consider the alignment of your dreams with your evolving journey.

If you like, as we navigate this phase, our dreams become powerful allies in our decision-making process. They illuminate the way forward, providing clarity and direction. We may find ourselves receiving guidance on specific courses of action or discerning the adjustments needed to stay true to our intentions. In essence, the First Quarter Moon serves as a touchstone for manifesting our dreams, offering us the insights and resolve to take decisive steps on our path of self-awareness and empowerment. This phase is a time of dynamic transformation and practical application, as our dreams guide us towards realizing our deepest desires.

Essentially, marking the midpoint between the New Moon and Full Moon, the First Quarter Moon is a focal point for action in our dreamwork. Dreams become more vivid and meaningful as our intentions begin to materialize. This phase prompts us to take tangible steps toward manifesting our aspirations, aligning our dreams with our chosen path. The First Quarter moon heralds a time of action and decision-making. Our dreams during this phase may offer guidance on the practical steps needed to manifest our intentions. It calls for a moment to assess our progress, make necessary adjustments, and take decisive action based on the insights gained from our dreamscapes.

First Quarter Moon Affirmation
"I am empowered to take action on my intentions."

First Quarter Moon Herbal Allies
Essential Oil: Peppermint. Peppermint oil embodies the vibrant and invigorating energy required for taking action during the First Quarter Moon. Its crisp and awakening scent can stimulate your senses and boost

mental clarity, helping you translate your intentions into practical steps. Peppermint motivates you to move forward with determination and purpose.

Flower Remedy: Elm (Bach Flower Remedy) or **Bush Fuchsia** (Australian Bush Flower Essence). Elm restores confidence and helps you handle increased responsibilities. Bush Fuchsia enhances adaptability and resilience in taking action.

Waxing Gibbous Moon: Dream Refinement

The Waxing Gibbous phase intensifies our dream experiences as the moon continues to wax. You may experience heightened awareness during this week. Dreams during this phase are characterized by their vividness and depth, often providing us with valuable insights and guidance. They act as a compass, directing us towards the most effective and meaningful ways to bring our intentions to fruition. It's a period of profound refinement, where the details are meticulously sculpted, setting the stage for the full manifestation of our dreams in the upcoming Full Moon phase. This the phase that calls for refinement, fine-tuning intentions, and

deepening our understanding of dream messages. Dreams during this phase offer valuable insights and guidance.

As the moon approaches its fullness, our dreams transform into invaluable instruments of refinement. They take on the role of discerning hidden obstacles, offering us insights for fine-tuning our plans, and assisting us in preparing for the fullness of manifestation. During the Waxing Gibbous phase, our dreams become like mirrors, reflecting the intricate details that require polishing and adjustment. During this transition, dreams serve as meticulous guides, illuminating the subtle nuances that may have gone unnoticed during earlier stages of intention-setting. They offer us a deeper understanding of the messages embedded within our subconscious, helping us refine our aspirations with precision. This phase is akin to an artist adding the final strokes to a masterpiece, ensuring that every element aligns harmoniously.

Dream Journal Update

During this time, reflecting on your dreams and refining your goals and intentions are important. This is because it helps you to stay focused and aligned with your goals.

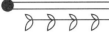 

They also give you the opportunity to course-correct and adjust as needed. When you take the time to reflect on your dreams and answer the questions as described in your dream that night, in your dream journal, you are engaging in an important process of self-evaluation and self-awareness. By acknowledging your progress, you are not only boosting your confidence and self-esteem, but also reinforcing positive behaviors and habits that have led you to where you are now.

At the same time, reflecting on your dreams you have journaled all week, and interpreting the main message received related to your question in your journal, can also help you identify areas where you may need to make changes or improvements. By being honest with yourself about areas where you may be falling short or struggling, you can take proactive steps to in "real life" by addressing those challenges. With the help of your dreams, you can overcome obstacles that may be holding you back. Lastly, by focusing on your successes, you are setting a positive tone for the future. Your past achievements can serve as a foundation for future growth and successful dreaming. By acknowledging what has worked well for you, you can build on that momentum and make further progress towards your goals.

Waxing Gibbous Moon Affirmation

*"I refine my intentions
with wisdom and insight."*

Waxing Gibbous Moon Herbal Allies

Essential Oil: Frankincense. Frankincense oil represents the refinement and deepening of your intentions during the Waxing Gibbous Moon. Its woody and resinous aroma encourages introspection and enhances the quality of your dreams. Frankincense is known for its spiritual qualities, guiding you to refine your aspirations with wisdom and insight.

Flower Remedy: Oak (Bach Flower Remedy) or **Bauhinia** (Australian Bush Flower Essence). Oak imparts strength and endurance during refinement. Bauhinia supports balance and creativity as you fine-tune your goals.

Week Two Affirmations

The Taking Actions lunar week calls for dynamic affirmations. Affirmations that propel you toward your goals. Phrases like, *"I am taking concrete steps towards my dreams,"* or *"Every dream empowers me to take action in my waking life,"* instill a sense of purpose and empowerment. They encourage you to actively engage with your dreams, seeing them as catalysts for real-world actions. By incorporating tailored affirmations into your bedtime routine, you harness the power of your mind to shape your dreams in alignment with each lunar phase. These affirmations serve as a bridge between your conscious intentions and the vast realm of your subconscious, creating a powerful synergy between your waking and dreaming selves. As you experiment with these affirmations throughout the lunar dream cycle, you may find that your dreamscapes become richer, more purposeful, and deeply connected to your lunar dreaming journey:

"My dreams guide me to making positive changes in my life every day."

"I am taking steps towards my goals and manifesting my desires."

"I trust in my mind's ability to provide the guidance I need through my dreams to overcome any challenges that arise."

"I am overcoming obstacles and making progress."

"I am harnessing the energy of the Moon to fuel positive transformations in every aspect of my life."

Crafting your affirmations in the way, resonates with the energy of progress and growth during the Waxing Gibbous phase, encouraging self-belief and forward momentum in your journey.

Week Two Dream Journal Questions

During the second week of the lunar dream cycle, we immerse ourselves in the energies of taking action and refinement. This phase prompts us to not only set our intentions but to also fine-tune them and take tangible steps towards our dreams. Here are some questions to guide you in your dream journal during this week:

"What specific actions can I take to manifest my intentions for this lunar cycle?"

"How can I refine my goals and intentions to align more closely with my true desires?"

"What insights can my dreams provide regarding practical steps I can take to achieve my aspirations?"

"What obstacles or challenges might I encounter, and how can I address them effectively?"

"How can I enhance my self-awareness and self-empowerment through my actions and intentions?"

"What aspects of my life require refinement and adjustment to support my growth and progress?"

"How can I harness the energy of this lunar phase to propel myself forward on my journey?"

Such questions stimulate and focus our subconscious to actively engage with our dreams. Seeking guidance on the concrete actions that we can take helps to bring their intentions to fruition. By recording your dreams and reflecting on these inquiries, they can refine their goals and make meaningful progress during the second week of the lunar dream cycle.

WEEK THREE:
FULFILLMENT AND
GRATITUDE

During the Full Moon phase, the Moon appears as a complete circle in the sky, fully illuminated by the Sun. The Full Moon, a radiant orb in the night sky, marks a moment of illumination both in the heavens and within our dreamscapes. The Full Moon shines brightly in the night sky, marking the culmination of the lunar cycle. Dreams during this phase are often profound and carry insights and revelations. It's a time to bask in the wisdom of our dreams and celebrate the manifestation of our intentions. Our dreams become exceptionally vivid and insightful, offering profound clarity on the culmination of our intentions. They provide us with a spotlight, casting light on our desires and their potential realization.

If you like, this phase is associated with fulfillment, clarity, and the realization of your desires. It is a moment to acknowledge and celebrate your personal growth, as well as reflect on your progress so far. Letting go of anything that no longer serves you, including negative thoughts or emotions which may be holding you back. It is a powerful spiritual practice during this phase, allowing you to make room for new opportunities and experiences.

The Full Moon: Illumination & Celebration
The Full Moon, radiant and resplendent in the night sky, marks a time of manifestation and abundance in our lunar dream cycle. It serves as a beacon of illumination, not only in the celestial realm but also within the realm of our dreams. During this phase, our dream experiences often shine brightly

with vividness and profound insights. These dreams hold the key to unlocking the culmination of our intentions, bringing forth clarity and deeper understanding.

During this week, take time to celebrate your accomplishments and acknowledge the fruits of your labor. As we pay close attention to the dreams that grace us during the Full Moon, we express gratitude for the wisdom bestowed upon us through these nocturnal journeys. Take stock of all that you have achieved thus far and to take pride in your progress. As you record your accomplishments in our dream journal, you allow the emotions of gratitude to permeate every cell of your being.

In this sacred space, we engage in visualization, a powerful practice that amplifies our connection to our dreams and intentions. We envision ourselves achieving even greater heights in the future, feeling grateful for the abundance that already resides in our lives. Ask your mind to grant you a dream that illuminates *"what it would look and feel like to achieve my intention this lunar month,"* and be ready to receive profound insights.

Full Moon Affirmations

In the radiant glow of the Full Moon, celebration and gratitude take center stage. Affirmations such as, "I celebrate my achievements and blessings in my dreams," or "Gratitude fills my heart as I dream of my accomplishments," align your dreams with a sense of fulfillment and appreciation. These affirmations encourage you to express thankfulness for the wisdom and abundance you encounter in your dreamscapes. Here a few examples to help you generate your own affirmations this week:

"I am grateful for all that I have accomplished."

"I am open and ready to receive for more success."

"I am in alignment with the abundance of the universe, and I welcome its blessings into my life."

"My intuition is a guiding light, and I trust it to lead me towards my highest purpose."

"I release all that no longer serves me, making space for new opportunities and growth."

"My dreams are powerful, and I have the courage to pursue them with unwavering determination."

"I am a beacon of positivity, radiating love and light to those around me."

"I am at peace with my past, present, and future, knowing that each moment holds valuable lessons."

"I am connected to the wisdom of my inner self, and I listen to its guidance with an open heart."

"I am worthy of success, and I chose to embrace it."

Full Moon Dream Journal Questions

Here are some examples of questions that can guide our dream exploration during the Full Moon:

"What have I accomplished during this lunar cycle that fills me with pride?"

"In what ways have I been blessed with abundance and positive energy during this phase?"

"How can I express gratitude for the people and experiences that have supported my journey?"

"What actions can I take to continue attracting positive energy and abundance into my life?"

"Which dreams have I manifested thus far, and how can I continue to bring them to life?"

"How can I utilize my unique talents and abilities to contribute to the well-being of others during this phase?"

Our dream journal becomes a treasure trove of reflection during lunar dreaming, a place to assess our progress and set intentions for the future. It becomes a potent tool for personal growth and development, a means of consciously integrating our subconscious mind. Through our journal, we celebrate our successes, learn from our challenges, and continue forging ahead toward our goals with unwavering purpose. Furthermore, as we embrace the Full Moon's luminance, we may even observe the colors we wear as the Moon progresses in its cycle and explore the emotions that rise within us. And should we encounter a dream that initially seems enigmatic or unrelated, we remember that it could hold the key to deeper exploration, guiding us toward a more profound understanding of the issues that matter most on our path of self-awareness and self-empowerment.

Full Moon Herbal Allies

Essential Oil: Sandalwood. Sandalwood oil aligns with the Full Moon's energy of illumination and clarity. Its warm and grounding fragrance helps you gain deeper insights into your dreams and intentions. Sandalwood encourages introspection and spiritual growth, making it a powerful ally for seeking profound revelations during this phase.

Flower Remedy: Wild Oat (Bach Flower Remedy) or **Bluebell** (Australian Bush Flower Essence). Wild Oat aligns with your purpose and vision during this peak phase. Bluebell enhances communication with your inner self and higher wisdom.

Waning Gibbous Moon

With the waning of the moon's brilliance comes a time for release and gratitude. Our dreams guide us in letting go of obstacles, fears, or patterns that hinder our progress. It is a phase for expressing gratitude for what we've achieved so far and for the wisdom gleaned from our dream journeys. As the moon begins to wane, dreams transition into a phase of introspection and integration. The Waning Gibbous phase encourages us to reflect on insights gained during the Full Moon and gradually release what no longer serves us. It is a time to distill dream wisdom into actionable steps for personal growth.

During the Waning Moon, the energy

is focused on reflection and introspection. In other words, this is the ideal time to go inward, meditate, and ask yourself what you need to release to move forward—you are preparing for a new cycle and a new beginning. Moreover, to make the most of the lunar cycle, generate and manifest your dreams; it is important to use a dream journal to ask yourself the right questions during each phase of the moon. For example, during the New Moon, write down what you want to achieve and set your intentions for the cycle ahead. During the Waxing Moon, ask yourself what you can do to act towards your goals. During the Full Moon, you expressed gratitude for what you have achieved and released anything that is no longer serving you. Finally, during the Waning Moon, ask

yourself what you need to release to move forward and let go of any negative thoughts or emotions.

Release any negativity and outdated beliefs and be aware that you are making space for something new to come into your life. Ask your mind for a dream on what you need to let go of to move forward. Write down what is holding you back and phrase your questions in a way that helps you to release them. For example, write similar questions in your dream journal: "what is important for me to release in order to create a new beginning?" or another example is "What do I need to let go of?" Once you receive your dream, write it down, then visualize yourself releasing these negative thoughts, emotions, and beliefs, around your issue and imagine yourself moving forward with a renewed sense of purpose and clarity. Your dreams might just give you insights or revelation on what is holding you back or how to release it. By using the dream journal and focusing on the energy of each phase of the moon, we can manifest our dreams and desires.

Waning Gibbous Moon Affirmations

The following affirmations can help you align with the energy of the Waning Gibbous Moon and facilitate personal growth and reflection during this phase. You can rephrase according to your goals.

"I release old patterns and welcome transformation."

"With each passing day, I gain deeper clarity and insight."

"I trust the process of growth and change in my life."

"I let go of what no longer serves me and make space for new wisdom."

"As the moon wanes, so do my doubts, leaving room for inner light."

Waning Gibbous Moon Dream Journal Questions

Here are some examples of questions you can ask yourself to help generate dreams:

"What do I need to release or let go off right now in my life to make space for new growth and abundance?"

"What can help me let go of what no longer serves me?"

"What can I let go of to create space for new growth?"

"What old or current habits or behaviors are holding me back from achieving my goals?"

"What emotions do I need to acknowledge and release to move forward?"

"What relationships or connections are draining my energy and how can I create healthy boundaries?"

"What can I do to simplify my life and focus on what truly matters?"

Waning Gibbous Moon Herbal Allies

Essential Oil: Eucalyptus. Eucalyptus oil embodies the cleansing and purifying energy of the Waning Gibbous Moon. Its invigorating and refreshing scent supports the release of what no longer serves you. Eucalyptus encourages gratitude for the lessons learned and helps clear away obstacles, making room for new growth and intentions.

Flower Remedy: Agrimony (Bach Flower Remedy) or **Pink Mulla Mulla** (Australian Bush Flower Essence). Agrimony aids in releasing inner tension and finding inner peace. Pink Mulla Mulla supports letting go and fostering emotional healing.

Affirmations for Week Three

During the Waning Moon phase, you are asked to let go of what no longer serves you. Affirmations like, "I release what no longer aligns with my path," or "Letting go in my dreams paves the way for new beginnings," guide your dreams towards shedding old patterns and beliefs. These affirmations support you in releasing the baggage of the past, making room for fresh intentions.

"I release anything that no longer serves me and make room for new growth and new beginnings."

"I am in tune with the gentle ebb of the lunar energy during this phase, allowing me to release with ease and grace."

"I am open to receiving the insights and clarity that come from letting go, allowing me to align with my true self."

Dream Journal Update:

Try to act on the guidance you receive in your dreams. Releasing what no longer serves us during this time in real life is essential, because it helps us to let go of what's holding us back and create space for what we want to manifest. It is like decluttering your life to make room for new possibilities. Remember that letting go and surrendering are important because they create space for new opportunities and blessings to come into your life. It also helps you to cultivate a sense of trust and surrender to the universe, knowing that everything is working out for your highest good.

Furthermore, the act of letting go is a dynamic dance of liberation. Moreover, it allows us to shed old patterns, beliefs, and limitations, ultimately lightening our spiritual load. This process is not one of loss but of liberation, freeing us from the shackles of the past and preparing us to embark on new adventures of self-discovery and growth. It nurtures a deep sense of trust and surrender

to the universe's divine orchestration, reminding us that everything is intricately connected and working in harmony for our highest good. Whether you want to gain insight into a particular situation or seek guidance on a personal issue, asking yourself specific questions before bed can help you direct your dreams towards your desired outcome. By consistently setting your intentions and recording your dreams, you can establish a deeper connection with your subconscious mind and gain a greater understanding of yourself and your life. So, take some time to experiment with different questions and see what insights your dreams may reveal to you.

WEEK FOUR:
RESET & RENEWAL

The Waning Moon phase, marked by the moon's decreasing illumination, offers a unique opportunity for introspection and self-examination. During this phase, the energy shifts from outward action to inner contemplation. During this phase, we are gently urged to turn inwards and engage in a deep and meaningful dialogue with our inner selves.

Moreover, the fourth and final week of the lunar dream cycle, is a phase of profound reflection and integration. This week is an invitation to embrace the art of surrender and reset our inner compass. In perfect harmony with the moon's graceful transition towards its new phase, where it becomes slimmer and wanes, we too are encouraged to shed the layers of old habits and patterns that no longer serve our highest good.

At the heart of this week lies the profound act of letting go. Use the guidance that came through your dreams to acknowledge and release what has become burdensome or stagnant in your life. Additionally, reflect upon aspects of yourself or situations that no longer align with your evolving path of self-awareness and self-empowerment. If you like, this process is life clearing out the clutter, making space for new growth and fresh intentions to take root.

Furthermore, in the quietude of this phase, reflect on what you have learned by referring to your dream journal:

What do you need to release to move forward on my journey?

What old beliefs or behaviors are holding you back from my fullest potential?

What does no longer resonate with the vision I have for myself?

These inquiries guide our inner work, offering clarity on what requires your attention and release. Write down below what pops up in your mind now:

Physical: _____

_____

Emotional: _____

_____

Mental/Beliefs: _____

_____

Actions/Behaviors: _____

_____

As you move towards the end of your Lunar dreaming cycle, the fourth week serves as a reset button. A moment of cleansing and rejuvenation for your inner landscape. Practices such meditation and mindful acknowledgment of what needs to be released, can be extremely helpful this week. These practices ready us for the upcoming New Moon, where we will plant new seeds of intention and pose fresh questions in our dream journal. So, in the spirit of renewal, we honor the cyclical nature of our journey, knowing that each lunar cycle brings opportunities for growth and self-discovery. This phase is our chance to cleanse the slate, reset our inner compass, and embark on the next leg of our journey with unwavering clarity and renewed purpose. We stand ready to set forth new intentions, pose new questions, and continue our quest for self-awareness and empowerment with hearts wide open to the mysteries of the lunar dream cycle.

Last Quarter Moon: Reflection & Preparation

The Last Quarter Moon is a pivotal point in our lunar dream journey. This phase marks the midpoint between the Full Moon's luminous radiance and the birth of the next New Moon. It serves as a reflective pause, a moment to assess our progress, and prepare for the forthcoming cycle of intentions.

During the Last Quarter Moon, our dreams often act as messengers, prompting us to shed old patterns, beliefs, or lingering doubts. This is the phase of inner reckoning, where we confront the aspects of our lives that require release and renewal. Dreams become allies in this process, gently guiding us towards a clearer path of self-awareness and empowerment. Moreover, the Last Quarter Moon offers an opportunity to distill the wisdom gained throughout the lunar cycle. Take time to reflect on the themes that have woven through your dreams in the past few weeks. Attempt to form a coherent narrative of our inner world. Perhaps even write a few paragraphs in your dream journal about what you have discovered or learned about yourself in the past three weeks. Do you recognize any themes emerging? These themes serve as signposts, guiding you towards a deeper understanding of your inner journey.

As we prepare ourselves for the imminent arrival of the New Moon, where fresh intentions will take root, we can sense a harmonious alignment between the lessons learned and the path forward. The Last Quarter Moon is a bridge that connects our past experiences with our future aspirations. It invites us to gather the pearls of wisdom from our dreamscapes, to release what no longer resonates, and to set our intentions with newfound clarity. In this phase of reflection and preparation, we honor the cyclical nature of our growth, knowing that each lunar cycle offers fresh opportunities for self-discovery and transformation. Our dreams, faithful companions on this journey, guide us through this process of release and renewal, ensuring that we enter the next lunar cycle with open hearts, clear minds, and intentions that align with our highest aspirations.

Affirmations for Last Quarter Moon

During the Last Quarter Moon phase, you are poised for reflection and assessment of your journey so far; acknowledging the valuable insights gained during this lunar cycle. Affirmations tailored to this phase, to signal your readiness to shed old patterns and beliefs help you navigate this introspective time. Begin with an affirmation like:

"I embrace the wisdom of my past dreams."

"I release what no longer serves my growth."

"I assess my dreams to prepare for new intentions."

Lastly, affirmations like, "I am prepared for the next cycle of intentions," instill a sense of readiness and anticipation for the fresh lunar cycle ahead—the phase of setting intentions.

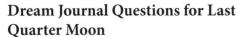

Dream Journal Questions for Last Quarter Moon

"What recurring themes or lessons have emerged in my dreams during this lunar cycle?"

"How have my dreams guided me in making positive changes in my life?"

"What aspects of my past experiences or beliefs am I ready to release, as revealed by my dreams?"

"What wisdom can I extract from my dreamscapes to apply to my upcoming intentions?"

"In what ways have my dreams prepared me for the next phase of my self-awareness and self-empowerment journey?"

"What specific actions or adjustments can I derive from my dream insights to enhance my life?"

"How can I express gratitude for the lessons and guidance received through my dreams during this phase?"

Last Quarter Moon Herbal Allies

Essential Oil: Clary Sage. Clary Sage oil complements the reflective and introspective nature of the Last Quarter Moon. Its earthy and herbal aroma encourages deep inner exploration and self-reflection. Clary Sage promotes emotional balance and insight, making it an ideal ally for gaining clarity and perspective on your dreams.

Flower Remedy: Crab Apple (Bach Flower Remedy) or **Flannel** Flower (Australian Bush Flower Essence). Crab Apple purifies and cleanses, helping you release old patterns. Flannel Flower enhances self-acceptance and inner reflection.

Waning Crescent Moon: Surrender & Rejuvenation

As we journey into the Waning Crescent

phase of the lunar dream cycle, we encounter a shift in the character of our dreams. The moon's crescent dwindles, casting a gentle, muted glow upon our nocturnal visions. During this phase, our dreams take on a serene quality, akin to a calm and healing embrace. This is a time of surrender and rest, a precious interlude in our spiritual journey. As the lunar cycle gracefully nears its conclusion, our inner selves yearn for solace and rejuvenation. It is a period of quiet reflection, a sacred pause before we embark on the next chapter of our dreams and intentions. In the arms of the Waning Crescent moon, we find the space to release the burdens of the past and recharge our spiritual energies.

Dreams during the Waning Crescent phase offer solace and healing. They become

like soothing balm to our souls, gently nurturing our inner landscapes. This is a time when we can surrender to the flow of the universe, knowing that rest is as vital as action on our path of self-awareness and empowerment. Moreover, as the moon approaches the end of its cycle, our dreams become quieter and more introspective. This phase encourages deep reflection, inviting us to dive into the inner chambers of our psyche. We integrate the insights and wisdom gained throughout the lunar cycle, preparing our inner selves for the journey ahead.

In this quietude, we are called to inner contemplation, a sacred communion with our inner selves. It is a time to honor our spiritual nourishment, allowing our souls to absorb the lessons, experiences, and growth of the past lunar month. As we rest in the tender embrace of the Waning Crescent moon, we emerge with a sense of clarity, purpose, and readiness to begin anew in the upcoming lunar cycle, setting fresh intentions and embarking on a continuous journey of self-discovery and empowerment.

Affirmations for Waning Crescent Moon

In the serene embrace of the Waning Crescent Moon, surrender and rejuvenation are paramount. Affirmations such as: "I surrender to the wisdom of my dreams," or "My

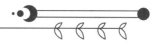

dreams rejuvenate my spirit and prepare me for the future," help guide your dreams toward offering solace and renewal.

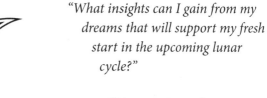

Dream Journal Questions for Waning Crescent Moon

In your dream journal, and as this is the last week, reflect on the following questions. Write your thoughts or write about the dreams that stood out in your mind. Remember to include any colors or symbols that came through for you. You can also tailor these suggested questions to induce dreams during this week:

"How have my dreams provided solace and healing during this lunar phase?"

"What recurring symbols or images have appeared in my dreams, and how do they relate to my need for rejuvenation?"

"In what ways have my dreams allowed me to surrender and let go of tension or concerns?"

"What insights can I gain from my dreams that will support my fresh start in the upcoming lunar cycle?"

"How can I use the rejuvenating power of my dreams to enhance my self-awareness and self-empowerment journey?"

"What practices or rituals can I incorporate before bed to maximize the soothing qualities of my dream experiences?"

"What aspects of my life can benefit from the sense of renewal and clarity that my dreams offer during this phase?"

These tailored affirmations and dream journal questions for both Last Quarter Moon and Waning Crescent Moon phases empower you to embrace reflection, release, and rejuvenation, paving the way for a new beginning in the upcoming lunar cycle.

Waning Crescent Moon Herbal Allies

Essential Oil: Chamomile. Chamomile oil represents the soothing and calming energy of surrender during the Waning Crescent

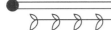 

LUNAR CYCLE END EXERCISE

At the end of your Lunar dream cycle, write down you answers to the following questions, to help you become aware of what you have achieved:

What lessons have I learned during this lunar cycle?

_____

_____

What challenges did I face, and how did I overcome them?

_____

_____

What self-care practices do I need to prioritize during this phase?

_____

_____

Moon. Its gentle and comforting fragrance helps you release tension and surrender to the natural flow of life. Chamomile fosters inner peace and serenity, allowing you to let go and prepare for the next cycle of intentions.

Flower Remedy: Pine (Bach Flower Remedy) or **Isopogon** (Australian Bush Flower Essence). Pine eases self-blame and fosters self-forgiveness during surrender. Isopogon supports inner peace and letting go of control.

Finally, when embarking on a new Lunar dreaming cycle, to take a few moments to sit in contemplation. Reflect on your current circumstances and where you stand in your life's journey. Consider what it is that you wish to nurture, develop, heal, or explore in the upcoming lunar month. Consider the season or the time of the year, for it often carries its own unique inspirations and needs. There is a profound connection between the ever-turning wheel of lunar cycles, the changing seasons, and the phase of life you currently live.

Each Lunar dreaming cycle holds the potential for different revelations and growth. You might discover that varying herbal allies are required, or perhaps just one for the entire four weeks. Trust your intuition and the wisdom you have gained about yourself as you attune yourself to each lunar dreaming cycle. To conclude each cycle, you may choose to engage in the following exercise, or feel free to craft your own, allowing the process to be a deeply personal and evolving journey.

By tuning into the cycles of the Moon, you can tap into its powerful energy of openness, renewal, intuition, and wisdom. These lunar cycles can help you become more aware of the rhythms and patterns within your own body, mind, heart, and spirit. With this awareness, you can work on healing and renewing yourself, and gain a deeper understanding of your innermost self. Moreover, each lunar month, you can focus on new intentions for inducing dreams, and customize your questions in your dream journal, as well as your affirmations during each phase in relation to your lunar intention. At the start if each lunar month, you can also refer to what you have discovered as you go through your dream journal. By using a dream journal and following the moon's phases, we can tap into our subconscious mind and induce dreams that help us manifest our deepest desires. Remember to set intentions, act, celebrate progress!

PLANNING YOUR ANNUAL LUNAR DREAMING CYCLE

An incredibly rewarding approach to connecting with your inner self, seeking guidance through your dreams, and synchronizing with the natural rhythms of the universe is to embark on an annual lunar dreaming cycle. This practical yet deeply enriching journey allows you to structure your personal growth and aspirations according to the phases of the moon. You have two primary options to consider. Firstly, you can opt for monthly themes or goals, with each month offering a unique opportunity for self-discovery and progress. Alternatively, you can break down your goals into four-week segments, aligning them with the four major lunar phases: New Moon, First Quarter Moon, Full Moon, and Last Quarter Moon.

The beauty of this approach lies in its practicality. By choosing monthly themes or breaking down your goals into lunar phases, you create a clear road map for your personal development. It is like having a supportive companion on your journey, guiding you step by step. This structured approach not only engages your conscious intentions but also taps into the power of your subconscious mind, forging a potent alliance that propels you toward your desired outcomes. Additionally, this deliberate alignment serves as a constant reminder, nurturing a deeper connection with your dreams and aspirations. It empowers you to cultivate self-awareness and instills a sense of confidence in your ability to shape your life according to your deepest desires. Here is how you can plan your next lunar cycle:

1. REFLECT ON YOUR GOALS

Begin by taking some quiet time to reflect on your aspirations, desires, and areas of personal growth you wish to focus on in the coming year to heal, resolve or achieve. Consider various aspects of your life, such as health, relationships, career, and spirituality. Find a quiet and peaceful space where you can sit comfortably without distractions. Ensure you have ample time to engage in this reflective process. Choose a moment when you can be fully present with your thoughts and feelings. As you begin your reflection, cast a wide net over various aspects of your life. Consider the following dimensions:

Health

Health represents a cornerstone of our overall well-being, encompassing both our physical vitality and mental equilibrium. During the planning of your lunar dreaming cycle, take a moment to envisage how you desire to nurture your well-being in the upcoming year. Ponder the elements of your physical and mental health that you wish to prioritize and enhance. You may aspire to adopt a healthier lifestyle by integrating consistent physical activity, balanced nutrition, or mindfulness practices into your daily regimen. Alternatively, you might aim to conquer particular health challenges or ailments, striving for increased resilience and vitality.

Mental well-being holds equal significance, and your lunar dreaming cycle serves as a transformative journey towards better emotional and psychological health. Contemplate your emotional landscape and psychological fortitude. Are there habits or strategies you seek to cultivate to elevate your emotional intelligence and inner strength? Perhaps you harbor an interest in exploring mindfulness or meditation techniques to manage stress and nurture mental lucidity. By integrating these intentions into your lunar journey, you align your dreamwork with your comprehensive well-being objectives. This conscious alignment empowers you to address health from a holistic perspective, harmoniously merging physical

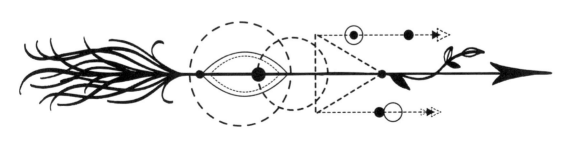

fitness with emotional and mental equi-librium, embarking on a journey towards holistic well-being. So, how do you envision your physical and mental well-being in the coming year? Are there specific health goals or habits you would like to cultivate?

Relationships

Reflect on your relationships with family, friends, romantic partners, and yourself. Are there areas where you seek growth or improvements in your connections?

Relationships hold a vital place in our lives, encompassing connections with family, friends, romantic partners, and the relationship we foster with ourselves. Within the framework of your lunar dream-ing cycle planning, set aside a moment for introspection regarding these relationships. Contemplate the nuances within each con-nection, and identify areas where you aspire for growth or enhancement.

Consider the dynamics of your family relationships. Are there unexplored opportunities for deeper understanding or improved communication within your familial bonds? Reflect on your friendships, pondering ways to strengthen these connec-tions or forge new ones that align with your aspirations. In matters of romance, assess the quality of your romantic partnerships and explore avenues for fostering greater intimacy and harmony. Additionally, delve into your relationship with yourself, as it underpins all other connections. Are there aspects of self-love and self-acceptance you wish to cultivate during your transforma-tive lunar journey?

Career

Explore your professional aspirations and ambitions. What career milestones or

changes do you hope to achieve? Are there skills you wish to develop?

Career forms a significant facet of our lives, shaping our livelihoods and aspirations. Within your lunar dreaming cycle planning, reserve time for contemplation regarding your professional journey. Dive into your career aspirations and ambitions, probing for the milestones and shifts you hope to attain. Reflect upon the skills you wish to hone or develop in the pursuit of your vocational goals.

Examine your professional trajectory and envision the career milestones that beckon on your transformative journey. Consider the prospects of change or advancement within your current field or the exploration of new avenues. Evaluate the skill set that is vital for your career progression, and lay the foundation for their cultivation during your lunar dream cycle.

This profound exploration of your career goals aligns your ambitions with the lunar rhythms, infusing your journey with purpose and direction. It is a pivotal step in your quest.

Spirituality

Delve into your spiritual journey. Are there spiritual practices or experiences you want to deepen? What connections do you wish to forge with your inner self? Take some time to reflect. Examine your spiritual journey and pinpoint the areas you want to explore in the upcoming year. Think about specific spiritual practices or experiences you'd like to dive into more deeply. Consider how you can strengthen your bond with your inner self. Moreover, reflect on your beliefs and what you hope to achieve on a spiritual level. Look for ways to sync up with the lunar rhythms to enhance your spiritual connection. This inner exploration not only deepens your spiritual awareness but also guides you towards a more enlightened and harmonious life ahead.

2. IDENTIFY TWELVE GOALS

Next, transfer these twelve goals onto the pages of your dream journal or onto a dedicated document. As you do so, take a moment to prioritize and organize them in a way that feels most intuitive to you. While reviewing your list, attune yourself to your emotions. Pay close attention to the goals that evoke strong feelings, whether it is enthusiasm, determination, or a sense of urgency. These emotional cues serve as valuable signposts guiding you toward the goals that genuinely resonate with your heart.

Make sure to express each goal with clarity and precision. Ensure that every goal is specific and actionable. For instance, rather than framing a goal vaguely as "improve my

health," consider specifying it as "commit to a regular exercise routine and maintain a balanced diet." This level of clarity empowers you to take tangible steps toward each aspiration. This is important as it will help you compose specific dream journal questions for each week or lunar month.

Alternatively, a practical approach is to write each of these twelve goals on individual sticky notes. Then, arrange them in a way that intuitively prioritizes one goal for each month of the upcoming year. This will also you to see if two or more goals come under the same theme, health, for example. The objective is to help you to establish a clear focus for each lunar cycle, ensuring that your goals align with the energy of the corresponding phase. Once you have determined the monthly priorities, you can then transfer them to your dream journal or a separate document. This method adds a tactile and visual dimension to your goal-setting, helping you stay connected to your aspirations throughout the year.

3. IMAGINE

Next, allow your imagination to wander freely as you envision your ideal life in the next year. What dreams and desires surface during this contemplation? Pay attention to the aspirations that ignite a sense of purpose and excitement within you. Once you have gathered these aspirations, organize them into categories or themes. This can help you see common threads or areas where goals might naturally align with each other. From your reflections, identify twelve specific and meaningful goals or issues you would like to work on during the next twelve months. These goals should be both attainable and significant to your personal growth journey. Identify your core values and passions. What truly matters to you? What brings you joy and fulfillment? Aligning your goals with your values ensures they resonate deeply with your authentic self.

4. ALIGN WITH LUNAR PHASES

Once you have identified your twelve aspirations for the year ahead, the next step involves a thoughtful alignment of each goal with the corresponding lunar phases. This intentional connection between your goals and the moon's energy can amplify your dream exploration and personal growth. For instance, you might want to start new endeavors during the New Moon phase, seek clarity during the Full Moon, and release obstacles during the Waning Moon. Tailor your goals to fit the energy of each phase.

For example:

Week 1

New Moon (Primary): This phase is ideal for seeking guidance through dreams about initiating new projects, setting intentions, and planting the seeds of your goals. If one of your goals is to start a new fitness routine, use the New Moon to commit to this intention by beginning your workouts or designing a workout plan, and of course asking for guidance in your dreams.

Waxing Crescent Moon: As the moon begins to grow, use this phase to nurture the growth of your goals. For instance, if you are working on improving your relationships, take small steps by seeking dream guidance on who from your connections of friends or family can you help or support you during this phase (and how).

Week 2

First Quarter Moon (Primary): This is a time for acting and overcoming obstacles. If you have a career-related goal, such as landing a new job or advancing in your current one, actively pursue dream guidance to spot opportunities and overcome challenges during this phase. Your dreams might feature challenges that need to be overcome, for instance.

Waxing Gibbous Moon: Refinement and fine-tuning are key during this phase. If your goal involves creative expression, like writing a book, use this time to edit and polish your work to perfection. You dreams may reflect skills you need to perfect, or how to fine-tune your creative process.

Week 3

Full Moon (Primary): The Full Moon is about illumination and celebration. If you are striving for personal growth, ask for guidance through your dreams on what would your desired goal look and feel like, or symbolic vision of how you would experience reaching that goal during this phase.

Waning Gibbous Moon: Use this phase for releasing and expressing gratitude. If you have a goal related to self-improvement, reflect on what you have learned and release any self-limiting beliefs or negative patterns. Your dream inquiry may involve letting go of past setbacks or limitations, expressing gratitude for progress made, and embracing a sense of inner freedom within your dream experiences.

Week 4

Last Quarter Moon (Primary): This phase is about reflection and shedding old patterns. If your goal is to break free from a habit, consider using this time to focus on overcoming it. During this week, your dream

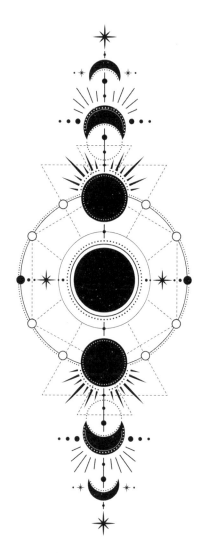

Waning Crescent Moon: In this phase of surrender, you can prepare for the next cycle of intentions. If you are looking to start fresh in any area of your life, use this phase for reflection and letting go of what no longer serves you. Your dream inquiry may involve themes of closure, relinquishing attachments, and embracing a sense of renewal and readiness for what lies ahead in their dreamscapes.

5. DESIGN YOUR LUNAR CALENDAR:

When you arrive at a final list, write it down in your dream journal, or create on a dedicated document or vision board of your twelve goals. **Prioritize and organize** them. Write them down clearly and concisely, ensuring each goal is specific and actionable. For example, instead of a vague goal such as "improve my health," you might specify, "commit to a regular exercise routine and maintain a balanced diet." Next, create your final lunar calendar that spans the next twelve months, with each month dedicated to one of your goals. Assign each goal to a specific lunar cycle, starting with the upcoming lunar month. This will help you stay focused and organized throughout the year (see table opposite as an example).

inquiry can delve into dreams that prompt self-reflection, highlight the shedding of old patterns, and offer insights into personal growth and transformation.

NEW MOON MONTH	ISSUE/GOAL/ PROJECT	SYMBOL	AFFIRMATION	QUESTION
1				
2				
3				
4				
5				
6				
7				
8				
9				
10				
11				
12				

12- month lunar dreaming plan

6. VISUAL REPRESENTATION

As you design your lunar calendar, consider creating a visual representation, a symbol, of it. You can use a calendar template or design your own, adding images, symbols, or colors that resonate with each goal. The goal is to involve all your senses to establish a deeper connection and generate dream guidance you seek. Moreover, visual aids can serve as a powerful reminder of your intentions.

7. DISPLAY YOUR CALENDAR

Place your lunar calendar in a location where you will see it regularly. For instance, the back of your bedroom or bathroom door, the inside of your wardrobe door, or any other space that you visit frequently. This constant visual reminder will help keep your goals at the forefront of your mind.

8. REGULAR REVIEW

Commit to reviewing your lunar calendar and goals regularly. Set aside time at the beginning of each lunar month to reflect on the goal assigned for that month and consider how your dreams may provide insights or guidance related to it.

9. DREAM JOURNAL INTEGRATION

Incorporate your lunar dreaming practice into this goal-setting journey. Use your dream journal to record dreams that relate to your current goal, pose questions to your subconscious mind, and track your progress in dreamwork.

10. ADAPT AND EVOLVE

Throughout the year, be open to adapting and evolving your goals as needed. Life is dynamic, and your aspirations may shift. Use your dream journal to explore how your dreams may reflect these changes and guide your path.

Following these steps, helps you create a structured and intentional approach to your self-awareness and self-empowerment journey, harmonizing it with the lunar cycles. This exercise empowers you to set clear intentions, stay focused, and cultivate a deeper connection with your dreams as valuable sources of guidance and insight.

Once you have embarked on your transformative lunar dreaming journey, it is crucial to establish a routine of regular review and reflection. Adopting this practice ensures that you stay connected to your goals, your dreams, and the profound insights they offer. Here's how you can integrate this essential step into your lunar dreamwork:

Consistent Lunar Calendar Check-Ins: At the commencement of each lunar month, mark a dedicated moment in your calendar to review the goal aligned with that specific month's lunar phase. This commitment to regularity ensures that you remain in sync with the moon's cycles, fostering a deep connection between your intentions and **the celestial rhythms.**

Reflecting on Dream Guidance: During these lunar calendar check-ins, dedicate time to reflect on your dreams from the previous lunar cycle. Pay keen attention to any dream symbols, messages, or emotions that may be related to your current goal. Dreams often hold valuable insights that can shed light on the path you are walking. By examining your dreams through this lens, you open yourself to a wealth of wisdom and guidance.

Journaling Insights: Record your reflections in your dream journal or a dedicated document. This practice solidifies your commitment to self-awareness and personal growth. Describe any dream scenarios, symbols, or feelings that resonate with your current goal. By documenting your dream insights, you create a tangible record of your journey, allowing you to track your progress and the evolution of your dreams.

Adjusting and Refining: Lunar dreaming is a dynamic and evolving process. As you gain deeper clarity and understanding through your dreams, you may find it beneficial to adjust or refine your goals. Embrace this adaptability as a powerful tool for personal growth. If your dreams indicate a shift in direction or a new perspective, trust in your intuition to modify your goals accordingly.

Celebrate Milestones: Take moments to acknowledge and celebrate any milestones or achievements related to your lunar dreaming goals. Whether it is a significant insight gained from a dream, progress made in your waking life, or a sense of personal empowerment, these victories deserve recognition. Celebrating your accomplishments reinforces your commitment to self-awareness and encourages continued growth.

By incorporating regular review into your lunar dreaming practice, you create a harmonious cycle of intention, reflection, and evolution. This mindful approach ensures that your dreams and goals remain intimately connected, guiding you on a transformative journey of self-discovery and empowerment.

CHAPTER 7

USING YOUR
DREAM
JOURNAL

Prior to starting to work with your dreams, establishing a firm foundation for your dream work is important. This groundwork commences with your trusted dream journal. Your dream journal functions as a steadfast witness to your nocturnal adventures in the dream domain. It functions as a special place where the fleeting stories of the night find a lasting home in ink and paper. Each morning, as you wake from your sleep, reach for your dream journal placed conveniently within arm's reach, right there beside your bedside. Capturing those delicate fragments of your dreams before they slip away into the waking world is crucial. Next, write down whatever you can remember, no matter how disjointed or fleeting it may seem. This simple act of recording your dreams not only preserves their essence but also conveys your appreciation for the messages they carry.

This practical journaling practice lays the foundation for deeper dream work, bridging the gap between your conscious and subconscious selves. As you accumulate more dream entries over time, you may begin to notice recurring patterns, symbols, and themes that offer valuable insights into your inner world. Your dream journal becomes a treasure trove of self-discovery, a mirror reflecting the hidden aspects of your psyche, and a guide on your path of exploration and growth. Furthermore, take a moment to revisit your responses to the exercises you have explored here in *The Book of Practical Dream Craft*. Make a dedicated entry for them in your journal. These answers serve as the building blocks for creating your personal dream dictionary and gaining insights into the inner workings of your own mind. Let your dream journal be your steadfast companion, always ready to capture the marvels unfolding within your dreamscapes.

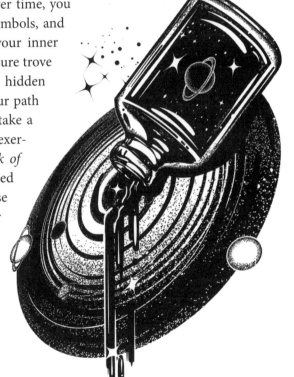

DREAMING RITUAL: UNVEILING THE POWER WITHIN

Your dreams are like a concealed gateway to our innermost thoughts, emotions, and desires lies dormant. Dreaming time represents a space where the ordinary constraints of reality yield to the extraordinary. To access this portal and tap into its potential for transformation, we delve into the practice of creating a dreaming ritual. Hopefully by now, you have resolved your dreaming attitude. And by engaging in a series of intentional practices, exercises mentioned before, and immersive sensory experiences, you can start practicing directing your dreams—that is asking your mind to guide you through your dreams by pausing specific questions.

Setting your intention to dream and remember your dreams, before you can write anything down in your dream journal; send a message to your subconscious mind.

Therefore, recognizing the significance of rituals in inducing dreams is elemental. These rituals act as keys to unlock the hidden chambers of our inner selves. They create a structured path to explore the extraordinary depths of our subconscious, where our thoughts, emotions, and desires take form. That is why embracing such rituals help our mind to gain access to the transformative potential that dreaming holds. Rituals, or methodologies and processes, train the mind, and enhance our connection with our inner world.

Furthermore, creating your own dreaming ritual, unlocks the dynamic connection between your dreams and your journal. This is not just about writing down dreams; it's about crafting an intentional and practical ritual that infuses your journal with the vivid

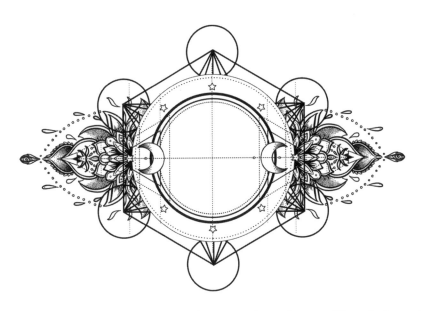

landscapes of your dreamscape. Through structured practices and sensory engagement, we learn to navigate the terrain of our subconscious with purpose, finding insights, setting intentions, and uncovering hidden truths that resonate in our daily lives.

Create Your Sacred Dream Space

Find a tranquil and private space where interruptions are unlikely. It could be a cozy nook in your bedroom, a comfortable chair near a window, or a serene corner of your garden. Ensure that the lighting is soothing, and think about adding a soft blanket or cushion to boost your comfort. Craft an environment that encourages both relaxation and introspection. You may opt to

introduce elements like calming colors, such as various shades of blue or earthy tones, to set the mood. Additionally, consider incorporating subtle scents like lavender or chamomile, which can further enhance the atmosphere of relaxation and contemplation (refer to herbal allies mentioned in the previous chapter). These fragrances can help create a sensory connection between your space and the act of introspection, signaling to your mind that it's time to delve into the inner realms of your thoughts and dreams.

Crafting the right environment, the soft glow of candlelight or the soothing aroma of essential oils can work wonders in setting the stage for relaxation and introspection. The calming colors and comfortable furnishings

envelop you in a sense of tranquility, making it easier to connect with your inner self and the world of dreams. Each element, from the gentle lighting to the cozy pillow, contributes to the ambiance of your sacred space, inviting you to immerse deeply in your intentional dream incubation ritual.

Indulge in Relaxation

As part of your relaxation routine, treat yourself to a warm bath infused with the soothing fragrance of lavender essential oil. Allow the comforting warmth of the water to envelop you, gently easing away tension from your muscles and creating a serene space for your mind to unwind. Alternatively, you can engage in a series of deep breathing exercises designed to quiet your thoughts and promote a state of inner calm. Inhale deeply for a count of four, hold your breath for four counts, and exhale slowly for another four

counts. Repeat this tranquil breathing cycle several times, with each breath carrying away any remaining stress or worries.

To enhance your relaxation further, consider incorporating gentle, nature-inspired sounds into your environment. These can be the sounds of a babbling brook, the rustle of leaves in a tranquil forest, or the soothing melody of birdsong. These auditory cues can transport you to a peaceful natural setting in your mind, helping you let go of any residual stress and prepare your mental canvas for the rich dreamwork that lies ahead.

Immerse in Pre-Sleep Ritual

As you step into your peaceful sanctuary, take a moment to adjust the lighting to a gentle, soothing level, casting a serene ambiance that invites relaxation and introspection. Enhance this atmosphere by igniting a scented candle or incense stick, choosing a fragrance that deeply resonates with your senses, whether it's the earthy warmth of sandalwood or the floral embrace of jasmine. If visual elements inspire you, consider placing a small table or altar nearby, adorned with objects that hold profound personal significance—a cherished crystal, a piece of artwork that speaks to your soul, or any items that symbolize your journey of self-discovery. These carefully chosen elements contribute to the sense of sacredness

enveloping your dream practice, creating a space where you can truly connect with the depths of your inner self.

Symbolic Sleepwear

Select a set of pajamas that you designate solely for your dream incubation nights. These sleepwear choices can encompass a range of preferences. Whether they are exceptionally comfortable, stylish, or decorated with symbols that carry profound personal meaning can prepare you for dreaming. When you slip into these special pajamas, it is like a deliberate signal to your subconscious that tonight holds the intention of purposeful dreaming. This small yet symbolic act serves as a powerful reminder to your inner self, reinforcing your commitment to explore the realms of your dreams with intent and mindfulness.

Formulate Your Question or Symbol

Dive deep into the theme or issue you have chosen for your dream exploration. Feel the sensations, visualize, daydream about the issue being resolved or questions answered. Then, craft a question that succinctly captures it. For instance, if your focus is on gaining insights into a specific relationship, your question could take the form of, "What actions can I initiate to enhance my connection with [person's name]?" Record this

question within the pages of your dream journal or on a sheet of paper that you keep within arm's reach. This tangible expression serves to anchor your intention, making it more tangible and reinforcing your commitment to seeking answers from your dreams.

This practice of framing your inquiry or symbol sets a clear direction for your subconscious mind, signaling that your dreams hold the key to unraveling the mysteries you seek to explore. It is like casting a spotlight on the specific area of your life that you're keen to understand better. By committing this question to paper, you are not only externalizing your intent but also forging a powerful connection between your conscious desire and the reservoir of wisdom residing in your dreams. This intention-setting process acts

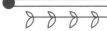
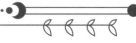

as a bridge, guiding you towards the insights and revelations that your dreams are poised to offer.

Sketch Meaningful Symbols

In addition to crafting your question, take the time to sketch symbols or images that hold deep significance for your dream inquiry. For instance, if your exploration centers around creativity, you might sketch symbols that embody the artistic journey, such as a vibrant palette of colors or a graceful quill pen. These visual symbols act as potent reminders of your dream's focal point, acting like beacons guiding your subconscious towards the specific theme you intend to delve into. These visual cues function as triggers, prompting your subconscious to channel its creative energies or insights in alignment with your dream objective. Much like an artist prepares their canvas with deliberate strokes, you are preparing the canvas of your mind for the vivid and purposeful dreamscapes that await exploration. So, before embarking on your dream rituals, etch

these symbols onto your dream landscape, ensuring that your dreams unfold with intention and resonance.

Sound Sensory Experience

Elevate your pre-sleep ritual by incorporating soundscapes that harmonize with your dream aspirations. If you are on a quest for inspiration, immerse yourself in the soothing melodies of instrumental music or revisit a cherished song renowned for kindling your creativity. Conversely, if your dream journey revolves around matters of love and relationships, engage in reading a beloved poem aloud or tune in to a guided meditation that explores the intricacies of the heart. Let these carefully chosen sounds serve as your guides, leading you deeper into the realm of your desired dream state. Through the resonance of auditory cues, your intentions are amplified, weaving seamlessly into the tapestry of your dream landscape.

Meditative Imprinting

As you meticulously sketch your chosen symbols and immerse yourself in contemplating

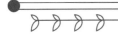

your question, embrace this process as a meditative practice. Concentrate your attention solely on your dream intent, releasing any extraneous distractions that may intrude. Visualize each deliberate stroke of the pen as a potent affirmation, a testament to your unwavering dedication to delve into the depths of this aspect of your life within your dream realm. This meditative imprinting technique serves to firmly anchor your intentions and fortify the bridge between your conscious and subconscious mind, ensuring a harmonious alignment between your waking desires and your dream's potential.

Personal Invitation to Dream

Recognize that this tranquil and deliberate ritual is your exclusive invitation into the realm of dreams. Embrace the notion that you stand prepared to embark on a journey through the enigmatic landscapes of your subconscious. As you transition seamlessly from this ritual to the world of slumber, retain the profound sense of purpose and unquenchable curiosity you have cultivated. Let these guiding forces accompany you into the dream realm, where they shall serve as beacons, illuminating the path to your dream's potential and revelations.

Engaged Senses

Recognize that all your senses have been engaged throughout this process. The soothing scents, the calming visuals, the focused thoughts, and the curated sounds have collectively primed your mind for dreaming. Your dream incubation ritual effectively bridges the gap between your waking and dream worlds, increasing the likelihood of your subconscious responding to your desires.

Essentially, incorporating such elements into your dream incubation ritual, you can create a comprehensive and immersive experience that connects you deeply with your dream world, enhances your dream recall and exploration, and strengthens your intention to delve into the realms of the subconscious.

DREAM RECALL

Dreams are the secret portals to our inner worlds, offering glimpses into our deepest thoughts, emotions, and desires. Keeping a dream journal is like collecting fragments of our subconscious, piecing together a puzzle that reveals the profound tapestry of our inner selves. However, to truly harness the power of your dreams, there is a crucial bridge that must be built — the bridge between the dream world and your waking consciousness. This bridge is dream recall, the ability to remember your dreams vividly and with clarity. Without it, your journal remains empty, and the treasure trove of wisdom that resides in your dreams remains locked away.

Nowadays, dream interpretation is regarded as important in mainstream disciplines such as psychology. The knowledge is available to all—not just the priests and oracles of the past. That is why keeping a dream journal can be a great way to access your own inner wisdom, exploring your conscious and unconscious blueprints, and gain insight into your everyday life. However, you might meet with an obstacle on your

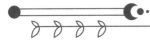 

journey — the unseen barrier: your dreaming attitude (refer to Chapter 2). The latter, stem from your beliefs and doubts regarding the significance of dreams, or your ability to remember them. This barrier can quietly undermine your dream recall, preventing you from fully tapping into the wisdom your dreams offer.

In the following section, we will dismantle this barrier by identifying what your blockages are, and then releasing them. This will pave the way for a deeper connection with your inner self, your dreams, and thus a heightened dream recall ability. Your dream journal will help you discover new insights and understanding. By dedicating some time to the following exercise, you will unlock true potential of your dream journal as a tool for self-discovery and growth.

TIPS FOR DREAM RECALL

Wake up slowly

When you wake up in the morning, to take your time and stay still, or in bed, for a few moments. This will help you to remember your dreams more clearly. If you jump out of bed and start your day right away, you might forget your dreams quickly. Taking a moment to stay still and quiet can help you to hold onto the details of your dream and prevent them from slipping away.

Resist the urge to get up and do

When you wake up, try to resist the urge to check your phone or start your daily routine right away. Instead, take a few deep breaths and try to recall any details of your dream. Pay attention to any images, sounds, or emotions that come to mind. By staying still and quiet, you are giving your brain the space it needs to retrieve the memories of your dream. You might be surprised by how much you can remember if you take the time to stay still and focus on your thoughts.

Write your dream down

Keep your dream journal by your bed side, so you can write down any details that come to mind before getting out of bed. Even if you can only remember fragments of your dream, write them down. This will help you to build a more complete picture of your dream over time.

Visualization

Visualization is a powerful tool that can help you to remember your dreams more easily. Before going to sleep, take a few moments to picture yourself waking up in the morning and remembering your dreams. Imagine yourself reaching for your dream journal and writing down everything you remember. Try to visualize as many details as possible, including the sights, sounds, and feelings associated with you writing your dream down. By practicing this visualization, you are training your brain to remember your dreams more easily.

When you visualize yourself remembering your dreams, you are creating a mental blueprint for your brain to follow. Your brain is incredibly powerful, and it can use this blueprint to help you recall your dreams more easily in the morning. Visualization is essentially a form of mental rehearsal. Practicing it regularly strengthens the neural pathways in your brain that are associated with memory and recall.

Remember, the more vivid and detailed your visualization is, the more effective it will be. When it comes to writing your dream down, try to engage all your senses when you are visualizing yourself remembering your dreams. What does the dream look like? What do you hear? What does it feel like? The more you can immerse yourself in the visualization, the more effective it will be.

In addition to practicing visualization, it is also helpful to set an intention to remember your dreams before you go to sleep or say an affirmation. By doing so, you are telling your brain that you value your dreams and want to remember them.

The Glass of Water Exercise

This technique used in the Silva Method, a self-help and meditation program developed by José Silva, for inducing dreams for problem-solving and goal achievement (see www.SilvaMethod.com). You can adapt the affirmation to remembering your dream.

- At night, before going to bed, take a water glass and fill it with water. As you drink approximately half of the water, close your eyes and turn them slightly upward. While doing so, repeat to yourself, *"This is all I need to do to find the solution to the problem I have in mind"* or *"… to remember my dream relevant to the question I have in mind."*
- Put away the remaining half glass of water and go to sleep. In the morning, upon waking up, drink the remaining half-glass of water. Then, close your eyes again and turn them slightly upward. Repeat to yourself, *"This is all I need to do to find the solution to the problem I have in mind"* or *"… to remember my dream relevant to the question I have in mind."*
- With this programming, you may awaken during the night or in the morning with a vivid recollection of a dream that contains information that you can use for solving the problem.

Alternatively, you may have a flash of insight during the day that contains information that can help you interpret your dream or remember it.

It is worth mentioning that in In the Silva Method's Glass of Water exercise, turning your eyes slightly upward while drinking the water and repeating the affirmation is done to help enter a relaxed and receptive state of mind by stimulating the pineal gland. This is because the upward eye movement is believed to activate the alpha brainwave state, which is associated with a relaxed, meditative state of mind. The alpha brainwave state is also associated with increased creativity, intuition, and visualization abilities.

Furthermore, the upward eye movement is also believed to activate the part of the brain responsible for visual processing and imagination, which can enhance the power of visualization during the exercise. By combining the upward eye movement with the affirmation, the technique aims to create a powerful mental association between the act of drinking water and the desired outcome, such as solving a problem or achieving a goal. It helps to induce a state of relaxation and enhance visualization abilities, which can lead to better dream recall and problem-solving or goal-achievement.

Use mnemonic devices

This involves creating a phrase or acronym that helps you remember your dreams. Mnemonic devices are memory aids that help people remember information more easily. They can take many forms, such as a phrase, acronym, rhyme, or image. Mnemonic devices work by associating information with something that is easier to remember.

In the context of remembering dreams, a mnemonic device could be used to help you remember key details of your dream. For example, if you had a dream about flying, you

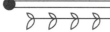

could use the acronym "F.A.S.T." to remember key details of the dream such as "Flying Above the Sky Tonight". Another example could be if you had a dream about a certain person, you could create a rhyme or phrase that helps you remember that person's name or appearance. The key to creating effective mnemonic devices is to make them easy to remember and relevant to the information you are trying to remember. The more unique and memorable the mnemonic, the easier it will be to recall the information associated with it.

Dream object integration

This is a technique that involves bringing elements from your dreams into your waking life through using symbolic objects that reflect elements you remember from your dream. Incorporating elements from your dreams into your waking life is a powerful way of tapping into the creative energy and wisdom of your dreams. The purpose of it is to integrate the wisdom of dreams into daily life and help you remember or recall other fragments of your dream; or simply bringing the wisdom of the dream into real like even when you do not consciously remember all your dream. For example, wearing a clothing or a certain color, or a jewelery item, that featured in your dreams. By doing so, you can carry the energy of the dream with you

throughout the day and remind yourself of the guidance it offered.

For instance, if you dreamt of a particular animal, you could wear clothing with an image of that animal on it to help remember the dream and its message; or make a simple drawing of it in your journal. This can help to reinforce the dream's significance and provide inspiration for problem-solving or creative endeavors.

Dream object integration can be a powerful tool for dream work and personal growth. By incorporating elements from your dreams into your waking life, you can tap into the creative energy and wisdom of your dreams. While this technique may not work for everyone, it is worth exploring to deepen your relationship with your dreams and use them as a source of inspiration and guidance in your daily life.

Over time, these simple techniques can help you to remember your dreams more easily and vividly. And the easier it will become to remember your dreams in the morning.

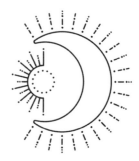

ELEMENTS OF DREAM JOURNALING

When writing in your dream journal, there are a few things you can do to help reveal the symbolism in your dreams:

Dream Date

Begin by recording the date of the dream. This seemingly simple step holds substantial importance in deciphering your personal dream language over time. Dreams often serve as reflections of the thoughts and experiences that have occupied your mind during the day or in the moments leading up to sleep. While the meaning or relevance of a dream may not immediately reveal itself, documenting the date serves as a crucial reference point. Dreams sometimes unfold gradually, much like a story told in installments. By noting the date, you create a timeline that can help you connect the dots and understand why certain dream elements recur. Furthermore, as your self-awareness deepens, you will observe shifts in your dream language and narrative. Keeping track of the date allows you to recognize these changes and the evolving layers of meaning within your dreams.

Real Life

Noting the dream date provides a temporal anchor that can reveal intriguing correlations between your daily experiences and dream content. Reflect on recent significant events or conversations in your life. Did you recently receive a promotion, start a new job, or move to a new house? Perhaps you engaged

in a thought-provoking discussion with a friend or partner about a specific topic that left a lasting impression. Even ideas and concerns that have occupied your thoughts for several days can play a role. Our minds often continue processing these real-life experiences during sleep, and dreams frequently employ symbols to explore and convey mess ages related to our waking life.

Very often, our brains are still processing happenings that we went through during the day, and it is likely that a dream what use symbols to help explore what was on your mind. Whatever is happening consciously in your real life filters into "dream life" and may come up as symbols to convey a message and attract your attention to.

So, directly beneath the date, create a section labeled "Real Life (R.L.)." This section acts as a bridge, connecting your conscious experiences to the symbolism within your dreams. By making this connection, you begin to weave together the tapestry of meaning that your dreams are attempting to convey. This integration process lays the foundation for a more in-depth exploration of your dream's elements, which we will delve into further in this section. Breaking down the elements of your dreams in this structured manner serves as a powerful tool for gaining insights as you journal. It allows you to gradually decode your unique dream

language, unlocking the hidden messages and symbolism that your dreams hold. As we progress, you'll uncover how the threads of your waking and dream life intertwine, leading to a deeper understanding of your inner world.

Dream Theme

Sometimes, upon waking, you may find that your dream slips through your fingers like sand, leaving only faint traces. In such moments, focus on capturing any lingering emotions or impressions that have etched

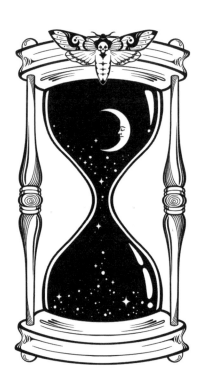

themselves into your waking consciousness. Write down these feelings or fragments, no matter how fleeting they may seem. Emotions can be powerful keys to unlock the deeper layers of your dream.

If your memory allows, and even if it is just fragments of the dream's narrative, jot down your initial impressions. What stands out the most? Is there a central theme or a vivid highlight that lingers in your mind? These first impressions serve as a starting point, a glimpse into the heart of your dream's narrative. They act as signposts that help you navigate the intricate details of your dream as you break it down into its various elements (refer to exercise on dream theme, in the Introduction). Moreover, if you remember your dream, before you get out of bed or speak to anyone, wrote your dream down without stopping to analyze. Keep flowing and then stop when you finished.

Dream Highlights

Having identified your dream theme and written whatever you managed to remember; start to break down your dream into elements that composed the dream. For instance, circle names of people, places, and objects that appeared in the dream, as well as any emotions or sensations you experienced.

Moreover, pay special attention to the emotions or colors that linger upon waking, as they can be your allies in later recalling more of the dream's details throughout the day. For instance, you might find yourself waking up feeling rejuvenated, as if you have just returned from a holiday. Or perhaps you recall that your dream transported you to the past, where you reunited with an old childhood friend, like X, in the familiar setting of your former home. Remembering emotions or colors you wake up with, can lead you to remembering more of the dream later during the day. Even if it seems mundane, jot down details like "X repeatedly called me on my mobile." Every fragment, no matter how small, contributes to unraveling your subconscious mind. Objects that appear in your dream have significance too. Consider elements like cars, planes, or trains, which might symbolize your journey through life, or bodies of water like pools, oceans, or lakes, which can represent the depths of your emotions. Similarly, the settings, such as a school, home, or hospital, hold keys to understanding the messages your subconscious is conveying.

Dream Story & Symbols

Next, write your dreams consider what each element in the dream might symbolize. For example, a house in a dream could represent security and stability, while a storm could symbolize conflict or turmoil. Reflect

on your personal connections with these symbols and what they represent to you on a deep, emotional level. These associations are uniquely yours and can provide profound insights into the messages your dream is conveying. Take those significant elements you've circled and create a list on the right-hand side of your journal page.

Now, for each element, write down one or two descriptive words that capture its essence. Ask yourself questions like "What does this mean to me?" or "What does this symbolize in my inner world?" Your responses might encompass various aspects of your life, such as past experiences, trusted individuals, cherished childhood memories, beloved animals, or even fears you harbor. Do not shy away from exploring these associations with an open and creative mind. Keep in mind that the language of the unconscious mind often operates in abstract and metaphorical ways. Therefore, the symbols in your dreams may not always offer a straightforward interpretation. Embrace the challenge of deciphering these symbols, for within their enigmatic nature lies the potential for profound self-discovery and understanding.

Preparing for Dream Direction

Directing your dreams mindfully is a fascinating way to tap into your subconscious. This approach not only provides insights into your inner thoughts but also empowers you to set intentions for your waking reality (see chapter 5 and Chapter 6). So, before bedtime, allocate a few minutes for this ritual. Seek out a serene and cozy environment that allows for undistracted concentration. Then, concentrate on crafting your specific dream question or intention. Make it well-defined and succinct. Consider the facet of your life that beckons for illumination or the predicament you are currently wrestling with. This might pertain to matters of relationships, personal evolution, profession, or any other facet of your existence. For instance:

"What can I learn from my recent challenges?"

"What is the best way to exploring my creative potential."

"Show me how to overcome my current obstacles."

Recording Your Question

Open your dream journal or a notebook dedicated to your dream practice. Write down your question or intention for the night. Make it precise and meaningful. Note down the date, and any significant or memorable events in your life that day. It might

also encompass a thought-provoking movie you watched, a melody from a song that lingered in your thoughts, or any issue or aspect of your life that commanded your attention. This thorough practice of recording not only forges a connection between your waking life and your dreams but also lays the groundwork for a more profound exploration of your dreamscapes. As you revisit these entries in the future, you will begin to discern patterns and connections between your daily experiences and the symbolic language of your dreams, enriching your dream work.

Upon Waking

As soon as you wake up, take a moment to recall any dreams you experienced during the night. Carefully transcribe these dreams into your journal, ensuring you capture not only the narrative but also the emotions, symbols, and intricate details that linger. As you engage in this morning ritual, consider the use of colors to enhance your dream journal. Colors possess a unique ability to convey emotions that sometimes words alone cannot express. Doing so using a palette of colors, infuses your dream journal with vivid memories of how you felt during those dreamscapes.

Furthermore, reflect on any connections between the dream elements. Once you have recorded your dream, consider how it relates to your question or intention. Explore the symbolism and themes within the dream that might hold answers or insights. If, for example, all you remember is dreaming of a red flower, wear something in red the following day. This delicate association brings the energy of the dream into real life. And you may remember more segments later.

Continuing the Practice

Make this mindful dream direction a regular practice. Experiment with different questions and intentions to explore various aspects of your life. Consistent mindful dream direction is key to unlocking the wealth of insights and guidance our dreams can offer. Each night presents an opportunity to delve into various facets of your life, from relationships and personal growth to career and creativity. By broadening your inquiries and remaining open to the diverse range of messages your dreams can convey, you further enrich your self-discovery journey and deepen the integration of your dream wisdom into your waking reality.

INTEGRATING A DREAM'S MESSAGE WITH REAL LIFE

When a dream unfolds in the realm of sleep, it often arrives with its own language and symbols. As dreamers, our first task is to decipher this unique code. This involves breaking down the elements of the dream, such as people, places, objects, and emotions. Each of these components may hold a hidden message, like pieces of a puzzle waiting to be assembled.

Once you have dissected the dream, the next step is to connect the dots between its symbols and our waking life. This requires a deep dive into our personal associations and experiences. For example, if a dream features a lighthouse, we might ask ourselves what the lighthouse represents to us. It could be a symbol of guidance, a beacon in times of uncertainty. Exploring these connections allows us to bridge the gap between the dream world and your daily reality.

 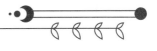
Moreover, as you decode the dream and make connections, keep recording your findings in your dream journal. Jot down the dream's details, your interpretations, and any insights gained. When you dedicate your dream journal to these reflections, it becomes a valuable tool in the integration the wisdom from your dreams into real life. Additionally, it serves as a tangible record of your journey towards understanding the dream's message and its relevance to our waking life. Even when you are not consciously aware of the meaning of dreams, your mind is! It will begin to apply what you learn in a practical way. For example, the decisions you make. This is where the true power of a dream lies: in its ability to inform and enrich our daily existence.

As you gain clarity on the dream's symbolism and its connection to our reality, you can begin to apply this newfound wisdom to our everyday challenges and aspirations. For instance, if a dream reveals a recurring theme of falling, you might explore whether this symbolizes a fear of failure or a sense of insecurity in your waking life. Armed with this insight, you can take proactive steps to address these feelings, whether through self-assurance techniques or by seeking support from others.

Furthermore, Dream integration can also be aligned with your personal goals. If you aspire to enhance your creativity, for example, and your dreams frequently feature artistic imagery or scenarios, you can view this as a nudge from our subconscious to pursue our creative passions more actively. This alignment between our dreams and our aspirations creates a harmonious synergy that propels us towards our objectives.

THE ROLE OF SELF-REFLECTION

Self-reflection is a pivotal component of integrating a dream's message into our daily life. It involves taking a step back and considering how the dream's insights align with our values, desires, and personal growth journey. This process of introspection helps us discern which aspects of the dream hold the most significance for us and how they can be applied practically.

Also, maintaining an open dialogue with your dreams involves a level of patience and receptivity. Dreams may not always offer immediate clarity, and some messages may unfold gradually over time. That is why it is important to approach this process with an open mind and a willingness to embrace the subtleties of the dream world. As you continue to engage in this ongoing conversation with your dreams, you will cultivate a deeper connection with your subconscious and unlock the full potential of their guidance in your waking lives.

Ultimately, dream integration calls for action. Once you have decoded the dream, made connections, and reflected on its relevance, it is time to implement what you have learned about yourself or your life through your dreams. Whether it is addressing a fear, pursuing a passion, or enhancing a relationship, the insights gained from your dreams serve as a blueprint for meaningful change in your lives.

Through this ongoing dialogue between the conscious and subconscious, we uncover the hidden gems of our inner world and embark on a journey of self-discovery that enriches every facet of our lives.

In closing, we have embarked on a journey into the realm of dream craft, where understanding the language of your unconscious mind empowers you. You have learned the significant influence of your thoughts and emotions in shaping your dreams and how the latter is shaped by the reality you experience. To foster this heightened awareness, remember that deliberate engagement with the language of your unconscious mind, as conveyed through dreams, becomes paramount.

Delving into your inner world, means assuming command of your life's direction, and forging a connection between your conscious and unconscious minds. Dream Craft then emerges as a powerful and self-empowering instrument for this synthesis.

As shared by my spiritual guide, *"Consciousness can only change through the application of consciousness."* This underscores the pivotal role of self-awareness as the driving force behind personal growth. It is not just about subscribing to intermittent healing techniques or modalities. But an unwavering commitment to empowering yourself by discovering your true unique identity, your authentic self. And this is what we hope The Book of Practical Dream Craft can support you. Discovering the "codes" of your unconscious mind is can truly enrich your life.

However, what often goes amiss on this journey is profound self-awareness—an unshakable connection to your authentic identity. Your consciousness, residing within your unique vessel, bestow upon you the self-empowering privilege of crafting the life of your dreams. Confronting your own "truth," therefore, directly through your own dreams is of paramount significance. There is no room for regrets as you reflect on your past experiences. Instead, focus on the essential dream inquiry and record your findings in your journal. For example, *"What can I improve?"*, or *"where does my true happiness lie?"* The phrase "let me sleep on it" will take a literal meaning.

Such questions serve as your compass, guiding the way toward self-improvement and a more fulfilling life. Moreover, self-awareness is your key to unlocking your fullest potential. No gimmicks here, only the joyful and conscious journey of dream interpretation. You have acquired practical skills—keeping a dream journal, inducing dreams, and deciphering dream language—to unveil the messages concealed within the narratives of your unconscious mind.

This connection, is your personal navigation system, helping you chart the course of your life's journey. Ignoring it can lead to feelings of exhaustion, hopelessness, and irritability. As Robert Moss sagely remarked, *"For me, the world is a forest of symbols."* Embrace this wisdom, interpreting dream symbols literally and waking life symbols metaphorically.

We hope that The Book of Dream Craft has been an enlightening exploration, sparking your zeal to craft your self-discovery book. May your dreams continue to serve as wellsprings of insight, empowerment, and self-awareness on your extraordinary life journey.

Happy Dreaming!

FURTHER READING

Dreaming Reality How Dreaming keeps us sane, or can drive us mad; Joe Griffin & Ivan Tyrrell (HG Publishing 2004)

The Interpretation of Dreams in Chinese Culture, by Fang Jing Pei & Zhang Juwen (Weatherhill 2000)

Pocketful or Dreams, by Denise Linn (Triple Five Publishing (1 Jan. 1988)

Psychic Powers Unlock Your Natural Intuition, by Sahar Huneidi Palmer (Sirius, 2022)

Your Dreams Spiritual Messages in Pajamas, by Ana Lora Garrard (Llewellyn Publications; Original edition 2010)

The Lucid Dreamer A Waking Guide for the Traveler Between Worlds Hardcover by Malcolm Godwin (Simon & Schuster; 1st edition, 1994)

The Secret History of Dreaming, Robert Moss (New World Library 2009)

The Secret Language of Dreams A Visual Key To Dreams And Their Meanings, by David Fontana.

INDEX